RAGE

RAGE

NARCISSISM, PATRIARCHY, AND
THE CULTURE OF TERRORISM

Abigail R. Esman

POTOMAC BOOKS
An imprint of the University of Nebraska Press

Portions of the introduction appeared previously as "If
I Could Close My Eyes, A Story of Love, Pain, Hope,
and Release," in *Diane, The Curves Magazine* (Fall
2006): 34–37. "Glory of Love": Words and Music by
David Foster, Peter Cetera, and Diana Nini. Copyright
© 1986 by Air Bear Music, Universal Music–MGB
Songs, EMI Gold Horizon Music Corp., and EMI
Golden Torch Music Corp. All rights for Air Bear
Music Administered by Peermusic Ltd. Exclusive Print
Rights for EMI Gold Horizon Music Corp. and EMI
Golden Torch Music Corp. Administered by Alfred
Music. International Copyright Secured. All Rights
Reserved. Reprinted by permission of Hal Leonard LLC.

Library of Congress Cataloging-in-Publication Data
Names: Esman, Abigail R., author.
Title: Rage: narcissism, patriarchy, and the
culture of terrorism / Abigail R. Esman.
Description: Lincoln: Potomac Books, an
imprint of the University of Nebraska Press,
[2020] | Includes bibliographical references.
Identifiers: LCCN 2020007865
ISBN 9781640122314 (hardback)
ISBN 9781640123977 (epub)
ISBN 9781640123984 (mobi)
ISBN 9781640123991 (pdf)
Subjects: LCSH: Terrorism. | Family
violence. | Narcissism.
Classification: LCC HV6431 .E747
2020 | DDC 303.6/25—dc23
LC record available at https://lccn.loc.gov/2020007865

Set in Adobe Garamond by Laura Buis.
Designed by N. Putens.

The most unfailing herald, companion, and follower of the awakening of a great people to work a beneficial change in opinion or institution, is poetry. . . . Poets are the unacknowledged legislators of the world.

—Percy Bysshe Shelley, "A Defense of Poetry," 1821

To my parents, Rosa and Aaron Esman,

and

To the poets

CONTENTS

AUTHOR'S NOTE

In presenting this book, a few small notes seem to be in order.

First, although all the events I describe in here are true, several names, along with some identifying characteristics, have been changed in the interest of privacy.

Second, while I refer throughout to abusers as "he" and the abused as "she," I am fully aware that there are women who abuse men and children. This is in no way meant to deny this painful fact.

And finally, I am not a clinical psychologist. Nothing I have stated in this book should be viewed as a diagnosis except for those diagnoses offered by professionals as cited. Rather I have attempted to apply the criteria of pathological narcissism, along with the expertise of those far more qualified in the field, to societal norms and to individuals as suitable. Where I have specifically identified anyone as a "pathological narcissist" I have done so based on the determinations of professionals who have examined, studied, or tested those individuals. Hence while I occasionally describe specific behaviors as narcissistic, not everyone who displays those behaviors is necessarily a pathological narcissist. These are small but important distinctions, and I have tried throughout this book to remain faithful to them.

ACKNOWLEDGMENTS

No book is written by its author alone. My deepest gratitude to those who contributed to the creation of this one.

First, my agent, Hilary Claggett, whose continual support of my work and belief in this project made its realization possible. No writer could have a better champion, and my gratitude is beyond measure.

Anne Manne was the first to know of my desire to write this book. It would not have happened without her insistence and encouragement, and to her, too, my deepest thanks.

Steven Emerson, for whose support I am always appreciative, went further, providing a generous grant from the Investigative Project on Terrorism that helped make writing the book possible.

To Keri Douglas, a woman I have never met, also my thanks. Her belief in this book helped keep me going, and her encouragement and enthusiasm helped to move me forward, though she can't possibly have known.

Those who contributed to this book by sharing their lives, their insights, their knowledge: Yasmine Mohammed, Shannon Foley Martinez, Mubin Shaikh, Anne Spekhard, Dov Cohen, Farhana Qazi, Otto Kernberg, MD. Your work, your lives, and your words make freedom—and peace—possible.

My eternal gratitude and love to Steven Peter and William Henry Byerly II, for their friendship, their love, and the courage that they gave me. You saved my life.

To Barbara Divver, whose wisdom, bravery, insights, generosity, and devotion inspire me in every aspect of my life and throughout the hours that I write: "thank you" is not enough. Your very being is a gift that makes so many of us strong.

I am also most deeply grateful to Yahsi Baraz, Can and Sevda Elgiz, and so many others like them in Istanbul and elsewhere who have devoted their lives to the promise of the arts—and the power of the truths that we believe in. I am so honored to call you friends.

To Kenyon College, for knowledge, for poetry, for freedom.

And finally to my husband, Peter Madden, who every day provides his loving, enduring, and valiant support—of my writing, of my work, of my vision. I am still amazed to be your wife and so proud to share my life with you.

Doubtless, more have contributed to making this particular book possible than I have named here; to them, too, my enduring gratitude.

INTRODUCTION

I am running on East Eighty-Ninth Street in the dark. Cannot breathe, cannot stop. In the streets kids are playing stickball I can hear them, but they are a blur of pink and brown, flesh and T-shirts, voices. *Keep running.* Behind me somewhere is the man who whispers to me in the night, but I cannot look back, can only run. *Keep running.* Air and night close around me, darkness at my throat, hair in my eyes, boots on the sidewalk, breathe, choke, a man asks, "Are you all right?" but I do not, cannot stop to answer. *Keep running.* Legs heavy; Eighty-Ninth Street going west is all uphill. Some nights it is whispers and some nights it is curses and tonight it was hisses, hot and filled with spit as a switchblade flashes to the corner of my eye and does not move from there, spit from his mouth spraying against cold steel, distorting the reflection. I am looking forward, only looking forward, do not dare to move my eyes. Until he drops the knife. "Too good for you," he mutters and turns to walk to where I know the gun is, and this is where I start to run, pull the lock open, the door, down the stairs and through two front doors. Surely he could have caught me by then if he'd wanted to. I am just five feet, and he is six foot one.

Run. Heels hard against the pavement, a hot June night, I still remember, *run.*

I turn left. Left is the obvious direction: toward home, not away. But I turn left, and he knows I will turn left and so he catches up to me, a hand on my shoulder, the lights stop, breath stops, footsteps stop, and I realize that deafening drumming in my ears has been the sound of my own footsteps because that, too, stops.

"What are you running from?" he says. "Come back with me."

Years later I still remember we are standing on Third Avenue in the dark in front of a deli between Eighty-Eighth and Eighty-Ninth Streets and he is wearing jeans and the pale brown hairs of his chest are visible beneath a denim work shirt that is two too many buttons unbuttoned, and I am seventeen years old and I am stuck. If I go home to my parents I will have to explain why I am back before 9:30 on a Saturday night. I will have to act as if everything is fine when it is not. I turn to face him. There does not seem to be a gun. "Don't be such a silly," he says and sweeps me into an embrace, the kind of embrace the good guy sweeps the frightened maiden in when he comes to save her from the evil king, the evil bandits. My head is spinning again but I am too confused and still too dumb with fright to argue.

Silly, he says again. Don't you know how much I love you?

* * *

It is thirty-five years later, and a glorious spring day. Two young men push their way along the crowded streets, sidestepping the toddlers darting underfoot. Around them people roar and cheer, but it is as if the two don't hear them; they converse privately and keep walking, the tall, muscular older one and the younger, smaller, handsome one. They are used to being noticed in a crowd—the younger, a star student, immensely popular in school; the older, a professional boxer, accustomed to the stage—but no one notices them now. They carry backpacks and wear caps to shield their faces from the sun. At the corner they part ways then melt into the crowd, half a million people strong.

There is a flash. And then another.

When the smoke clears men and women lie scattered across the Boston Marathon finish line, legs blasted far away from the bodies they only seconds ago had given motion, helped to run, or walk, or stand; arms shorn from shoulders, blood and bone and horror, and a small boy, lying lifeless at his father's feet.

* * *

In 2017 more than twenty-six thousand people were killed in terror attacks around the world, most of them in the Middle East.

That same year over ten million men, women, and children became the victims of domestic violence in America alone. Over fifteen hundred of them died.

These two facts are not unrelated. Neither are the stories of domestic abusers and terrorists, and the experiences of their victims. The weapon is fear; the laurel, power. Fists, bombs, words, rape, airplanes, sarin—it's all the same. You know there will be something. You don't know when. You don't know quite where. You don't know if you are safe, or if you ever will be.

This is what the fear is.

This is what terrorism does—in our homes. In our streets. In our lives.

This book is about understanding these two deadly forms of violence—domestic abuse and terrorism—and the many links between them: the cultures—both public and private—that breed terrorism, that breed abuse, the mutual cause-and-effect relationship between them, and the personalities of those behind the terror.

I want to be clear: this is, ultimately, a book about terrorists and terrorism—not about domestic abuse itself. But the ties between them—the terrorist and the abuser, the terrorized and the abused, the terrorist and terrorized—are such that, as Susan Heitler, PhD, has written, "terrorism is a large-scale version of domestic violence."[1] (It is also worth noting that the U.S. Department of Justice defines "domestic violence" in part as "any behaviors that intimidate, manipulate, humiliate, isolate, frighten, terrorize, coerce, threaten, blame, hurt, injure, or wound someone.")

And so this is a book really about what domestic violence—from the perspective of both the batterer and the battered—can teach us about terrorism: how we live with it, and how we can defeat it.

Because in truth, in the post-9/11 age, we do live with it. All of us. Indeed the complex interrelationships between domestic violence and terrorism form a web that captures much of our current sociopolitical life, from economic patterns and political debates in America and Europe; to suicide bombings and massacres in Paris and in Boston and in Charleston, South Carolina; to the atrocities taking place across the Middle East: the stoning of women in Saudi Arabia, sex slavery and beheadings in the Islamic State, the shooting of Malala Yousafzai in Pakistan's Swat Valley. *Rage: Narcissism, Patriarchy, and the Culture of Terrorism* unravels that web—first by exposing the threads that bind it together, and then by offering tools that may help us to untie the knots—before they catch us in their fatal grip.

And fatal it is: numerous studies, many reviewed in these pages, reveal that cultures where women are more oppressed and violence against women is tolerated tend to be more violent in general, and more inclined to engage in warfare. Indeed, as Soraya Chemaly wrote in an article in the *Huffington Post*, "The greater the polarization of gender in a household, the higher tolerance there is for violence and oppression and the greater the violence experienced by women and girls in those households, the greater the likelihood of militarization and national violence."[2]

This book is a step toward ending that violence for the future.

* * *

On September 11, 2001, I was visiting my family in New York. I'd grown up there. This was my city.

It was also the city where I'd lived through two violent love affairs— one at age seventeen, the other twenty-one years later. In 2001 I was still recovering, not only from the second affair but from the ghosts of the first that the second had released, that lurked now in the corners of my days. I startled easily. Sudden movements caused me to recoil. Raised male voices made me shiver. Few nights passed without nightmares.

Yet even so, I hadn't released the more recent lover—call him Rick— completely from my life. He demanded contact. I didn't dare refuse. More, I didn't want to face so fully what I already really knew: that this man, who had so long been my partner, my ally, was in truth my enemy; that a wish to trust someone isn't quite enough to make you safe; that sometimes there are no part-way measures—you're either safe, or you are not; that sometimes, even when you do not see the danger, it is there.

And that I couldn't control any of it because it was not, in fact, my fault. This is important.

On September 12, 2001, I watched my friends, my neighbors, my city, become like me. A car door slammed. We trembled. A truck backfired: our muscles ignited, prepared to run. Newspapers asked: Why do they hate us? On television, pundits enumerated America's many sins. We searched our souls for answers: What had we done to deserve this slaughtering of thousands? What would we need to do to keep it from happening again? What were the rules we had somehow failed to follow?

"Why are you doing this?" I asked Boris once, not long after the evening with the knife. Bruises colored my arms and legs. Fear colored my days and nights.

"Don't be silly," he had laughed. "Everybody does it."

Everybody does it. For the abuser as for the terrorist, this is how life is. Both Rick and Boris were battered in their childhood homes. And "in cultures and countries that produce terrorists," writes Susan Heitler, "rates of domestic abuse are very high. . . . The belief that dominating others via violence is a legitimate way to act pervades homes, the religious arena, and the behaviors of governments toward both their citizens and toward neighboring countries."[3]

Everybody does it.

This is why, in the end, domestic abuse, be it physical or emotional, affects not just women but children: sons who grow up to shoot children playing on the island of Utoya, Norway; who plant pressure-cooker bombs in Boston; who behead off-duty soldiers in London and shoot filmmakers in Amsterdam; or who travel to Syria and join the Islamic State, kidnapping Americans and Jordanians and Englishmen and burning them alive, or capturing women by the thousands and selling them as sex slaves to one another. Or they become the fathers of such sons, or they become the fathers of young girls they kill for honor—in Pakistan, in Montreal, in Texas.

And it affects not just wives but daughters—daughters who become the mothers of such sons, or the mothers of the mothers of such sons, or daughters who run off to become jihadi brides in Syria—and are often raped or killed there, too.

But it is not simply a matter of repeating learned behavior: Daddy hits, Baby hits. Rather the child who grows up in an abusive home tends to develop a specific personality, marked by a sense of shame, a (pathological) concern for honor, and what psychiatrists call "pathological narcissism,"[4] all bound to one another and to a patriarchal machismo, to visions—romantic, political, literary, and socioeconomic—of men as warrior-heroes, knights on powerful white steeds, brave, all-protecting, and ever victorious. All three of these traits—shame, pathological (malignant) narcissism, and an honor culture—have been linked by psychiatrists, sociologists, and others to violence, and specifically to terrorism. The "honor culture" that characterizes Muslim societies, for instance, is—not coincidentally—also often attributed to the American South, where domestic violence rates are the highest in the country and where right-wing terrorist and extremist groups such as the Odinists, the League of the South, and the Council of Conservative Citizens, which has been linked to white supremacist mass murderer Dylann Roof, find most of their membership.

Indeed studies have shown these traits in common among the cultures and homes that breed abusive behavior and terrorism, leading to what writer Anne Manne, author of *The Book of I*, a study of narcissism, calls the "shame-rage spiral of the narcissist who reacts to failure with other-directed humiliated fury."[5]

The terrorist.

The abuser.

Little surprise, then, that Tamerlan Tsarnaev was charged with assault and battery in 2009 for beating up his then-girlfriend, and was later known to have abused his wife, Katherine Russell; or that he was also known to have hit his sisters; or that Mohammed Atta, one of the masterminds of the 9/11 attacks, was mollycoddled by his doting mother while his father, according to a *Frontline* report, "was a domineering figure and a strict disciplinarian"—a combination that, according to narcissism expert Otto Kernberg,[6] often results in a malignant narcissistic disorder in the child, who is at once slammed with shame while at the same time made to feel, in one way or another, "special."

Not all child victims of domestic violence become terrorists, of course, nor do they always become abusers (though research indicates they usually do). Many become violent criminals. According to a 1998 report by the Cuyahoga County Community Health Research Institute, "One study of 2,245 children and teenagers found that recent exposure to violence in the home was a significant factor in predicting a child's violent behavior."[7] Others go on to lead normal, healthy lives; but too often a child's mind is formed by a dangerous culture that resides either within or outside the family—and sometimes both: a culture based on principles of machismo, shame, and honor, and in which malignant narcissism breeds, infecting thought, tradition, and daily life.

And the terror starts.

How does this happen?

And when it does, who will go beyond interpersonal violence in the private sphere, as Tamerlan Tsarnaev did, and take their vengeance to the streets? Who will emerge so scarred, as Mohammed Atta did, that he will plan and take part in a massacre of thousands? What motivates them, if anything, any differently than the man who beats his son, the wife who beats her daughter, the husband who slams his new bride's head against the bathroom sink because she wasn't quick enough to say hello? Who will find a false salvation, a false heroism, in religion and martyrdom? Who will use that religion, too, to murder a wife or daughter? And what can we do, the rest of us, to stop it? More urgently—how in an age of increasing narcissism (a phenomenon only partly explainable by Facebook and Instagram) do we protect our sons, our daughters, and our communities from what counterterrorism expert Raffaello Pantucci, author of *We Love Death As You Love Life*, terms "jihadi cool"?[8]

I have tried, in the pages of this book, to examine these questions, not just from a psychological perspective but from sociological and sociopolitical ones, as well. The forces that breed terrorists, we now understand, are not a question of what America and the West have "done wrong," easily remedied by fixing our own behavior so they will no longer "hate us." They come, instead, from the societies and families of the terrorists themselves—young men (and often young women) raised not only with specific worldviews but with specific self-views that lead them to become the Joel Steinbergs, the O. J. Simpsons, the Tamerlan Tsarnaevs and Mohammed Attas and Anders Breiviks and Osama bin Ladens of our age.

Yet like the web that binds together terrorism and abuse, untying the strands of shame and honor and abuse and violence and terror is not a simple task: the knots are intricate and tight, like the designs on a Turkish carpet, where the background and the pattern often are the same.

Interestingly, "background" in the case of terror and abuse is also often inseparable from pattern, from patterns of behavior repeated over generations, in cultural mores, in societal traditions. (It is, for instance, in part because of this that arguments continue about such things as female genital mutilation, and whether they are part of culture or religion or whether there is even any difference between the two.) Add to this the influences of patriarchy and male-centered traditions and the mix becomes even more complex and intertwined. How to begin to unwind the threads so that a new and brighter fabric can be woven?

* * *

In her groundbreaking classic *The Demon Lover: The Roots of Terrorism*, author Robin Morgan speaks of "the eroticization and elevation of violence as the expression of 'manhood.'"[9] It is this, she says, that accounts for the allure of terrorism; and it is this, surely, that accounts for the successes of al Qaeda and now ISIS and their ability to recruit young men and women from all walks of life—from Moroccan immigrants in Brussels or Paris to African American Christian converts in small-town Mississippi.

"The terrorist (or depending on one's view, the freedom fighter)," she writes, "is the ultimate sexual idol of a male-centered cultural tradition that stretches from pre-Biblical times to the present; he is the logical extension of the patriarchal hero/martyr. He is the Demon Lover, and society is (secretly or openly) fascinated by him. He walks with death and is thus inviolate; he is an idealist but a man of action, a fanatic of dedication and an archetype of self-sacrifice, a mixture of volatility, purity, severe discipline. He is desperate and therefore vulnerable, at risk and therefore brave, wholly given over to an idea. His intensity reeks of glamour. Women, we are told, lust to have him. Men, we are told, long to be him. He is sexy because he is deadly; he excites with the thrill of fear."[10]

It would be hard to imagine a more compelling image for the young woman, the young man craving honor and respect, desperate for attention, eager to take power (take, not achieve). And while Morgan is focused on public terrorism, the portrait she draws depicts, too, the terrorist in our bedrooms, the man who wants to make clear "who rules," "who wears the pants" in his family, the king of his castle, demanding to be loved.

* * *

A critical purpose of this book is to create a deeper awareness of domestic abuse and violence against women and children as part of an effort to reduce rates of "national violence and militarism"—and terror. That violence exists not only in the desert sands of Islamic State territory and in the mountain villages of Afghanistan but also in American school shootings, mass murders at movie theaters, and terrorist attacks on the streets of Boston, at Christmas parties in San Bernardino, at military recruitment centers in Tennessee, in a synagogue in Pittsburgh, on the sidewalks of New York City; and at a café in Sydney, Australia, a conference in Copenhagen, a restaurant in Paris, on the London Metro, on the cobbled streets of Amsterdam, and far too many more.

And so, along with explanations of the concepts of shame, honor, and malignant narcissism and the profiles of terrorists and abusers, I have included here my own experiences as a survivor of abuse, along with the experiences of others. The parallels to the experiences of Western cultures at large as the terrorist threat deepens are striking. But if we are going to understand the larger picture, if we as a culture are going to avoid making the mistakes in the face of terrorism that so many abuse victims have made with their abusers, we need to understand those parallels—and the paths that lead to freedom.

This, too, is important. In a post-9/11 world, and as terrorism tightens its grip across the globe—from Aleppo to Paris, from Bangladesh to Boston, from Charleston to Christchurch—the atrocities that once left us reeling with horror have gradually become an accepted part of our reality. Where the beheadings of James Foley and Steven Sotloff and others shocked the Western world with their barbarism and execrable savagery, we now react to news of such inhuman, barbarous brutalities much as we do to the news of any murder: dismayed, distressed, perhaps, but no longer quite so shocked, so sickened.

And this is exactly what happens to the victims of abuse: eventually we hardly feel the pain. Eventually we enter a "new normal." Our vision of the world around us changes. We question our former values. We rebuild context, reframe our perspective. Michelle Knight, one of three girls held captive for eleven years in the home of convicted kidnapper and sexual molester Ariel Castro, explained her situation in an interview after she was freed, having spent years, as she put it, often tied up "like a fish" and chained against a wall—usually naked.

"What happens is hard at first," she told CNN. "You don't really want to adapt to it. You don't want to comply. You don't want to do anything at first.

"But then you find yourself saying, why not? I'm here, just let him get it over with. So you slowly end up saying, 'OK, whatever, just do it, go.'"[11]

* * *

This is the story of life with a terrorist.

It comes without warning. His fist against your cheekbone cracks like the tearing of branches from a tree. You don't even notice the pain. It is the sound that echoes in your mind.

For the rest of the day your cheek burns. Wearing dark glasses, you walk along the street, conscious of your skin, and you shrink from anything—a lamppost, a passerby—that comes too near. Footsteps pound beside you, behind you, a roar inside your head.

Any man, woman, or child who has ever experienced an attack out of nowhere, the unexpected thundering of a fury we do not understand, knows what this is. Suddenly we are on high alert. Everything frightens. For a moment nature overcomes us: *fight*, we think, *or flee*. We consider leaving. We consider hitting back. We consider calling the police. But in the end we do none of these. A consciousness with fears all its own intervenes. It is incomprehensible that something like this should happen to us. All these ideas start to seem melodramatic, hysterical even. We must have done something to provoke it. Or something. Why else would someone do such a thing?

We will figure out what the problem was. We can work this out.

Weeks, even months pass. Things become, if not quite the way they were before, quite nearly so. And so we retreat. As incomprehensible as the idea of him doing it once is the idea of him doing it again. It won't happen. We know that. We'll be careful.

And this is our often-fatal error.

People often ask me why I stayed, why women stay. The answer to this is difficult and complex, but it is rooted, I have come finally to believe, in one central truth: we don't. In some crazy, convoluted, callisthenic of our psyche, a portion of our mind escapes, running from the horror and the betrayal and the fear, a fear that follows us everywhere we go, that hangs over us in the shower, shadows us along the street, sits beside us on the subway, sleeps within us as we sleep, until, exhausted, we flee for refuge on an island called denial before our more rational selves can stop us.

* * *

I would try to reason with him. "You don't have to hit me," I'd say. "If you don't like something, just tell me."

Whack.

And then there are the innocent victims to think of. And we do. If we have children, friends remind us that a child needs a family. Why punish the children for the sins of their fathers? (And, so, too, we consider: are we to punish the Afghan people for the sins of the Taliban and al Qaeda? The Syrians for the atrocities of the Islamic State?)

Others warn us that our partner will be devastated if we leave, will never be able to manage without us.

Guilt.

We are trapped. Either we face the pain of life with an abuser, or we take the risk of hitting back, or we face the pain of what it means to leave, to even think of leaving. There must, we decide, be another way—if only we can find it. And we do: we determine to act as if we do not know what we in fact do know. We refuse it. Things like that do not happen to us. They most certainly do not happen to us again.

And so we sit.

And we forget.

We are so wrong.

Because when we forget, or pretend to forget, or fear remembering, when forgetting becomes the only way to stop the nightmares and the trembling and the nerves that fire at every unexpected sound, at every movement, we lead ourselves right back into the jaws of danger. I know this. Any one of us who has lived with a terrorist in the bedroom knows this.

For as long as we are fearful, we are careful. As long as we allow ourselves to feel the unbearable, to acknowledge the unthinkable, we are safe. It is only when things become too terrible to deny any longer that we leave. But by then it often is too late. By then we have been hit and hit again, by words, by fists, by books and bats and billiard balls hurled across the room, and sometimes, most of all, by our own reluctance to defend ourselves and our lives.

* * *

There is more danger in this than it even first appears. Patricia Evans, an expert on emotional and verbal abuse, has compared the process of abuse to a frog placed in hot water. Place a live frog in a boiling pot and he will leap right out. But place him in cool water and slowly raise the heat and he will gradually boil to death.[12]

If we are going to escape that kind of slow and painful end, we will need to understand far better than we do what it is that sets the fire burning beneath the pot. These accounts, these reminiscences, are not just about memoir; they are an effort at building that understanding.

Which is why, while this book examines domestic violence and terrorism in varied sociopolitical arenas, I've placed a particular focus on Islamist terrorism and the treatment of women and young boys in the Muslim world and Muslim family life. In an age when the West is increasingly under threat from Islamist extremism, understanding how Muslims radicalize, the effectiveness of ISIS recruiting (especially in the West), the growth of lone-wolf Islamist terror, and the rising rates of honor violence against Western Muslim women and girls is not only crucial but urgent. Because as Somali-born activist Ayaan Hirsi Ali told me years ago, sitting in a restaurant on an Amsterdam canal, "If you look at Middle Eastern society—the way they live, the way men and women relate, the way fathers and sons, mothers and daughters, even mothers and sons relate in private life—you can see that the public chaos and the public crisis in which these countries find themselves is a reflection of the crisis in the home, and the helplessness, and the terror. Only if we see that is peace possible. And the end of terrorism."

RAGE

CHAPTER I

THE NARCISSIST

It is the afternoon of September 11, 2001. Silence weighs thick on the Upper East Side of Manhattan, dark and heavy, like thunderclouds you cannot see through. We have all stood still and stunned, watching our TV screens, watching the smoke downtown rise up into view, waiting for phone calls that do not come. Most of us fear going out, fear the streets, even as we hear the roar of military jets circling above the city, forming a sort of safety net from the sky. Others rush to hospitals, offering aid, offering blood, or hoping to find the wife, the husband, the father, the daughter, who hasn't yet come home.

Mostly we tremble.

And we wait.

The largest city in the United States, the financial capital of the world, was virtually closed down. Transportation into Manhattan was halted, as was much of public transport within the city. Parts of Lower Manhattan were left without power, compelling Mayor Giuliani to order Battery Park

City to be evacuated. Major stock exchanges closed. Primary elections for mayor and other city offices were cancelled. Thousands of workers, released from their offices in Lower Manhattan but with no way to get home except by foot, set off in vast streams, down the avenues and across the bridges under a beautiful, clear sky, accompanied by the unceasing sound of sirens.

While doctors and nurses at hospitals across the city tended to hundreds of damaged people, a disquieting sense grew throughout the day at other triage centers and emergency rooms that there would, actually, be less work: the morgues were going to be busiest.

A sense of shock, grief, and solidarity spread rapidly through the city. There was the expectation that friends and relatives would be revealed among the victims. Schools prepared to let students stay overnight if they could not get home, or if it emerged there was no one to go home to.

New York Times, September 12, 2001[1]

By morning America awakens not only to a changed world but to the discovery of new words, new concepts, new names: Jihad. Al Qaeda. Osama bin Laden. "Jihad," we learn, means "holy war," subject to various interpretations we will continue to argue about for years to come. "Al Qaeda" is a terrorist group we have dealt with in the past—most recently in October 2000, with the bombing of the navy ship USS *Cole*. Seventeen U.S. sailors were killed, and thirty-nine injured.

But who was Osama bin Laden?

The world today knows well who bin Laden was, knew long before he was killed in a U.S. Navy SEAL operation on May 2, 2011: the mastermind of the 9/11 attacks, the leader of al Qaeda, the spiritual master and inspiration for thousands of radical Muslims around the world, a demigod, in fact, even years after his death.

But he hadn't always been a terrorist leader. What had happened to turn this once-shy, soft-spoken youth, the son of a Yemeni Saudi billionaire, into a mass murderer, a religious warrior prepared to destroy the world for Islam?

As much as is known about Osama bin Mohammed bin Awad bin

Laden, even now many details remain sketchy. He was born in either 1956 or 1957 (some say 1955), either the eleventh or seventeenth of Mohammed bin Awad bin Laden's children and his only child with Hamida Ibrahim, a Syrian beauty who is said to have been the last of his four wives. (Osama's father, according to Adam Robinson's 2002 biography *Bin Laden: Behind the Mask of the Terrorist*,[2] circumvented the Islamic rule that allows only four wives by regularly marrying and divorcing, so that he ultimately fathered over fifty children from ten or eleven wives.) Bin Laden père, a Yemeni who immigrated to Saudi Arabia in 1931, amassed an enormous fortune in construction, eventually being granted all construction projects commissioned by the kingdom; consequently he, and therefore all his children, enjoyed a close, privileged relationship with the royal family.

Hamida, on the other hand, was spurned by Mohammed's other wives and children, largely for her Syrian heritage. The nickname they gave her, "the slave" (*al abida*), carried down also to Osama, whose half siblings referred to him as *ibn al abida*, or "son of the slave." (He, after all, had no Saudi parentage; their mothers were all of Saudi blood. He was an outsider, and an inferior one at that.)

Hamida, however, was by all accounts proud, independent, and distant—all perhaps reasons why she and Mohammed divorced shortly after Osama was born—a development that the young boy, on top of the sting of ostracization and bullying by his half siblings, may well have experienced as further rejection.

Nonetheless, even after the divorce Osama spent much time with his father and is believed to have greatly revered him, making Mohammed's sudden death in a helicopter crash in 1967 all the more traumatic to the then ten-year-old Osama. That the pilot of that flight was an American may or may not have played a role in the adult Osama's profound hatred for America and its people.

But Osama's reaction to his father's death surely also was filled with conflict and confusion. His father, however devoted, was also known to beat him cruelly. Was young Osama then, in the face of his father's death, relieved as much as he was grief stricken? Did he come to enjoy his privileged position as the man of the family, even at that young age? (There is a certain poetry in the fact that this son of a builder made his name in the history books by destroying two of the tallest buildings in the world—a kind of castration, you might say, right in line with Oedipal theories.)

Osama did, however, inherit an enormous fortune; the reported amounts vary, but it was in any case many tens of millions of dollars—certainly more than enough to subsidize his high-flying life as a late teenager at school in Lebanon, where he zipped around in a chauffeur-driven Mercedes and partied, according to Robinson, at chic nightclubs with a wild group of "playboys" and the occasional prostitute or two.

But the outbreak of civil war put an end to the festivities, and Osama, now seventeen and married to the first of his four wives (though still evidently living it up as a bachelor would), was called home and sent to university in Jeddah.

It was here that bin Laden first found his deep religious faith. He became involved with the Muslim Brotherhood and formed a strong personal bond with Abdullah Azzam, a radical Islamic scholar who has been called the "godfather of jihad."[3] Azzam's ideas later, according to a *New York Times* obituary of bin Laden, "would underpin Al Qaeda."[4]

Beginning in 1979, with the start of the Soviet-Afghan War, Osama became involved in the Afghan resistance, helping to support the mujahideen both with weaponry and jihadist recruits. With Azzam he organized groups of Arab fighters, naming the operation "al Qaeda," or "the Base." "To would-be recruits across the Arab world," the *Times* reported in 2011, "Bin Laden's was an attractive story: the rich young man who had become a warrior. His own description of the battles he had seen, how he had lost the fear of death and slept in the face of artillery fire, were brushstrokes of a divine figure."[5]

It was a long way from being "the slave's son."

And he reveled in it. What's more, he seems to have matched the two identities together, creating an even more magnificent myth: this "slave's son"–cum–royal prince, now a warrior king—it was the kind of story one might spin about the birth of the Messiah. And as the years passed, it seems, Osama bin Laden increasingly adopted that story as his own.

Indeed with Russia's retreat from Afghanistan in May 1988, bin Laden was already riding high on his own legend: he returned to Saudi Arabia prepared to take his jihad further.

In 1990 the Iraqi army invaded Kuwait. Still convinced of his prowess as a military hero, bin Laden offered his services to the Saudi royals, certain he would repeat his success in driving back the Iraqi enemy and protecting the kingdom. They turned him down. According to the *Times*, "'He was shocked,' a family friend said, to learn that the Americans—the enemy, in his mind—would defend [the kingdom] instead. To him, it was the height of American arrogance."[6]

The truth is, for bin Laden, it was personal. America had again asserted its strength and power as greater than his own. Worse, they had done so in collaboration with the Saudis—those very people who had, in the personification of his own Saudi half siblings, bullied and insulted him as a child. The rejection—by his own nation, no less—was a slap in the face Osama could not, and never would, forgive. He fled to the Sudan and soon began his plot against America. He made his first strike at a hotel in Yemen that housed American troops—though the soldiers had in fact already left for Somalia when the bomb went off. A year later he celebrated the 1993 bombings of the World Trade Center in New York.

In 1995 Saudi Arabia revoked his citizenship. He was now a man without a father, and without a fatherland.

But he was still, at least in his own mind, a great and noble warrior, a leader of brave armies that had conquered the Russian superpower in Afghanistan. While plotting further attacks and strengthening his armies, he began speaking of "My Islamic Nation" and writing speeches directed to "my people."[7] And while he lived an increasingly ascetic life by this time (his family was not permitted to use air conditioners or refrigerators, for instance, let alone wear fancy clothes as his Chanel-loving mother had done), he remained ever aware of the swarthy, exotic figure he had cut as a young man in Beirut: in 1997, when interviewed for CNN, the *New York Times* later reported, he had his team of media advisors edit out any "unflattering shots."[8]

Now fully committed to his mission to lead a holy war for Islam, bin Laden began writing fatwas. The first, dated February 1998, states, "We—with God's help—call on every Muslim who believes in God and wishes to be rewarded to comply with God's order to kill the Americans and plunder their money wherever and whenever they find it."[9] The wording is noteworthy: as counterterror expert and political psychologist Jerrold Post observes in his 2002 paper "Killing in the Name of God," "According to bin Laden's fatwah, it is not bin Laden, but God, who has ordered religious Muslims to kill all the Americans, God, for whom bin Laden speaks with authority."[10]

That sense of authority only grew. That same year he told *Time* magazine's John Miller, "I am confident that Muslims will be able to end the legend of the so-called superpower that is America."[11] "In its place," reports the *Times*, "he built his own legend, modeling himself after the Prophet Muhammed, who in the seventh century led the Muslim people to rout the infidels, or nonbelievers, from North Africa and the Middle East. Just as Muhammed saw the Koran revealed to him amid intense persecution, bin Laden regarded his expulsions from Saudi Arabia and then Sudan in the 1990s as signs that he was a chosen one."[12]

Osama bin Laden, in other words, had become, in his own mind, the messenger for God. It was perhaps the final phase in his development as a pathological narcissist.

Most people think of narcissism as a kind of extreme vanity; and indeed Osama bin Laden was quite vain, as videos of him found after his death revealed: concerned about his appearance to his followers, even in reclusive exile he dyed his beard black and carefully rehearsed his speeches on video before broadcasting them.

But pathological narcissism—or what psychoanalyst Otto Kernberg also terms "malignant narcissism"—goes further, often becoming what Post describes as "the most dangerous political personality."[13] The pathological narcissist is characterized as much by his craving for attention and acclaim as by his fury—both of which stretch far beyond his grasp.

Many is the woman, after all, who gazes into the mirror in the morning, hoping to see a beautiful reflection gaze back at her; but only one evil queen set out to kill Snow White for being more beautiful than she.

"The usual conception of the 'malignant narcissist,'" explains psychoanalyst and Cornell Medical College professor emeritus Aaron H. Esman, MD, "would be one who is totally self-concerned to a criminal extent (of manipulating or harming innocent others). It would be essentially equivalent to a psychopathic character."[14] Jerrold Post and others have described the syndrome as being characterized by "grandiose self-importance, a messianic sense of mission, an inability to empathize with others," and as Anne Manne puts it, "their susceptibility to feelings of humiliation, their desire to retaliate after suffering a narcissistic wound. This rage after a wound or blow to self-esteem is natural to the narcissist—if things don't go their way, the world will pay."[15] The rage of the pathological narcissist is fierce and often deadly.

That narcissism-violence link involves complex twists: shame, psychiatrists agree, frequently begets violence (as will be discussed in a later chapter); violence begets respect. In the same way, shame is a key ingredient in the cocktail that creates narcissism; from that shame comes fury; from fury, violence; from violence, again, the respect that the narcissist so deeply craves.

Psychiatrist and author James Gilligan describes shame as "the pathogen that causes violence just as specifically as the tubercle bacillus causes tuberculosis."[16] By contrast, in interviewing violent criminals, he says, he would "start to hear comments like 'I never got so much respect before in my life as I did when I pointed a gun at some dude's face.'"[17] Again: shame begets violence; violence begets respect. This is the paradigm these criminals live with. It is the paradigm that defines the lives and minds, too, of terrorists and of domestic abusers.

"Respect," of course, is a common goal, but the more so for those for whom honor holds a sanctified position. More, it is self-affirming when won through a kind of conquest, a form of establishing power-over, not simply power-alongside (as opposed, say, to the respect one might attain for having good table manners, or performing a difficult Mozart piano concerto without a single sour note, or saving the life of a drowning child).

Not surprisingly "respect" is particularly treasured also by those who feel (often rightly) they've never received their fair share—people who, like the man with his gun in "some dude's face," know only a lifetime of shame. Sometimes—often—that shame comes from the bullying of siblings or parents or peers. Sometimes—often—it comes from society: through racial discrimination, poverty, educational disadvantages. And as Anne Manne writes, "One response to the shame of exclusion and marginalization is violence, which enacts revenge at the same moment that it lifts the person out of oblivion."[18] Or put another way, in the words of James Gilligan, violence is about getting attention.

And attention, in turn, is what the narcissist craves most. Fail to pay it and he will grow enraged. In his humiliation—his sense of invisibility, of insignificance—he takes a stand: he will humiliate you back, you, the Other—and fill his soul with the power that this brings: the truck bomb on the street corner, the gun in the man's face, the knife to his wife's throat, his fist into her pregnant, swelling belly, until they beg for a mercy only he can give. He is king. He is a demigod. Entire nations come to him, asking for a prisoner's release. He demands his ransom. He calls the shots: even to presidents, even to dictators; and in this brave new internet-ed world, he can speak and everyone will hear him. They will tremble. Millions will watch as he holds the sword to the young man's neck. They will pay attention. They will know who he is, and they will fear him. Yes, they will.

And should the armies defeat him? He assures himself of God's praise, of his place in paradise. He deserves that, after all. And so he will not die. He is beyond death. As gods are.

Take Anders Breivik.

It was an idyllic sanctuary, an island surrounded by a gentle lake, where children gathered, playing guitar, hiking, laughing in the summer sun. On the afternoon of July 22, 2011, they had come as they did every year, the children of political leftists, for a few days of intense debate and equally intense leisure, away from their families, with few rules and much freedom.

And then the man arrived. He wore a uniform. He was handsome and heroic. He was strong.

He had a gun.

For more than an hour he pursued the campers across the island of Utoya, chasing them into the lake when they endeavored to escape, shooting into trees, bullets flying as he laughed, as if it were all a game, a camper's game, like "Capture the Flag." When he himself was finally apprehended, led away, the Norwegian Anders Breivik had taken the lives of sixty-nine children. Their bloodied bodies colored the lake, littered the fields, shook the world.

Psychiatrists were quick to diagnose Breivik as a pathological narcissist, a conclusion reached in part through interviews with the killer and in part through his online activities before the massacre, including a fifteen-hundred-page manifesto, "2083: A European Declaration of Independence," and his pronouncement of himself as a Knight of Templar. Extremely self-conscious and vain, Breivik, then thirty-two, had undergone plastic surgery in his twenties to change his nose and chin. He wore makeup, took testosterone supplements, and spent many hours bodybuilding at the gym. When police tried to take his mug shot, he complained the photographs were unflattering. He insisted, at the very least, on posing as a bodybuilder would, flexing his muscles for the camera. This was the image he wanted the world to know.

On the face of it, with the exception of their terrorist activities, Breivik and bin Laden couldn't be more unalike.

But in fact their lives were not so dissimilar at all.

The childhoods of those who go on to become malignant narcissists tend to follow a consistent pattern, usually involving "inadequate parenting," as Post puts it. Often there is an absent or semi-absent father. There may be a rejecting mother, or an overly indulgent one. According to Kernberg and others, among the many variables that produce a pathological narcissistic personality disorder are a combination of distant, un-loving parents (usually the father) or an overly doting, indulgent parent counterbalanced by an emotionally withholding one. This creates something of a conflicted self-identity: on the one hand, the child feels unworthy, shamed, rejected; on the other, he is assured that he is special, valuable, beyond all others.

Or the child of an abusive or distant parent may have an extraordinary talent, says Kernberg, either "a special quality which he exaggerates, or a source of admiration that replaces the lack of love and compensates for all the cruelty around him."[19]

Remarkably, studies by Patrick Amoyel, a French researcher involved in (Islamic) deradicalization efforts in France, show similar patterns. "The youth we follow come from all layers of society," he told *Le Point*, a French news magazine. "There is only one thing they have in common: a non-functioning family. They have experienced a dramatic divorce, they were abandoned, fathers have disappeared or abused their children. That leaves an existential void that becomes filled with ideologies."[20]

Bin Laden, of course, had his great wealth as a resource, which bought him power in Afghanistan, and a (probably mythical) heroism on the battlefields there that brought him admiration. Breivik had, in its place, a bizarre relationship with his mother, who at once repelled him but with whom he was at the same time pathologically intimate, literally climbing on top of her to kiss her. As a child, even by the time he was four, social workers had intervened twice, concerned about possible sexual abuse by his mother, who slept with him in her bed. And yet that same mother was also known to hurl verbal abuse at her son, telling him (frequently) she wished he were dead.

Like Osama, Anders grew up without his father's presence; his parents had separated when he was barely a year old. And like Osama, whose father died when the boy was only ten, Breivik's father cut off contact in Anders's early teens, a response to the boy's arrests for graffiti—the first signs, clearly, of his need for the world to remember his name. (The elder Breivik has disputed this, however, saying that it was Anders who cut ties.)[21]

Absent a father figure, Breivik, like bin Laden, sought guidance and power where he could, struggling for recognition and respect. Ironically, where bin Laden did indeed rule armies, Breivik was a one-man show. The Knights of Templar he led existed only in his grandiose, deranged mind.

Nonetheless both men saw themselves as the future leaders of the world, a world that, until they could fully conquer it, would remain evil, corrupt, and heading to self-destruction. They alone—the Islamist and the white supremacist—could save it.

Similar family patterns can be found in the lives of other terrorist leaders—and many jihadist foot soldiers. Tamerlan Tsarnaev's father was secular, but according to a lengthy investigative report on the family, he was also "deeply traditional" and known to beat his children on several occasions—daughters as well as sons. Yet to his mother, Zubeidat, Tamerlan could do no wrong: a friend told the *Boston Globe*, for Zubeidat, "Tamerlan was idolized. Anything he said was right. He was perfect."[22]

Like Breivik, Tamerlan Tsarnaev planned on being famous. And as with other malignant narcissists, somewhere in the workings of his mind, the "perfect boy" his mother called "handsome as Hercules" with a "masterpiece physique" clashed against his father's punishing demands and disappointments.[23] When he began boxing semiprofessionally in his teens, the *Globe* reports, "It was no mere matter of sport. For the Tsarnaev family, it was their passport to respectability and their ticket to success."[24]

For Tamerlan, who had arrived in the United States with his parents from Kyrgyzstan in 1993, boxing was also a chance to grasp the limelight, and he did. He dressed flamboyantly, showing up in silver high-tops, snakeskin pants, and with his shirts unbuttoned to the waist. He turned cartwheels in the ring.[25] And he fought hard, winning the Golden Gloves championships in 2009 and 2010.

But in 2009, now twenty-three, Tamerlan learned that as a non-U.S. citizen, he was ineligible for the national Golden Glove Tournament of Champions—a contest his family had always believed would send him to Olympic glory.

It was a crushing blow, and one he may well have received much the way Osama bin Laden took the news of Saudi's choice of America, not al-Qaeda, to defend them against the growing military threat posed by Iraq.

Or, for that matter, as does the evil queen, told by the mirror that not she, but Snow White, is now "the fairest in the land."

It was then, friends and acquaintances of Tamerlan Tsarnaev have said, that he began to radicalize, and started to turn against America.[26] Three years later, on a sunny Patriot's Day in 2013, in the heart of the "Cradle of Liberty," he did his best to destroy it.

* * *

But pathological narcissism and the patterns that create it are true characteristics not only of terrorist leaders but of their followers as well. Perhaps the most notable distinction is in the motivations: terrorist leaders (and especially Islamist terrorist leaders) view themselves as messianic, responsible for instituting change in the world. They are the power. The foot soldiers who follow them, by contrast, merely aspire to that kind of power and prestige—or to be part of it.

Indeed, it is a notable point in the trajectory of malignant narcissism: the fixating on a hero figure, a mentor of sorts, as Azzam was for Osama bin Laden. Through this figure they absorb their future power. As author Christopher Lasch notes in his classic *The Culture of Narcissism*, "Narcissistic patients, according to Kernberg, 'often admire some hero or outstanding individual' and 'experience themselves as part of that outstanding person.'"[27] In addition he writes, radicals generally "display, in exaggerated form, the prevailing obsession with celebrity and a determination to achieve it even at the cost of rational self-interest and personal safety."[28]

Think, for instance, of the typical suicide bomber. Generally raised in a lower-to-middle-class family and one of many children, he is frequently characterized as "shy" and "insecure" or "angry" (all words that have been used to describe Mohammed Emwazi, the ISIS terrorist also known as "Jihadi John," as a child). He may have fought against social ostracization and discrimination—a particular problem for Muslim youth living in the West—or he may have joined a gang, gotten involved in drugs, perhaps spent time in prison.

For the terrorist recruiter, such a youth presents an open target: promise him absolution for his sins, promise him revenge, promise him immortality, yes; but more, promise him fame. The suicide bomber, like the terrorist leader, is not forgotten. He can change the course of history. They will remember his name. Or hers.

In this, a little-noted dynamic between narcissists takes place. Lack of empathy stands as one of the more prominent characteristics of pathological narcissism—and it is seen over and over again in the response terrorists have to the destruction they cause. (Oklahoma bomber Timothy McVeigh, for instance, who killed 168 people—including nineteen children—in the 1995 bombing of Oklahoma City's Alfred P. Murrah Federal Building, told his biographers: "I understand what they felt in Oklahoma City. I have no sympathy for them."[29])

But the men who send youth into restaurants, or soccer stadiums in Paris, or young women into wedding halls in Amman,[30] strapped with explosives around their bodies and prepared to blow themselves up for Allah, show just as little empathy for their disciples. Unlike the victims of such attacks, who are strangers to the plotters, who are in theory the enemy, the suicide bombers and soldiers on the battlefields of terrorism are neither enemy nor stranger. No matter. For the pathological narcissist, other people are little more than tools, utilities to be used in acquiring whatever it is the narcissist may want. Osama bin Laden regularly beat his children. He experimented with poisons and chemical weapons on their pets.[31] And when seeking suicide bombers for the 9/11 attacks, Osama bin Laden urged his own sons to volunteer.[32]

Instead as it turned out he found nineteen other hijackers, dutifully bound to their hero and ready at any cost to attach themselves to his celebrity and power as a warrior for Allah. Think of the stardom, the literal immortality that awaited them in martyrdom, and the "existential void" filled by their mentor-hero's approval, the promise of celebrity and greatness.

Mohammed Atta, for instance, the hijacker of American Airlines flight 11 that crashed into the World Trade Center's North Tower, was pampered and adored by his doting mother; he was her only son and, in a fashion that recalls Anders Breivik, reportedly "continued to sit on her lap until enrolling in Cairo University."[33] By contrast, his father, Mohammed Senior, was a harsh disciplinarian who urged him to "be more of a man" and to achieve great academic heights. Like many other suicide bombers and lower-level soldiers for jihad, Atta was considered "shy" and "polite," suggesting both a desire for social approval and a notable lack of self-confidence. He was a perfectionist, eager to please his macho father without losing the love of his emasculating mother.

Bin Laden and al Qaeda offered an alternative: a way to prove his manhood to his father, reward his mother with his martyrdom, and be celebrated by the father surrogate, the "outstanding individual" who was Osama bin Laden.

Interestingly, while Atta was raised in Egypt, similar patterns appear in the radicalization of Western Muslim youth as well. An extensive study by Hans Werdmölder,[34] a Dutch criminologist and professor of law at the University of Utrecht, though it dates to the 1980s, remains relevant and eye-opening even now—or maybe now more than ever. With Muslim immigrants, largely from Morocco, streaming into the Netherlands and Belgium in the 1970s, problems emerged between the native Europeans and the immigrant cultures—conflicts that went beyond those of other immigrant groups of the past. Crime among Moroccan boys was significantly higher than the norm: 33 percent of all those between the ages of twelve and seventeen had had trouble with the law.[35] Unemployment, school dropout rates, drug abuse—figures for all of these were alarmingly high, not just in the Netherlands but in France, Sweden, Germany, Belgium, and the UK as well.

And the problems did not go away. Rather, as native Europeans began despairing of the "troublemaking Muslim boys," and as their jobless rates subsequently increased, racial tensions by the time of the 9/11 attacks had already led to a growing radicalization through the mosques. Aiding in this effort were the Saudi-funded imams and Saudi-sponsored schools, which taught Wahabbist—or extreme—interpretations of the Koran. Saudi funds also subsidized the production and distribution of booklets like "How to Be a Good Muslim," which teaches (among other things) the best way to beat one's wife.[36]

Most of these boys had come to Europe through family unification policies, joining their fathers who had arrived first as guest workers. In the years between, they had lived with their mothers in small rural villages with low literacy rates and strong traditional religious values. In the small towns and cities they lived in—unlike the European metropolises they later moved to—they were known to their neighbors, familiar faces in the local mosques and local streets. They had, in that small-town way, recognition.

Yet with their fathers gone, the boys ran the households. They commanded their mothers, their sisters, their younger brothers. Even mothers willing to try to discipline their sons, according to Werdmölder, largely failed.

Until their fathers came home on visits—or until the young men joined their fathers in Europe. No longer free to make the rules, many of these boys clashed with their authoritarian fathers as much as they did with the customs, values, mores, and unaccustomed anonymity of life in their new countries.

Those who were in their teens at that time are mostly in their forties today. Some have mellowed. Many have become significant figures in their new countries—politicians, authors, artists. Yet others have unwittingly become the fathers of a newly radicalized generation of young men who continue to clash with the cultures in which they live. And still others have become the new leaders, pushing these youths deeper into their radical Islamist visions.

This is by no means to say that every European Muslim is either radicalized or criminal. Those who are, in fact, form a small minority of the European Muslim population. But it is, however, to accentuate a pattern within the Muslim communities in Europe (and to a lesser extent, in America) that has helped facilitate narcissistic pathologies. And as these youth search for meaning, structure, and above all, paternal figures, some find themselves joining (radicalized) mosques, adopting a religious fanaticism among recruiters for jihad. Indeed, as psychologist Daniel Goleman noted in the *New York Times* in 1986, many children who grow up to become terrorists find strength and "solace" in joining these radicalized groups. "The group and its leaders play the psychological role of a strong, protective parent," he says.[37]

Put another way: stripped of their machismo, their power, their manhood, by their reduced status in their new society and the reappearance of their fathers as authority figures in the home, many such young men turned to other sources of power: terror—in the world, in the home, and far too often, both.

Decades later, they—and their children—still do.

* * *

On March 29, 2016, Seif Eldin Mustafa slipped into his seat on Egypt Air flight 181 from Alexandria to Cairo. He sat quietly, settling in, until drinks were served throughout the plane. Then in a quick, small gesture, he opened his jacket, exposing to flight attendants the suicide vest strapped on beneath. The plane, he said, would now change course and head, instead, for Cyprus—or he would blow the whole thing up.

His reasons were complex and occasionally confused: he wanted political asylum in the EU. He wanted Egyptian women prisoners released. He wanted to speak to his ex-wife.

Hours later, Mustafa surrendered to police on the tarmac of Lanarca International Airport in Cyprus. By then most of the passengers had either escaped or been released. The suicide vest, it turned out, was a fake, made of iPhone cases neatly bound with fabric.

But what had decidedly been real had been Mustafa's insistence on speaking to his former wife, Marina Paraschos, whom he had not seen, by his own account, in twenty-four years. In the course of that time he had been convicted on charges of fraud and forgery, escaping from prison during the 2010 uprisings against Hosni Mubarak. He returned to prison in 2014 and was released a year later.

Now he wanted to see his former wife again. But with his passport blacklisted, he later said, he did the only thing he could. And when the plane landed he dropped an envelope on the runway, saying it was a "love letter" to Marina.

It is hard to fathom the workings of such a mind, the thought patterns of someone so hard-bent on having his way that he would terrify dozens of innocent strangers, let alone ignore the highest levels of international laws against hijacking, kidnapping, hostage-taking, and terrorism.

But as it turned out, Seif Eldin Mustafa had that kind of mind: one empty of empathy, certain only of his entitlements and his complete innocence of all wrongdoing. His ex-wife put it succinctly: "He was a man who knew how to inflict fear and to create misery around him."[38]

The marriage between the two was brief, but Paraschos described those seven years as "a marriage of hell with threats, beatings, torture, and fear." That he might have hijacked the plane to see her and their children, she said, was simply not credible. In fact when their daughter Sofia was killed in a car accident in 2002 at the age of seventeen, Marina had called to let him know.

"What do I care?" he answered.

He did not attend the funeral.

Rather, Marina Paraschos told reporters, her ex-husband was only using her and her family as instruments, an excuse, a way of garnering sympathy, when his only real purpose had been to get to Cyprus. (The "love letter," it turned out, repeated the demand for sixty-three female prisoners in Egypt to be released.)

But clearly there was more to it than that. Mustafa, with his background in fraud and forgery (not to mention a hot market in false Syrian passports), could just as easily have found a way around the blacklisting of his own passport. What he wanted, at least as much as a flight to Cyprus, was fame. He was going to do this, and he was going to do it big. That he even posed, his face unmasked, while passengers on the flight took "selfies" next to him makes this all the more apparent; and so, as he was driven off after his first court appearance in Lanarca, he flashed a "V" for victory at the cameras—and the public.

Seif Eldin Mustafa was not a terrorist. He was a domestic abuser—and a pathological narcissist desperate for attention—and for power.

* * *

It was called the "trial of the century": the murder case against football legend and actor O. J. Simpson, accused of killing his ex-wife and her friend. From the famous pre-arrest chase that had the world watching as police pursued Simpson, who sat in the backseat of a white Bronco holding a gun pointed to his own head—the entire event broadcast on live TV—until the live coverage of the trial, it was not just a laying bare of issues around justice and race, around domestic abuse and the celebrity of heroes. It was the world's first reality TV show, and O. J. Simpson was its star.

Which was perfectly all right with him. As long as he came out the winner.

And he did.

Orenthal James Simpson always said he would one day be rich and famous. At his induction ceremony to the Pro Football Hall of Fame, his mother, Eunice, recalled, "He always said 'One of these days you're going to read about me.' And my oldest daughter would always say, 'In the police report.'"[39]

Eunice Simpson raised O.J. and his three siblings on her own: their father left when O.J. was only four, returning, according to a *New York Times* profile, only now and then "to punish his son with a belt." He "resented his father's absence," O.J. later said but made up for it in the close bond he formed with Eunice. The day he was arrested for the murders of Nicole Brown Simpson and Ron Goldman, the intensity of that bond became clear: before surrendering to the authorities, the forty-five-year-old football superstar insisted on calling his mother first.

He was not a model child. The leader of a gang called the Persian Warriors, and of a social club of boys he named (tellingly) "the Superiors," he amused himself as a young man with petty thievery and street fights.

He was a poor student, and as a result of childhood rickets, walked with bowed legs that made him move awkwardly.

Still, he set his sights early on a career in football and struggled both athletically and academically to succeed. Stardom finally came when he played for USC, where he won his Heisman Trophy in 1968 and married his first wife, childhood sweetheart Marguerite Whitley.

But while it is not known whether O.J. ever abused his first wife, he was—as he was later with Nicole—frequently unfaithful. The rules of life's games did not, after all, apply to Simpson, the Superior. Indeed it was this fact that so often seems to have ignited his rages against Nicole: he was accustomed to getting what he wanted—even if he had to steal it or fight for it, or, as it turned out, to kill for it. He could not abide Nicole gaining weight in pregnancy, which made her less of a "trophy" on his arm. (That the trophy-winner saw his own wife as a trophy is not, perhaps, insignificant: inanimate, an object without feeling, with no purpose or being but to announce his own greatness and glory.) He could not tolerate her speaking with her friends. And he could not tolerate being found at fault: when Nicole found an earring in their bed that was not her own, she accused him of having an affair. "He threw a fit," she wrote in her diary, "chased me, grabbed me, threw me into walls. Threw all my clothes out of the window into the street three floors down. Bruised me."[40]

When Simpson was ultimately exonerated for the murder in a decision most Americans, if not the rest of the world, found suspect, the verdict confirmed in the footballer's own mind what he had already always believed: that he was untouchable, a man above the rest. (Years later psychologist Patricia Sanders of the Metropolitan Center for Mental Health in New York would tell ABC News: "OJ is almost a textbook definition of what psychologists call a narcissistic personality."[41])

And in fact whether or not Simpson actually killed Nicole Brown Simpson and Ron Goldman on the night of June 12, 1994, he had certainly threatened to kill Nicole. And he had come close before, beating and kicking his then-wife so violently on New Year's morning in 1989 that when officers arrived on the scene she ran to them in terror, screaming: "He's going to kill me!"[42]

~~But she dropped the charges the following day, despite severe bruising, a black eye, and other injuries. Simpson was fined $700 and there was no more talk about it.[43]~~

But there were records. Documents introduced in the court case included a statement from Eddie Reynoza, who acted alongside Simpson in the film *Naked Gun 2½*, in which he claimed that the Heisman winner had threatened to behead his ex-wife's boyfriends if he ever caught them driving any of his cars—including the white Ferrari he had bought Nicole.[44] In addition, a limo driver recalled seeing O.J. smack her. ~~In a call to a battered women's shelter days before Nicole's murder, a woman named "Nicole" told a woman on the line that her husband—whom she described as "high-profile"—was threatening to kill her.~~

And Nicole Brown Simpson's own diary, uncovered after her death, recounted countless other incidents, including being thrown out of a moving car and beaten during sex. In a letter she wrote O.J., also uncovered after her killing, she described many of his barrages of abuse, both physical and emotional: She didn't dress well enough. Her pregnancy made her fat. In her moments of despair, she wrote:

In between [the births of] Sydney & justin, you say my clothes bothered you—that my shoes were on the floor that I bugged you—Wow that's so terrible! Try I had a low self esteem because since we got married I felt [alone]. There was also that time before Justin & after few months Sydney, I felt really good about how I got back into shape and we made out. You beat the holy hell out of me & we lied at the X-ray lab & said I fell off a bike . . . Remember!??[45] (Spelling and grammar as per original text.)

* * *

Let me tell you something about living with that kind of terror.

There are times when life is normal. There are times of happiness and laughter and romance. You think that it is over. You think you are protected. You think that you are safe.

And then like a bomb exploding in an airport, like men firing Kalashnikovs into a bustling Paris brasserie, it begins again. And even if you survive the beatings, the shootings, the bombs, you do not escape the fear.

This, too, is what abusers and terrorists have in common. It is not like, say, mass murderers, people like James Eagan Holmes, who killed twelve and injured seventy innocent moviegoers at a showing of *The Dark Knight Rises* at a theater in Aurora, Colorado, in July of 2012, or Adam Lanza, who massacred twenty children at the Sandy Hook Elementary School in Newtown, Connecticut, that same December. Like the terrorist, the domestic abuser uses violence to create change. He believes in the moral righteousness of his purpose. While he may deny the entire episode to the police, he will boast about it to his friends: "She had it coming," he'll say, or "I beat that bitch up bad," or maybe simply mention he "taught her a little lesson," "reminded her who wears the pants."

And she—we—wonder, shaken and confused, if maybe he is right.

We wonder, shaken and confused, if maybe we have not given him enough.

Or the terrorists enough.

If only we would give them what they wanted. If we only hadn't treated them that way.

"Why do you do this?" I asked him.

"Why do they hate us?" asked America after 9/11.

And so we tell stories. Nicole Simpson "fell off a bike." I "walked into a piano." "Fell down the stairs."

We do this because we live our lives powered largely by a sense of hope, of faith: that the beating will stop because he promises it will. That the attacks will stop because our security systems are strong enough. That we are safe because we've finally moved out. That we are safe because there are soldiers on every street.

Somehow, we believe, it will stop. It all will be okay.

And indeed it does stop—many times. Before it starts again.

Or we console ourselves with denial. It's not that bad, we say. We say it to ourselves, to one another.

"It's only a small minority of Muslims who are radicalized," the multiculturalists of Europe reassured us, largely before the rise of ISIS and its recruiters. "You can't really say that there's a threat." When confronted with O. J. Simpson's history of abusing Nicole Brown Simpson, his lawyers said, "Any attempt to characterize Nicole Brown Simpson as a 'battered wife' based upon isolated and widely separated incidents ignores the substantial evidence of a loving relationship which spanned 17 years."[46]

What, then, is "enough"?

We keep forgiving, keep forgetting, keep looking away. And still it happens, over and again; because unlike the perpetrators of other forms of violence, the terrorist and the batterer thrive not just on the violent act itself, on the revenge. They thrive most on the fear that they instill, on the trembling, on the power. ISIS did not, after all, need to videotape Jihadi John's executions, or the live burning of Jordanian Air Force pilot Muath Safi Yousef Al-Kasasbeh. These things they did, in part, to star in their own movies, for celebrity; but even more, it was to leave the world to shiver at their feet.

And yet—millions of men (and women) around the world are raised without fathers, or with strict fathers and overindulgent mothers. Some (but not all) become pathological narcissists. And of those, some, but certainly not all, become terrorists, or beat their children or their wives.

What is it that makes the difference?

CHAPTER 2

THE SHAME AND THE POWER

Anders Breivik was obsessed with his face—its imperfection, its too-feminine chin, its proportions—and so he paid a surgeon to fix it. What is fixed, you may say, is repaired. What is repaired, is saved.

"Saving face" is what the massacre at Utoya was really all about.

For Breivik, Muslims and the left-wing non-Muslims who forge much of their political support threatened the supremacy of the white male Christian culture of his homeland. And if it threatened them, it threatened him: not because of any particular violent action—there had been no Muslim terrorist attacks on Norwegian soil—but by numbers, by the growth of a non-white, non-Christian population; and by their influence on such things as school holidays, the presence of halal butchers, and similar "assaults" on his society (and for all this he blamed the leftists). White Christians were losing power, losing ground: and a man who loses power, loses face.

According to James Gilligan,[1] in a 1977 study by criminologist David Luckinbill of seventy murders that took place between 1963 and 1972, "in all cases, the murderer had interpreted his violence as the only means by which to save or maintain 'face' and reputation and demonstrate that his character was strong rather than weak in a situation that he interpreted as casting doubt on that assessment of himself." School shooters, too, have almost universally indicated a desire to prove themselves in some way, to someone: if not to "save face" then perhaps to achieve it, to be known, admired, recognized, to be "the face of" power, or heroism, or victory, or strength.

* * *

It is a complicated word, "shame." We speak of "having shame" and "feeling shame"—denigrating, punishing terms that somehow suggest scandal or malfeasance; and then we ask of those whom we call out for scandal: Has she no shame? As if shame would have made her better behaved, was needed, was a trait to be aspired to.

~~Indeed in many Middle Eastern, Southeast Asian, and North African cultures—Muslim cultures—shame is what women are required to have; they must avert their eyes and cover their bodies and their hair and even sometimes their faces, but should they bring shame to their families, culture (and sometimes law) demands that they be punished heavily, even killed.~~

Here is where "shame" becomes a synonym for "dishonor." But they are not always the same thing.

In French, for instance—the language of *Charlie Hebdo* gunmen Saïd and Chérif Kouachi and of the seven terrorists responsible for the November 13, 2015, Paris attacks—one of many words for "shame" is *le dommage*, which parallels more the use of "shame" as ~~"pity" or "unfortune," as in: "what a shame"—*quelle dommage*.~~ We've all known moments of such shame, shame that is painful, that bruises the edges of our pride: the time we lied about not going to school and got caught; the time we shoplifted a candy bar and our mother marched us back into the store to return it and say I'm sorry; the time the prettiest girl in school teased us about our shabby clothes, or the captain of the baseball team said "we don't want to play with you."

This is *le dommage.*

But *le dommage* also has other meanings: "hurt," for instance, or "damage."

It is this kind of existential shame—soul damage—that can shape violence and narcissistic rage. It is the profound humiliation that inspires a feeling of worthlessness, of being viewed with utter contempt, defiled and stripped of human value. It is a shame like no other.

* * *

Among the remarkable qualities of shame, of shamefulness, is the fact that, unlike so many other emotions, we do not all respond in the same way. When something amuses us, we laugh. If it saddens us, we cry. But there are those who will respond to shame, to that profound sense of humiliation and "damage," by turning inward, hiding, escaping to a safer, inner place. Many become depressed or even masochistic, certain that the good of things is far too good for them. So deep and so all-encompassing is their shame that it becomes self-loathing. Or they loathe the shamer. And still others loathe both, alike.

The first two become violent, acting out their rage—either against themselves or others; BBC correspondent Bridget Kendall found, for instance, that female terrorists, particularly suicide bombers among the Sri Lankan Tamil Tigers, turned to terrorism "after they had been raped and wanted to end the shame to themselves and to their families."[2] Similarly, former white supremacist Shannon Martinez joined neo-Nazi groups in her American town of Temperence, Michigan, after being gang-raped at a party when she was fourteen, because, she says, "I hated everything; I hated everyone. Part of me was like, *They gotta take me in! Who's worse than the Nazis?*"[3] And Farhana Qazi, author of *Invisible Martyrs* and the first Muslim woman to serve in the U.S. government's National Counterterrorism Center, also notes that some women choose to become suicide bombers after suffering trauma. "Suicide terrorism is a choice," she writes, "explained by feelings of helplessness; a tendency toward risk-taking; and an intense anger, resulting in harm to others as well as self-harm."[4]

Finally, those whose disgust and loathing are directed both at others and the self can become easy fodder for terrorist recruiters, who promise not only revenge but redemption: martyrdom, heroism, greatness. They are the ones most likely to turn specifically to terror, seduced by its lure of purpose, brotherhood, and meaning. Together they forge an army, a community, a fraternity of brothers who reinforce one another's importance and the valor and supremacy of their shared mission. White supremacist groups in the United States therefore take on names like "Global Crusader Knights," "Confederate White Knights," or "American Renaissance." Islamists highlight the sacredness of their missions with a shared mythos of heroism in martyrdom.

This especially—the sense of a greater cause with the promise of redemption, even admiration and glory—is what most makes the shamed a threat to the rest of us: if not redemption through martyrdom, if not power through destruction, then the heroism of the fight for a greater good—for example, the power of white men, the resurrection of the South, the freedom of Palestine, the rise of a global caliphate, and onward.

Few people understood this so well as ISIS leader Abu Bakr al-Baghdadi—and he used it as perhaps his most powerful weapon, recruiting the young Muslims of the world to his battle and his cause. Even in proclaiming the establishment of the Islamic State, he seduced men—and women—with a call to their deepest longings, and the promise to fulfill their most romantic, power-craving dreams. Victory, and so the world, he vowed, would soon belong to them:

The time has come for those generations that were drowning in oceans of disgrace, being nursed on the milk of humiliation, and being ruled by the vilest of all people, after their long slumber in the darkness of neglect—the time has come for them to rise. The time has come for the ummah of Muhammad (peace be upon him) to wake up from its sleep, remove the garments of dishonor, and shake off the dust of humiliation and disgrace, for the era of lamenting and moaning has gone, and the dawn of honor has emerged anew. The sun of jihad has risen.[5]

"Dishonor." "Humiliation." "Disgrace." And the rise of "honor" through jihad.

The kind of shame that drives violence, then, drills well into the core of a person's sense of self. It forges, from the earliest years of life, the psychological mechanisms, the character and impulses, that he (or she) needs simply to endure a childhood of abuse and humiliation. It is, in other words, what builds the pathological narcissist he becomes.

This is why shame matters.

* * *

But it isn't always a matter solely of personal humiliation and abuse. Even more frequently it is societal, an element so carved into the culture that it shapes the sensibilities of every person in it. A CIA profile of Arabs, for instance, observes, "Blame, fault, or error accruing to an Arab personally brings his immediate fall from social grace and a loss of dignity or face. He therefore feels revulsion and bitterness for anything that tends to compromise him in this way. . . . Knowledgeable Arabs realize that their people and countries fall in some measure short of the progress and development that some other nations have achieved. Unable to find themselves at fault for this, they are naturally led to seek the cause of their troubles in outside sources—the will of Allah, the imperialists, Israel, family and personal obligations and many wrongs which have been done them. This saves the collective face from appearing defective and allows those who can accept subjectively-interpreted facts to maintain their sense of personal dignity and self-confidence."[6]

Similarly, even in writing of shame and its influence on violent criminality, Gilligan quotes Eyad Sarraj, a founder of the Palestinian Independent Commission for Citizen's Rights: "What propels . . . Palestinian men, and now women [to blow] themselves up in Israeli restaurants and buses . . . is a long history of humiliation and a desire for revenge that every Arab harbors. . . . Shame is the most painful emotion in the Arab culture, producing the feeling that one is unworthy to live. The honorable Arab is the one who refuses to suffer shame and dies in dignity."[7]

One has only to look at the conflicts between Israel and Palestine, where, some experts say, it is a combination of cultural envy and humiliation bred by Israel's economic successes and technological sophistication that (partly) inspires Palestinian suicide bombings.[8]

Hence Arab culture's shame in the face of Western progress; hence the resentment of downtrodden or oppressed Muslim immigrants in the West; hence the violent fury of so many Muslim boys treated as kings by their mothers, beaten by fathers whose manhood they threaten simply by their own, or shamed by unspoken sexual abuse that takes place among Arab and Muslim men.

Enter the recruiter, who promises him eternal honor and manhood, who calls him a warrior for Allah.

Not coincidentally it is precisely these same feelings of "humiliation" and "disgrace"—and indeed "saving face"—that are key ingredients in the building of the narcissist (just think of the myth of Narcissus himself, and his desire to save the image of his own face). Hence what the CIA describes doesn't define the role of honor and shame only in Arab culture. It reflects, too, the importance of honor (and fear of humiliation) among white supremacists, who tend to blame immigrants, feminism, liberals, and (often) Jews for their communities' higher levels of joblessness, poverty, and inability to adapt to socio-technological changes. It is, in fact, the essence of honor culture, and honor cultures have no single geography or religion. As Joseph Burgo, author of *Shame: Free Yourself, Find Joy, and Build True Self Esteem*, puts it, "Narcissism is the flip side of shame. . . . Someone who becomes a narcissist decides 'I am not going to be this shame-ridden damaged person, I'm going to be this winner.' These defenses take hold, and the more shame they feel the more they defend against it."[9]

In fact narcissism "is the primary defense against shame," Burgo maintains. "When people suffer from an unbearable sense of shame, they often seek to elicit admiration *from the outside*, as if to deny the *internal* damage." In the end, he says, "They will battle to the death to defend that sense of self whenever it is challenged."[10]

"Battle to the death." And if that death brings martyrdom and glory, all the better: the sense of self as grand and all-important, as immortal hero, triumphs, after all.

It is, then, the narcissist for whom the notion of fault, inadequacy, imperfection, is too painful to bear—just as it is for terrorists and abusers. This basic fact underscores the essentially narcissistic character of honor cultures. The "inability to find themselves at fault" makes projection—even at the expense of fact—their most loyal weapon in the "battle to the death to defend that sense of self whenever it is challenged." It is the magic sword the narcissist carries in his rage against his perceived assaulter-insulter-demeaner, a sword imbued with the extraordinary power to reclaim his fallen honor, restore his manliness, his "face."

As it was for Anders Breivik.

And as it was as well for American-born terrorist Anwar al-Awlaki, one of the most successful recruiters of Western Muslims to al Qaeda, who inspired countless lone-wolf terror attacks and of whom the Combatting Terrorism Center at West Point declared, "No figure in jihadist propaganda has eclipsed his well-established brand."[11] As described in Scott Shane's *Objective Troy*, al-Awlaki frequently patronized prostitutes, even after his marriage—an activity that bred what Paul R. Pillar describes in the *New York Times Book Review* as "a kind of self-loathing that took the form of 'fury' at his native country for producing the sinful sexual culture that had so enticed and entangled him."[12] (It was also a prostitute who tipped al-Awlaki off to the fact that the FBI was investigating him; surely the realization that even the FBI knew of his "sinful acts" would have added both to his shame and "fury" at America: their fault, not his.)

It is the echo of a refrain heard across the playgrounds of the world: the taunting schoolchildren and the victim who warns of his revenge: "I'll get you," he snarls, perhaps aloud, perhaps only to himself; but the shame-revenge chain has already begun.

Al-Awlaki may or may not have understood French. But he was fluent in Arabic. And while the French *dommage* can be a synonym for damage, in Arabic, the word for "shame," *fadiha*, is far worse: not just "dishonor" and "disgrace," but "outrage."

And so the fury—the outrage—that it breeds, such as the violent global response to the so-called Mohammed cartoons, which Muslims worldwide denounced as an insult to—shaming of—the Prophet of Islam.

On September 30, 2005, Danish newspaper *Jyllands Posten* published a series of twelve cartoons of the Prophet Mohammed, including one depicting him in paradise, standing on a cloud, hand raised, and crying, "Stop! We're running out of virgins!"

Though most of the sketches were in no way derogatory, images of Mohammad are banned in Islam, and many Muslims therefore view such images as an affront to them and to their faith.

Condemnation was swift, with reprimands from the leaders of the countries of the Organization of Islamic Corporation and the Arab League. Within months two hundred people had died in violent protests worldwide and attacks on Danish and other Western embassies in Syria, Lebanon, and Iran. More than a decade later the *Jyllands Posten* cartoonists continue to face attempts on their lives; the editors of French satirical magazine *Charlie Hebdo*, which produced its own Mohammad cartoons, are now dead—killed in a terrorist attack on their Paris offices in January 2015; and in May of that year two Muslim men stormed a "Draw Mohammad" contest in Garland, Texas, shooting and injuring a security guard before being shot dead by police.

Insult. Outrage. Disgrace. Shame.

Violence.

Redemption.

* * *

It is, again, crucial to understand the nature and experience of this particular breed of "shame." It is not the shame of embarrassment. It is not defined by episode—that mortifying moment when your skirt flies up in the wind, or you discover a "kick me" sign taped to your back, or you've had too much to drink at the office party and everyone is staring at you on the dance floor—but by an existential sense of worthlessness, a nearly sadomasochistic self-hate so excruciatingly painful that only refusal to recognize or accept it makes living with it possible. One compensates—or rather, overcompensates—with a mask of self-love, a carefully and elaborately crafted costume designed to convince not just the world, but oneself, of his or her extraordinary superiority and worth. Tear into that costume at your own risk; its wearer will fight "to the death" to re-establish its credibility—and so, his own. And he will kill you for the injury, if he must.

What "shame" is not—what "shame" in this sense can never be—is guilt. To the contrary guilt cultures—which describes most Western cultures—are defined by a sense of personal responsibility and a capacity for empathy often absent in cultures of shame or honor. The humiliation that narcissists, and especially violent narcissists, experience requires audience, as "saving face" does—how one looks to others. Notes Mark Zaslav, PhD, "Unlike guilt, in which we feel regret about an action that caused harm to another person, shame is a private, self-focused experience in which we feel bad, deficient or inadequate. In the parlance of modern psychology, guilt is about *doing*, while shame is about *being*."[13]

What creates that state of being?

* * *

Gilligan and others point primarily to a child's experience of physical or emotional abuse or both. Swedish researchers found that "men who have been subjected to serious violence in childhood are more prone to feeling shame. When being violated they tend to react more directly with aggression towards both sexes."[14] In his doctoral thesis Peter Jansson of the School of Health and Welfare at Jönköping University observed that "violence and aggression are often preceded by feelings of shame. Shame is one of the strongest and most painful emotions that can affect a person. Instead of directing the anger inwards, against oneself, the aggression is directed towards others. It is a protective mechanism."[15] Often, say the researchers, that shame is converted into actions that reflect "the influence of masculinity norms with toughness, aggression and violence."[16]

The damage done increases in the worst cases when a parent attempts to disguise that abuse as "love": "I'm only doing this because I love you so much and want you to be safe," they say, while locking a child in the closet, or as a father beats his daughter for leaving the house without her *hijab*, or scarf. Still others might offer the more commonplace, and unfathomably confusing, "it's for your own good."

As if pain and punishment were to be valued, as a gift.

In Arab culture, and that of most Muslim societies, however, this is an established norm. "The principal technique of childrearing in [feudal-bourgeois Arab families] is shaming," writes Halim Barakat in *The Arab World*, "while the learning process emphasizes physical punishment and *talqin* (rote-learning) rather than persuasion and reward. . . . Furthermore, children learn to link love and certain expectations, and they consequently experience guilt feelings whenever they annoy or fail to perform their duties toward their parents."[17] (I would, however, replace the word "guilt" here with "shame.")

It is important to note that this is not unique to the Arab world. Writing under the name "Umm Salihah" ("Mother of Salihah") one woman described child rearing in her native Pakistan to the *New York Times*: "It was the norm to be smacked by your parents, extended relations and anyone else that happened to be around and in a bad mood. It was also okay to be given a smack 'round the head for doing something you shouldn't have, for watching someone else doing it, maybe for not stopping them or maybe again because someone was in a bad mood."[18]

The name "Umm Salihah" is telling: Muslim women often change their name after the birth of their first son to show that they are the boy's mother: "Umm Salihah" means "Mother of Salihah," for instance, as "Umm Osama" would be "Mother of Osama." No longer is she her own person, with her own name, or even her husband's wife; from the moment of her son's birth, a (traditional) Muslim mother wraps her entire identity in the personhood of her son in what Barakat calls the "morbid" nature of mother-son relationships in Muslim families.[19] ("Your Paradise," according to one hadith, "lies at the foot of your mother.")

But such overbearing, saccharine mothering, when a child feels smothered (as with Tamerlan Tsarnaev) or even sexually intimidated (as with

Breivik), can also engender confusion in the child, both inside the familial dynamic and in the larger world. The messages it gives are filled with contradiction. If the child is so lovable, why is he being assaulted and punished? If he is so bad, how can he be so lovable? Does showing someone you love him include insults and beating? If you love me, why do you hurt me? If I'm so terrible, how can I ever be good enough for you to love me again? And if his mother so adores him, what is wrong with her?

Against this is the punishing, contemptuous father, the father who beats his son while assaulting him with words targeted to destroy his self-esteem, his sense of worth, even as the mother dotes on him, as O.J.'s did, or Breivik's, bin Laden's, and Tsarnaev's. If he is both Beauty and the Beast, then surely, he decides, his father's abuse is a sign of jealousy. He is better than the father. He must be. He is more handsome. He is more brave. He is godlike in his manliness.

And yet: the gnawing voice will not grow silent, the echo of his father's wrath, telling him again and again that none of this is true, that he is nothing, he is worthless. Sheer physical truth makes clear his father is the more powerful.

"Please," we say. "I love you." We hope the words will melt his heart. We hope he will forgive us, just because we love him. "Please don't hit me. I did nothing wrong, and if I did I didn't know, but I love you and I'm sorry and don't you still love me?"

"Please," Americans asked after the attacks on 9/11. "Why do you hate us so?"

Consequently, notes Seth Meyers, PsyD, in the cases of what he calls "sadistic narcissists," "the most important point to understand is that the drive to punish or upset others on a regular basis typically stems from an individual having been on the receiving end of confusing, mind-twisting behavior from a parent early in life."[20] Love is violence. Violence is shaming. Is pain. And yet it is love that is so desperately wanted.

* * *

Before he shot and killed forty-nine people at the Pulse nightclub in Orlando, Florida, one warm June night in 2016, Omar Mateen had a habit of picking on girls in elementary school.[21] The son of Afghan immigrants, Omar was the only boy among four children, with a history, by the time he was a teenager, of bullying and fighting that he would come to wear as a badge of honor in adulthood: according to the *Washington Post*, he was expelled from school and charged with battery in 2001, and though the school ultimately never prosecuted, "Mateen listed the incident on job applications as an adult."[22]

It made him, after all, more of a man.

As, apparently, being connected to terrorists did, at least in his own mind. When the Twin Towers were struck on 9/11, ~~Omar announced to his classmates that Osama bin Laden was his uncle. His father, however, whom the *Washington Post* describes as bearing his own "grandiose notions" of outside influence in Afghan politics, soon put an end to that talk: when called to fetch Omar from school, a classmate recalled, he walked straight over to his son "and in the courtyard in front of everyone, the dad slapped him right across the face."~~[23]

Did he feel degraded? Probably: within a year he was working out prolifically and by 2006 he was taking steroids. At the same time, he was frequently getting himself into bar fights, as if testing the power of his masculinity—that manhood so publicly assaulted by his own father in the schoolyard.

He soon found a different way to channel his masculinity: to join law enforcement. In 2006 Mateen took his police officer's oath—only to be dismissed from the force six months later. Undeterred he found a job as a security guard with one of the world's largest security firms, G4S—with a license to carry a gun.

All he needed now was a wife.

Mateen and Sitora Yusufy wed in April 2009. The trouble between them began early. "He beat me," Yusufy later told reporters. "He would just come home and start beating me up because the laundry wasn't finished or something like that."[24]

It is so often like this.

* * *

Yasmine Mohammed, a Canadian ex-Muslim activist, had many such days. In her memoir *Unveiled: How Western Liberals Empower Radical Islam*, she recalls the moment just a week after she wed her first husband, whom she later learned was a member of al Qaeda.

She had opened up the curtains on a sun-filled afternoon.

Then he came home.

"Are you a whore?"

"What?" I had no idea what he was referring to.

"You want the whole world to see you parading around here with your hair uncovered?"

"I haven't left this apartment all day."

"The windows! You don't think people can see you? Do you think it's only one way? Are you stupid? Walking around here like a stupid, naked, whore."

"It's the 17th floor!"

I finally understood his issue. "No one can see 17 floors up and in! Are you worried about someone in a helicopter flying—"

And then he hit me.[25]

* * *

The first time I read Yasmine's words, I tremble. I cannot find my breath. Then I start to laugh; but it is a crazy laugh, uncontrolled.

I, too, have written about the curtains. As I catch my breath, I search my files for the story that so closely echoes hers.

He comes home as he usually does, shortly after six. I am still at my desk in a nook beside the living room.

"Why are the curtains open?"

"Um . . . because I like the sun?" I am suddenly searching for answers, for the right answer, for him not to be angry. And I can see that he is angry, even if I don't know why. "The view?"

"Neighbors can see in."

"Not really," I say, and hope I sound reassuring. "You really can't see that far in—look how little we can see in the apartments across the street. You can barely see beyond the windowsill."

"They can see," he says. "What do you do, stand in the window all day? Did you close them when you got dressed this morning, or did they see that, too?"

The truth is, I don't remember.

I tell him that I closed them anyway.

But I am now on guard. The next day I draw the curtains shut before he returns home.

This time, he is glowering before the front door even shuts behind him. "What the fuck?" he says.

"What?"

"The curtains."

I look at him, and then at the curtained windows.

"Did you spend the whole day like this?" He is screaming now, his face inches away from mine. "It looks like a drug den, like a crack house in here. What the fuck is wrong with you?"

I am without words. Seeking peace, I go to open them again. He stops me as my hand touches the raw cotton, the creamy cotton curtains we hung together when we first moved in, the first gesture of a home—our first home together. When he pushes me, my back slams against the wall.

"Just leave them," he says. His face is dark and furious. The curtains move, just so slightly, in a passing breeze.

* * *

Mateen's machismo went beyond his wife abuse: he returned to his earlier boasts of having family connections to al Qaeda and associations with the Boston bombers Djokar and Tamerlan Tsarnaev.[26] In many ways these claims were not just a way of strutting his imaginary power and fame; they were a means of identifying with his father, the self-proclaimed leader of the "Islamic Revolutionary Transitional Government of Afghanistan"—an organization that does not, in fact, exist.

But just as bin Laden had destroyed buildings when his father had constructed them, Omar could do his father one better: he could be a real revolutionary, a real warrior, for a real government that would, he believed, one day rule the world. On June 10, 2016, he pledged allegiance to the Islamic State.

That night, he went to war for them.

* * *

For Omar Mateen, destroying the gay nightclub where he had, to his own shame and self-loathing, gone in search of male company was a matter not just of religious righteousness or a phallic competition with his father—though it was certainly both of these. More, with every bullet that he fired, he put a wound into the shame that so ensnared him.

Notes Gilligan, "a . . . precondition that enormously increases the chance that shame will lead to violence exists when the individual has been socialized into the male gender role that, in our patriarchal culture, means he has been taught that there are many circumstances in which one has to be violent in order to maintain one's masculinity or sense of masculine sexual identity and adequacy, and in which a nonviolent man would be seen as impotent and emasculated, a coward, wimp, eunuch, boy, homosexual or woman, a man who has 'no balls.'"[27]

Omar Mateen killed for Allah; but most of all he killed to be a man.

It was a matter of honor, after all.

CHAPTER 3

HONOR SOCIETY

Honor. On your honor. On my honor. The highest honor.

We live in a world where honor holds power, where we honor the powerful; a world where honor, as it were, is honored above almost anything. We honor our fathers. We honor our gods; we bow to our leaders; we speak of Your Majesty, Your Excellency, and Your Honor. We bestow honors. We give our word of honor. We will fight for our honor: in the hit song "Glory of Love," Peter Cetera promises, "I am a man who will fight for your honor; I'll be the hero you're dreaming of."

The "hero" is the man who "fights for honor." This is more than a romantic conceit, more than a fairy-tale icon (though it is that, too). The archetype of the warrior defending honor is responsible for the killings of more than five thousand women every year globally (so-called honor killings), for a significant part of ISIS's success in recruiting Western Muslims, and for the rise of white supremacism in Europe and the United States.

Honor cultures exist in a private universe, one increasingly alienated from our own society, with moral codes and values that in many respects defy liberal democratic ideals. The CIA reports on Arab culture point, for instance, to the importance of maintaining honor and dignity even above truth[1]—a frequent source of misunderstanding and conflict even in the course of diplomatic discussion. Similarly, patriarchal values that view men as the guardians of women—and their honor—are reflected not only in countries like Saudi Arabia and Iran but also in the honor culture of the American South. Notably, men in such societies are more alert to personal threats and more likely to use violence when feeling their personal honor is at stake. (This would also likely account for the fact that eight of the ten states with the highest rates of domestic abuse, based on homicide statistics, are located in the South.[2] Accordingly the rise of white supremacist groups in these states might also be a function of the "proud American" mentality, and the narcissistic injury—dishonor—carried down through generations, brought on by the South's historic loss in the Civil War.)

"Victims of violence, loss, and betrayal . . . struggle against powerful feelings of shame, guilt, grief, and the desire for revenge, and the death-like numbing that often accompanies prolonged exposure to trauma," psychiatrist Sandra Bloom, MD, reports in "Reflections on the Desire for Revenge."[3] "As victims, they have been helpless against the powerful perpetrator and their inability to protect themselves and others leads to both shame and guilt. Honor, pride, identity can only be restored by reclaiming competence—and yet reclaiming a perceived sense of competence often means unwittingly assuming the mantle of the perpetrator."[4]

It isn't just the Middle East and the American South where powerful concerns about honor color the mores of societies and families; honor similarly shapes social customs and conduct in much of Latin America, for instance. But it is, according to the late journalist Sandra Mackey, a specialist in the culture of the Middle East, there where honor most dictates culture. "Honor is the driving force of the Arab psyche," she writes in the classic *Passion and Politics: The Turbulent World of the Arabs*. Among Bedouins, she says, "all different kinds of honor from bravery in battle to generosity extended to guests to the sexual chastity of his sisters and daughters interlocked to surround the Bedouin ego like a coat of armor.

The smallest chink in that armor threatened to unhinge it, leaving the individual exposed to the greatest of all threats—shame. . . . In the end, and at any cost, honor had to be restored."[5]

Narcissism. Shame. Honor. In his shame he seeks to shame the Other. If the Other is contemptible, then he stands, he must stand, higher. The important thing is not to be below, beneath, even if it comes through force. Respect becomes confused with obedience, force with power, and power, honor.

And so the violence begins.

And so, the terror.

These interlacings are the knot that finally ties machismo together with the narcissist, abuser, and the terrorist, and form the noose that threatens to choke anyone who ventures close.

"There's a saying in my tribe," writes Pakistani women's rights activist Khalida Brohi, "Izzat mare, pen mare te maf: 'Even if I have nothing, I should have honor.'"[6] For this, she notes, one thousand women are killed in her country every year, their fate for having caused dishonor to their families, and above all to their husbands or their fathers, having caused them humiliation in the public square. A woman who does not succumb to the power and control of her master—a father or a husband most often, but occasionally a brother, even if he is younger—forces him to demonstrate, as if in rebuttal, the very power of his authority and strength. Beatings will inevitably follow, either in private or on the street. Family conferences will be called to decide on punishment. The woman's own mother may take part, not only in the discussions but in the vengeance; she, too, knows the importance of obedience. She, too, worships power. She, too, reflects her husband's honor. And if shame and humiliation drive violence, if violence restores power, power will restore honor, and all will be right again.

Aiya Altameemi understood this, even as burns blistered her body and the ropes that held her to the bed dug twisted bruises in her arms.

A nineteen-year-old Iraqi immigrant, Aiya Altameemi was living with her parents and younger sister in Phoenix, Arizona, when her father happened to see her chatting with a boy from her class outside of school. According to news reports, he grabbed Aiya and forced her into his car. Once home, he began to beat her, then held a knife against her throat before her mother, Yusra Farhan, intervened—but not to save her. Instead Farhan, with the help of Aiya's eighteen-year-old sister, padlocked Aiya to her bed before burning her across her face and chest with the back of a hot spoon. The girl remained tied to the bed until the next day.

What Aiya Altameemi recognized, what she in fact later defended, was that her father's—and so, her family's—honor was tied directly to her and her behavior. She had spoken to a boy—and as she explained later to the media, "We are Muslim. Our culture says no talking to boys, no boyfriend."[7]

There is a saying in Arabic: A man's honor lies between the legs of a woman. It's a powerful and far more complex idea than it may first appear. If a man's honor, after all, lies between the legs of a woman, then keeping his honor means maintaining control of her body—not just her sexuality but all her interactions with the world. Everything she does is a reflection on him; and so in large part his honor lies not only in her actions but in his power to control her actions, in any way he must: forcing her to wear concealing garments; forbidding her to leave the house; prohibiting contact with her family or friends; and when all else fails, the violence of his fist, of rape, of gunfire.

How better, after all, to prove his manliness? And how else, anyway, should he react to shame?

This, too, is what the curtains were really all about. (What is a veil if not a curtain?) Indeed "curtain" (or "covering") is the origin of the word "shame."[8] For my fiancé, for Yasmine Mohammed's husband, the exposure of our bodies—bodies that belonged exclusively to them—undercut their masculinity, betrayed their lack of full power and control over what we did, where we did it, and with whom. More, it allowed other men—even if only potentially—to have a part of what they saw as theirs and theirs alone. And what humiliation for another man to perceive them as so weak! (The lurid word "pussywhipped" comes to mind.)

And so the open curtains were a call to show the full force of his muscle, of his power, to make others tremble. Fear. Honor.

Like an angry god.

Notably Muslim groups aimed at protecting the rights of women make precisely this comparison. "In the most abusive homes, the father believes and socializes his wife and children to believe that whatever he wants the family to do is the same as what Allah wants them to do," explains the National Resource Center on Domestic Violence on its website. "He, in effect, makes himself into something of a god."[9]

* * *

Ironically in many cases of domestic abuse such violence often ends in sex—usually forced, but by no means always. He grows hot with the eroticism of his own manhood, a primitive, animalistic pride of conquest and of subjugation. But it isn't the woman he is making love to. He stands in his own glory, enthralled by his own manliness, and his orgasm is the medal of honor he confers upon himself.

So, as well, for the terrorist, who ties his honor and his manhood to a cause—particularly those who martyr themselves in the expectation of entry into paradise and Allah's eternal love. If they survive, they are heroes, celebrated as demigods, as bin Laden was after 9/11; if they do not, their mothers praise their memory. The Palestinian Authority even goes so far as to provide the families of suicide bombers lifetime financial support, a gift of gratitude for their sacrifice, given in their dead son's honor. For the terrorist, more than the death of the enemy, he seeks the glory of his act.

But in most cases there is even more. The terror act is personal, a way to prove themselves to their fathers, to their communities, to rid themselves of shame by making the ultimate act of valor. If Mohammed Atta's father considered him too feminine, too soft, Mohammed would show him just what a man he really was. He was not just brave; he was a fighter, he was a martyr, a savior of his people, and of their eternal honor.

"He walks with death and is thus inviolate; he is an idealist but a man of action, a fanatic of dedication and an archetype of self-sacrifice," writes

Robin Morgan. "His intensity reeks of glamor. Women, we are told, lust to have him. Men, we are told, long to be him. He is sexy because he is deadly; he excites with the thrill of fear."[10]

Herein lies the other vision of honor, the romantic vision, the hero vision, the one about patriarchy and machismo, where men protect their womenfolk not only from themselves but from those who would steal their "honor," their purity—which belongs, after all, not just to the women but to their men.

In this lies, too, the image of the warrior hero, the knight in shining armor, Sir Lancelot with his fierce and able sword, the prince who scales the tower to rescue the fair princess after he has slain her evil captors; and as he lifts her high in his strong arms and tosses her on the back of his powerful white steed, she wraps her arms around his muscled waist, and they ride off together, into a golden world where he will ever act as her protector, and she will love him tenderly in return.

He is the man who has fought for her honor.

He is the hero she's been dreaming of.

When ISIS recruiters approached Western Muslim men, this was the story that they told—a fairy tale expressly made for young men in search of love and glory. Come to the Islamic State, they promised, and find your pure young maiden here. She will love you for your courage. She will support you in your battle. You will be a man of honor, immortalized by your deeds.

* * *

But it isn't only the men. The same fairy tales drive many of the women who join the Islamic State and other extremist groups. "Every woman involved in terrorism is a romantic," a lawyer defending female Palestinian suicide bombers told Middle East expert Daniel Pipes, founder of the Middle East Forum.[11] Scholar Anat Berko, in her landmark study of these women, quotes one failed bomber in prison in Israel, who described her "perfect" husband as "muscular and strong . . . who would rule me and not be ruled by me." Another told Berko she had expected to go to paradise, where "I will be like a queen and sit in my kingdom and marry anyone I want to. I will marry someone who is handsome . . . and Allah will receive me."[12]

Similarly Safaa Boular, who was convicted of plotting an attack in the UK along with her sister and mother in 2018, was radicalized largely by a man she met online, Naweed Hussain, a British Muslim then living in the Islamic State. He flattered her, she told the court after her arrest. "He was very caring, very sweet, very flattering. It was the first time that I had received this kind of attention from a male."[13] He, too, wooed her with fantasies of honor and glory, telling her, "[Suicide] belts . . . are a must, even with you. Don't even be hesitant to pull da pin ok. Your honor is worth more than any kaffir's [unbeliever's] life."[14] The two wed in an online ceremony as they fantasized about their joint suicide bombing, and plotted an attack on the British Museum in London.

It is no different for white supremacists. Writing on the AltRight.com website in 2017, for instance, Wolfie James, an alt-right woman with a strong online following, posted "Seven Reasons Why Alt-Right Men Are the Hottest."

"The Alt-Right male believes he has a duty to perfect his physique and appearance in accordance with the inherent potential afforded him by European genetics," she explains. "As such, he is more likely to lift heavy weights, run fast, eat well, wear properly fitting clothes, and fashily cut his hair in a nod to Germany's golden age. There are no pajama boys in the Alt-Right, and the masculinity they exude is positively intoxicating. . . . [The Alt-Right man] fights for recognition of his identity, to secure the existence of his people and a future for white children. Rebels have always held irresistible allure, and Alt-Right men are no exception."[15]

* * *

We grow up on princess stories. We grow up in search of the man who will come to our rescue. We do not understand, just as children who are beaten do not understand, that our abusers are at once the evil prison guard and the prince who finally saves us. The little boy runs to greet his father every night—the good father, the kind father, the one who tosses him high up in the air and catches him, safe in his strong, fatherly arms. The rageful, senseless man who filled his father's body yesterday is gone, no longer exists, forgotten, his very being so horrific the boy decides he never will come back again.

Aiya Altameemi wept when her mother went to prison. "I want her to come home," she cried during the trial.

But of course she did: this was her mother, the mother who makes her dinner every night, who soothes her forehead when her body sears with fever, who sees she says her prayers, the mother who kisses her before she goes to bed, who smiles when she reads from the Koran, the mother who held her hand when they first landed in America from the war-ravaged home they'd departed in Iraq. She has already forgotten the mother who whipped her, who told her she should die.

I refused to understand the beatings hadn't ended.

Too often we who are the targets of terrorism refuse to understand: it hasn't ended either.

* * *

In the fall of 2014 two Austrian Muslim girls who had made *hijrah*—the pilgrimage—to the Islamic State announced that they wanted to come back home. Sabina Selimovic and Samra Kesinovic, ages fourteen and sixteen, had left for the Caliphate that April, lured by the dream, as they wrote in their farewell note to their parents, that they would "serve Allah and . . . die for him."[16] At least one of the two was pregnant, both having been married off to ISIS fighters when they arrived.

"I think they should be allowed back," I write a friend in an email.

"They made their beds," she answers.

I argue back: they are living with strangers they were forced to marry, men they do not love and who certainly do not love them; they are watching these men rip the heads off other women, crucify young men and leave them there to die.

"Look at these girls," I want to tell her, staring at the girls' photographs online, photographs taken before they had left home. "These beautiful girls with their brushed hair long and tied back behind their faces, their blue eyes articulated by liquid liner like they teach you on YouTube." I have seen the messages exchanged between teen girls in the West and female recruiters in the Caliphate, how from Europe to Aleppo they ask questions like 'can I bring my curling iron?' thinking they will be living in domestic bliss with their own houses and their own tied-back curtains and marble baths and no schoolwork and no one to tell them when it's time for bed. They do not anticipate losing their virginity to a stranger, or being beaten when dinner is not on time, or not well made, or not what he had wanted.

"They are in danger," I tell my friend.

"I have no sympathy for them," she says.

But I was one of them once. I chose to live with him. I chose to follow his dreams. I chose his fantasy. It seemed so romantic, just us in a two-room trailer, far from my upper-class Manhattan life, where I would write novels and poetry and he would work in a local gas station fixing cars, and we would have a garden. It would be like Hollywood.

We are mesmerized by such fantasies, by the Hollywood dreams. We want to save the men who need us, want to be good and kind; a good woman obeys her husband, is patient and loving and forgives. This is what we learn. This is who we want to be.

But when I had to run, when I needed to escape, I had someplace to go. These girls did not. They never do.

In 2015 reports came that Kesinovic had been killed trying to escape sex slavery in Raqqa, beaten to death with a hammer. She was just seventeen years old.[17]

* * *

If honor must be defended, so must honorability. For most men, whatever their cultural background, this includes their ability to support a family, the honorability of honest work. But in an honor system, psychologist

Dov Cohen, coauthor of *Culture of Honor: The Psychology of Violence in the South*, tells me, "your worth and your virtue and virility are all tied together."[18] Any man without work feels little worth and little virility; in an honor culture he also faces a kind of deep humiliation, a sense of weakness in his failure to provide, in his being, as it were, impotent—emasculated. As one former autoworker told the *New York Times* after losing his job at the GM plant in Lordstown, Ohio, in 2019, "People are going to get hungry, and when I mean hungry, I don't mean just for food. I think, once you get pushed to a point that you have nothing left. . . . Without the ability to feed my family and pay for my children and feed my children, what am I as a man?"[19]

In study after study Cohen and Richard Nisbett, the codirector of the Culture and Cognition program at the University of Michigan at Ann Arbor, have found that this kind of psychological injury is handled differently in honor than in non-honor, or what they call "dignity," cultures. In experiments "Southerners were made more upset [than were Northerners] by the insult, as indicated by their rise in cortisol levels and the patterns of emotional responses they displayed. . . . [They] were more likely to believe the insult damaged their masculine reputation or status in front of others. . . . Were more likely to show physiological preparedness for dominance or aggressive behaviors, as indicated by their rise in testosterone levels. . . . [and] were more likely to actually behave in aggressive ways"[20]

But consider how much more demoralizing it would be to recognize this loss of employment as the consequence of one's own failings, like dropping out of school, say, or drinking on the job, or doing imperfect work. For the narcissist, who makes no mistakes, the very idea is as unfathomable as it is terrifying, a threat to the shield of denial he wears over his own underlying self-doubt, the roar of applause he plays in his own mind to drown out the shaming words of his father, his classmates, his mother.

Instead he comforts himself with the knowledge that it is not his fault but that of the other guy, the immigrant, the Hispanics, the blacks, the Jews, the Other. Through their presence, and—worse—their continued procreation, they form an existential threat to the continued power of white men: those filthy black folk he—*he*!—is required to check in with at the unemployment office, who show up in his local park; those Spanish-speaking Mexicans who are taking all the jobs, while his tax money supports their families and not his own. And not just them: also those women, those feminists, who demand equality in place of servitude. Them.

They—*them*—now become the target of his rage. He will force them into submission, violently, if necessary, until he has emerged again victorious—virile, virtuous, heroic, a man of honor once again.

This is the pattern that imprints itself on the minds, superimposes itself over the visions, of white supremacists across the world—including former white supremacist Christian Picciolini, whose Italian immigrant parents worked long days, making him feel ostracized from his classmates. As he recounts in his memoir *Romantic Violence*, because they worked so much longer than his friends' parents did, he was always the last one to be picked up at school—a fact he experienced as a disgrace.[21]

Then he found the skinheads.

Suddenly everything made sense. "Honest, hardworking white people like my parents were being forced to work day and night just to make ends meet to support their families, while the minorities sat back collecting unemployment and pumping out more crack babies to boost their monthly welfare checks," he writes.[22] From the skinheads he learned that none of this was coincidental. And it wasn't mere misfortune. Rather it was part of a careful, greedy, insidious Jewish plot to promote integration, immigration, and abortion as part of a program of white genocide (a theory also championed by Breivik). It wasn't his parents' fault at all; it was the Jews'.

And so fighting against it, even if the "Jewish-run media" made the skinheads look like "violent thugs," was laudable, something to be proud of, even noble, Picciolini decided. It was "for the good of a cause. An honorable cause. Protecting the white race."[23] Within little time he had gone from being the shamed, bullied kid to a member of an elite society. "I was somebody now," he writes. "I belonged. Was valued. Honored. And feared."[24]

* * *

Picciolini was part of an early wave of white supremacy in America, but he shares much with those who joined later, as he does with extremist Muslims and domestic abusers, whose stories are told throughout this book. His mother adored him, thought him brilliant, encouraged him to be a doctor.[25] His father, however, tended to smack him one from time to time, until, at the end of his freshman year in high school, Christian finally hit him back. So, too, with Tamerlan Tsarnaev, whose mother doted on his every move, his every word (his body was a "masterpiece," she said), while his father was a strict disciplinarian.[26]

By contrast, interestingly, before their radicalization, the British terrorist Safaa Boular and her sister Rislaine suffered regular abuse from their mother, Mina Dich, with whom they lived after their parents divorced, though they maintained a good relationship with their father. According to the BBC, "Their Moroccan-French parents split up acrimoniously when Safaa was aged six. While she maintained a good relationship with her father, the 18-year-old accused her mother during the trial of being violent and vindictive—the head of a chaotic home where the girls had to fend for themselves." Their mother was often brutal and uncontrollable, throwing objects, cursing and insulting the daughters. "And then the next day," reports the BBC, "she would act as if nothing had happened and say she loved her children deeply."[27]

In between, it seems, she paid little attention to the girls at all. When Safaa was first diagnosed with Type-1 diabetes, her mother doted on her. "She treated me like a little princess," Safaa said at her trial. But "after maybe a month or so, my mum got used to it."[28] The feeling of being cast aside, of having lost her place at the center of her mother's life, her throne, made her especially vulnerable to Naweed Hussain's endearments, his flattery and charm.

Picciolini was valued. Safaa Boular was loved.

Indeed in all these cases, and so many more, the internal battle between feelings of enormous worth and utter worthlessness worked to build pathological narcissistic characters that could only be made to feel whole through insisting on honor—prestige, worship, obedience, call it what you ~~will—cost what it may~~. He will slaughter the woman who forsakes his honor. He will annihilate the man who steals it. And he—or she— will exterminate those who attack the honor of his people: his race, his gender, his country, his faith, his god. Only then can the debasing words be silenced, the humiliation, destroyed.

"When a man feels his reputation, person, family or property is being threatened, the honor code dictates that he has the right to defend his interests, even to the point of violence," according to Ryan P. Brown, managing director for measurement at the Doerr Institute for New Leaders at Rice University. "Indeed, he is *expected* to do so if he wants to be known as a 'real' man."[29]

This then becomes yet another thread that knots terror directly to abuse: ~~if honor is the most precious thing in a Muslim man's life, and if indeed he will kill to claim it—if, in fact, the feeling of dishonor raises his physiological readiness for aggression and violence—then the dishonor imposed on him not only by a woman, but by the West, by American power, by the mere fact that even to communicate his ideology, to spread his call for vengeance, he needs the help—the *help*!~~—of American inventions like personal computers and cell phones and YouTube and Twitter and encrypted message systems that run on cellular technology, this alone is a humiliation. Wh~~at causes him dishonor can only be—must be—destroyed; and he must be the one to do it. Only then, beating his chest and roaring into the wild over the enemy's dead body, can his own honor be restored, and with it, his return to power.~~

The will, as it were, to power.

~~Hence the only solutions available to him: if it is his wife or daughter who humiliates him, shames him, then inevitably she must~~ be beaten, ~~even put to death; but so, too, must those who seek to destroy his people, the *ummah*, through warfare, through racism, through their insistence on another god, through the unbearable truth of their power.~~

"In a typical honor culture," Brown and his colleagues write, "reputation is everything. . . . More specifically, men in honor cultures strive to build and defend reputations for strength, bravery, and an intolerance for disrespect. Women in honor cultures typically strive to build and protect reputations for loyalty and sexual purity."[30]

* * *

Likewise the notion that a man's honor "lies between the legs of a woman"— even the wholesale oppression of women in the Arab world—finds its match in white supremacist culture (betraying yet another link between white supremacist states and those areas where domestic abuse festers). Indeed Nisbett has found that articles written by students in Southern college newspapers "describe honor-related killings in ways that are more sympathetic to the killer."[31]

The role of women is crucial here. In the end misogyny is not just among the cornerstones of domestic abuse; in such cultures, it is a vital part of male honor, and its presence in families and cultures perpetuates the cycle of honor, machismo, oppression, humiliation, anger, rage, and violence.

There are even socio-scientific explanations for this. Being the family leader, the support to his family, the caretaker, as part of the machismo identity of men from every culture, Western and non-Western, is rooted in our ancestral past. The man hunted. The woman cooked and cared for the house (or cave) and children. The higher levels of testosterone, the more powerful musculature, of males of all species makes clear that this is part of our evolutionary chain. But with it, over millennia, has come the socialization of roles: A man supports his family. A man feeds his family. A man is the patriarch.

It is a position of dominance. Of control. Of power.

Of honor.

Yet increasingly men in the West are feeling that power, that honor, being pulled out from under them. And in trying to right themselves, according to a 2018 Anti-Defamation League (ADL) report that links misogyny with white supremacy, many have found a place in white supremacist groups, which they often first encounter online in conversations about the sluttiness, the arrogance, the disrespect, the impertinence, of women.[32]

"There is a robust symbiosis between misogyny and white supremacy;

the two ideologies are powerfully intertwined," according to the ADL. "While not all misogynists are racists, and not every white supremacist is a misogynist, a deep-seated loathing of women acts as a connective tissue between many white supremacists, especially those in the alt right, and their lesser-known brothers in hate like incels (involuntary celibates), MRAs (Men's Rights Activists), and PUAs (Pick Up Artists). This cross-pollination means the largely anonymous outrage of the men's rights arena acts as a bridge to the white supremacist and anti-Semitic ideology of the alt right. After all, it's not a huge leap from 'women's quest for equal rights threatens my stature as a man' to 'minorities' and women's quests for equal rights threaten my stature as a white man.'"[33]

These men vehemently repudiate the feminist movement and decry any progressive laws it may have fostered. The notion of women working outside the home threatens their position as the ruler of the house, the lord of the castle, as it were. It is the princess story once again, and a good princess, in a proper castle, should be devoted to her king, her lordship, as they say in all the fairy tales.

Remarkably (or maybe not so remarkably) women in alt-right, white supremacist groups tend to feel the same way. Women, "especially in romantic relationships, and even when they are mistreated by their romantic partners, are encouraged to 'stand by their man' so as not to shame the family name or suggest that their partners are *not worthy of respect*," says Brown (italics mine).[34]

It's an identity so tied to who we are as women, particularly in America, that Tammy Wynette's crooned "Stand By Your Man" became of the most successful songs in the history of country music.[35]

* * *

Shannon Martinez and I first meet on Skype, introduced by an assistant to Chris Picciolini. Also a former neo-Nazi, Martinez was a co-founder, with Picciolini, of the Free Radical Project, a nonprofit that counsels people who are starting to question their radical views. Immediately I like her—her fast pace, her energetic determination. And I am moved by her story, so similar and yet so different from my own: Shannon was raped by two boys at a party when she was just fourteen. Her fury, her debasement, were what set her forth on her path to violence and hate. As she described it in a 2018 interview with *Quartz*, "Within six months, I was so consumed with rage, and self-loathing and self-hatred. I needed somewhere I could be angry, and the angriest people in my subculture were the skinheads. They started fights at every show, and I loved that. I wanted to fight. I hated everything; I hated everyone. Part of me was like, *They gotta take me in! Who's worse than the Nazis?* All I had to do was espouse this ideology, which was almost a relief to me, because I had this ineffable hate. To be able to just say, *I hate all these types of people*—it was almost kind of a relief to have that hate have a focus, instead of just being all-consuming. And eventually, I got further and deeper in, and only associated with other skinheads."[36]

Yet while she found strength in the white supremacist community, in many ways it also reaffirmed much of what she had experienced as a rape victim—and at the same time, ironically, made the rape easier to accept. "When I was inside the movement," she tells me, "many of the relationships I had, interpersonal relationships, were very violent, abusive. It's an entire ideology based on objectifying people perceived as weaker, so naturally women didn't fare well. At the same time, I associated all of that toxic masculinity with strength. I felt strength and protection from it." Women in these mind-sets, she says, "attach themselves to the power associated with the aggressor."[37]

This is true; but it only tells part of the story. To accept what we have endured—as the targets of battery, as the victims of rape—holding to the idea that this is in some way a confirmation of your place as a woman within the system, that good women submit and forgive and stand behind their men—helps us regain a sense of our dignity, at least within ourselves. However the experience left us, whatever self-hate we may have felt, whatever fury we have no place to unleash, whatever confusion spins our sense of reason, there is this, given us as an absolute: This is how it is supposed to be. It's okay.

It's okay.

Compare this with the systemic oppression of women in Saudi Arabia, in Pakistan, in Afghanistan, and the willingness of fundamentalist Muslim women to submit to it—their insistence, even, on perpetuating that same imbalance of power through the ways they raise their daughters and their sons.

As white supremacism spreads in our part of the world, experts are becoming more alert to these connections as they shape our own communities. "More and more," Heidi Beirich, director of the Southern Poverty Law Center's Intelligence Division, declared in June of 2019, "we see misogyny as the gateway drug for extremists."[38]

She was right, except for one thing: This is nothing new. It's the way it's always been.

CHAPTER 4

EMPATHY

For eleven years Cleveland bus driver Ariel Castro kept three young women locked inside his house, chained to their bedroom walls or to a pole in the basement floor. "Like a fish," Michelle Knight, the eldest of the three, recalled after she and the others had been freed. Every single day of those eleven years, he raped them. To quiet their screams he put a motorcycle helmet on their heads so nobody could hear. When one of the women became pregnant, he beat her, stomping on her abdomen, pounding her face and body with dumbbells. She miscarried five times.

When the girls escaped on May 6, 2013, police arrested Castro; at his sentencing three months later, he turned and faced the court.

"I am not a violent person," he said. "I am a happy person inside. . . . There was harmony in our home. I was a good person."[1]

For twenty minutes, he carried on this way, insisting over and over, "I am not a monster." He was a victim, he said, the victim of childhood sexual abuse and sexual addiction as a result. None of it had been his fault. And anyway, "There was harmony in our home."

Castro wasn't telling the truth, but he also wasn't lying: what he told was the truth as he knew it. It was no different, really, than my boyfriend calmly handing me a tissue to soak the blood that ran from my face onto the floor, hot and sticky in the summer heat, as if the crashing of his fist and a broomstick across my face had not been what set it flowing, as if none of it had even happened, and as if, if it even had, it wasn't really a big deal.

Empathy is one of the wondrous traits that, like imagination, distinguish us as human. It is what makes civilization possible. It is, as Sandra Bloom writes, an "essential prerequisite for social and moral development."[2]

But children who are raised in violence and shame often grow up with an abyss in their characters where empathy should be. Think of the man they call Jihadi John, stroking the blade of his knife across the necks of his victims as they kneel helpless at his feet. Think of Dylann Roof, who shot nine people dead at a church in Charleston, South Carolina, in 2015 and later told psychiatrists he had no regret: "You don't feel sorry for people that you don't identify with," he said.[3] Think of Mohammed Bouyeri, who shot and stabbed filmmaker Theo van Gogh on an Amsterdam street then calmly pinned a note into his body with a fileting knife before walking casually away. Later he would tell Van Gogh's mother, "I don't feel your pain."[4]

"I don't feel your pain." It's the shoulder shrug of every terrorist, the twisted sneer of the abuser.

In fact much of the time he doesn't even recognize what he's done as harmful. "The single best predictor of children becoming either perpetrators or victims of domestic violence is whether or not they grow up in a home where there is domestic violence," according to a 2006 UNICEF report. "Studies from various countries support the findings that rates of abuse are higher among women whose husbands were abused as children or who saw their mothers being abused. Children who grow up with violence in the home learn early and powerful lessons about the use of violence in interpersonal relationships to dominate others, and might even be encouraged in doing so."[5]

And so: "Everybody does it," Boris, my boyfriend at seventeen, insisted. "Even if you don't see it, your father hits your mother behind closed doors." It was reality as he knew it, reality as he had seen and felt it all his life; he, too, knew the force of his father's angry, heavy fist.

And Ariel Castro, who claimed he was severely physically and sexually abused as a child, was so fully immersed in his own pleasure, he did not feel the pain he caused his victims; everything was "harmonious" because he was simply incapable of recognizing the situation from any standpoint but his own.[6] In the life that he'd created for himself—anything he wanted, any time he wanted it—he couldn't even notice the suffering of his captives. The motorcycle helmets didn't only silence their screams for the neighbors; they silenced them for him, lest the sound penetrate his consciousness, and so, what little left he had of conscience. No wonder he was "happy."

But something else happens in the face of so much violence and pain, a survival response of the psyche: you grow numb. For a child it becomes "normal." For an adult, at least in the West, the first time leaves you bewildered, shocked, dizzy—not from the blow but from your efforts to understand it. (Did I do something wrong? Am I that unaware? Or is it his fault, his wrongdoing? Is he crazy, is this a side of him I never knew, and what do I do now?) The second time you are stunned again, not only because of the pain, not just because it's happened, but because now it's happened twice.

But he is sorry now, he is so sorry, will you please forgive him, he begs, and you say yes, of course you will, because you love him after all, and you'll try not to annoy him in the future, and it won't happen again *and anyway it's not so bad.*

And now neither of you can feel.

* * *

Something similar happens on the battlefield, a known element of the PTSD that so many soldiers experience after war. The first time you kill, there are nightmares. There is horror. But it isn't long before it's just

another day on the job, another challenge that you meet. ~~You grow numb.~~
~~Compassion no longer stands in your way.~~

Shannon Martinez refers to this as a "sociopathic break": she, too, had no sense of the cruelty of her acts as a radical supremacist during the time that she was active in the movement. It is a phenomenon she is still trying to understand. "I was highly empathic before I joined the movement," she tells me, "and I really am now; but while I was in it I was not empathic at all."[7]

~~Which is why ISIS leaders began putting nine-year-old boys through jihad training, having them count the lashes of a person being whipped, or watch beheadings and the mass assassinations of firing squads as part of their normal days at school—consciously and deliberately destroying each child's ability to comprehend the magnitude of the violence—and so, his capacity to feel another's pain.~~[8]

The same occurs in the face of trauma such as violence in the home, or rape. Remember, for instance, the words of Michelle Knight, after being freed from eleven years of captivity and torture with Ariel Castro: "What happens is hard at first. You don't really want to adapt to it. You don't want to comply. You don't want to do anything at first.

"But then you find yourself saying, why not? I'm here, just let him get it over with. So you slowly end up saying, 'OK, whatever, just do it, go.'"[9]

She could have been speaking for millions of other women.

She could have been speaking for me.

* * *

Because they themselves are so much shaped by just this kind of trauma—emotional, physical, or both—narcissists, too, are numb, their emotions frozen in the depths of their cold-hearted, self-absorbed soul. ~~Trapped within their own battle between self-loathing and self-aggrandizement, they have little left to feel for others, to feel what another person feels, the abstract capacity to "walk in another man's shoes." The fact is, they don't care what the other person feels.~~ It's immaterial: other people, after all, exist only as objects whose purpose and value is no more than to satisfy their (narcissistic) needs, the demands of their own ego. ~~The narcissistic rage that they unleash should others fail to do their part is what fuels the violence; but it is the fact that the narcissist does not feel, cannot capture, the agony he inflicts on others that makes the violence possible.~~

And because he is numb; because no one else is fully human; because he is driven to fulfill his own needs with a hunger that makes all obstacles, all critics, into enemies to be destroyed; because his own pain and inner shame is more than he can bear, he feels nothing. He doesn't dare.

As Ariel Castro could not listen to the screams of his captives when he raped them.

* * *

~~In some ways it would seem that remorse is one quality that distinguishes the terrorist from the domestic abuser: the abuser is always sorry, always apologetic.~~ Although not generally true for those in honor cultures (particularly Islamist) who ma~~y view violence against women as necessary, even religiously mandated, in the West that apology is so frequent and predictable it has become part of a recognized paradigm, true even of abusers who go on to commit terrorist acts~~. After every episode a "honeymoon" begins. He begs forgiveness. He buys her flowers. The romance rekindles. He takes her out, the bruises hidden behind sunglasses and Dermablend, to dinner. He makes promises.

~~But he is not sorry for her pain, a pain he doesn't understand.~~ He rather ~~is consumed with his own hurt, and the fear that she might leave him, the abandonment (or banishment) that so terrifies him (and perhaps also tormented him as a child).~~ Incapable of feeling for another, he is focused only on himself and the chance to grasp back his power, on the declaration of his place. He will do whatever he needs to do.

Still, in the beginning, we believe him. Boris brought me roses. Rick bought me a ring. Or he would climb into bed beside me, stroking, kissing. I didn't want him there. I didn't want him near me. But he was titillated by his own display of manliness, the flex of his own muscle, just as much as he feared that I would leave him in the morning.

Later I understood, as we all eventually come to understand: ~~The apology was never about remorse.~~ It never grew from a root of empathy; and ~~it had nothing to do with me.~~ He could look at me directly in the face, blood across my cheeks, and only shrug his shoulders. The roses, the ring, were to soothe himself, insurance against losing me, a strategy of self-preservation. ~~The only pain he felt then was his own.~~

This isn't always the case, of course. Actor Charlie Sheen, who has a long history of domestic abuse (such as "accidentally" shooting his then-fiancée Kelly Preston with a .22; throwing furniture at and threatening to kill ex-wife Denise Richards; and strangling third wife Brooke Mueller, whom he also allegedly held at knifepoint), remains entirely unapologetic and does not seem ever to have tried to hide it. Like the *Charlie Hebdo* terrorists, he blames his victims: he has called them money-hungry, exploitative, liars.[10]

Here, too, honor comes into play. A woman who announces to her husband she is leaving; a Muslim daughter who talks to a boy outside of class; a young girl who rebuffs her employer's flirtations—all are nothing when put against his honor. She becomes, as it were, "collateral damage" in the war to protect his place, restore his mastery.

So, too, for the wife who smiles at a man who is not her husband—or the man who smiles back; the boy who loses the sculling competition; the young man who tells his father he is gay.

~~To be clear, this is~~ not merely about revenge, ~~especially for men: once more, it is the manhood he regains through violence, alongside reclaiming honor, that matters.~~ "Much of the 'mystique' of the culture of honor is tied in explicit ways to concepts of manhood," Richard Nisbett and Dov Cohen explain in *Culture of Honor: The Psychology of Violence in the South*. "Who a man is in such cultures has everything to do with how much of a man he is—defined in terms of toughness and respect. Honor in this sense is based not on good character, but on a man's strength and power to enforce his will on others."[11] Dishonor me and I will dishonor you; I will take back my strength, my pride, by causing you to fear me.

~~But for women, too, honor matters. Many of the women in prison for terrorism in Israel~~—most of them suicide bombers whose missions

failed—took up their missions as a way to redeem themselves after a rape
or divorce. "Sometimes," writes Anat Berko, "women are raped and forced
to blow themselves up to expunge the shame."[12]

Similarly when Yasmine Mohammed's husband beat her the first time,
she ran to her mother, whose apartment was just downstairs, seeking solace
and support. Sitting comfortably in the study of the home where she
lives with her new husband, the nightmare of those years finally behind
her, she recalls, "I said, 'He beat me up! Look at my bruises! Look at my
eye!'" But her mother only answered, "That's his right. Allah gave him
the right to hit you."[13]

Telling this story now, Yasmine pauses. "I couldn't believe it," she says.
She is holding her coffee cup, solid, warm, between her hands. "I said,
'Yes, but it wasn't justified. He did it for a stupid reason.' But she only
said, 'Okay, but look: you've only been married a week. If you divorce
now, everybody in the community is going to think he divorced you
because you're not a virgin. You will have tarnished your reputation, you've
tarnished my reputation.' So even that—the idea of honor was the bars
on the cage. It's what keeps you in line the whole time—this fear of dishonoring the family."

"So then, it wasn't about you, then," I say. "Your pain didn't matter.
It was about how she looked—to others. To the community. And in the
mirror." Like Narcissus.

* * *

On an August afternoon in Jerusalem, the sidewalks steamy with the
heat, families and friends enjoying a late and lazy lunch crowd the tables
at a Sbarro pizzeria. There is chatter, children laughing, teenagers leaning
into a conversation. A rabbi orders a baked ziti, then sends it back to be
rewarmed. When a man and woman enter, no one notices. No one notices,
either, when she leaves, and he remains.

Then the explosion. It rocks the restaurant, pulls the walls down, turns
the daylight dark. Later the rabbi, Binny Freedman, will recall, "And then
the screaming began. An awful, heartrending sound. . . . A woman was

lying near the steps to the back. Her eyes were staring straight at me, following me. So full of pain and longing, sadness, and despair. I dropped down beside her trying to elicit a response to see if she could speak. And then I watched the life just drain out of her. I tried to get a pulse, to no avail. She died there, on the steps in front of me."[14]

Outside a woman stood sobbing beside a stroller, her baby covered in blood, lifeless.

Four small children, three teenagers, and eight adults, including a pregnant woman visiting from the States, were killed in the attack. It was a month and two days before the horrors of 9/11 would bring the dark shadow of Islamist terror to the West.

The man and woman who entered the restaurant just before the blast, Izz al Masri and Ahlam al-Tamimi, were both members of Hamas. The guitar case they carried with them was filled with ten kilos of explosives, and hundreds of nails, nuts, and bolts to maximize the damage. As planned, al-Tamimi left the restaurant before the bomb could be set off, allowing her to escape safely. Al Masri died in the blast, another suicide bomber hoping for paradise and glory.

But fate had other plans for al-Tamimi. Arrested shortly after the attack, she was sentenced to sixteen life terms before being released prematurely in 2011, part of an exchange deal between Israel and Hamas to secure the freedom of Israeli soldier Gilad Shalit. She now lives in Jordan, avoiding extradition to the United States.

~~Eighteen years later, she has no regrets.~~

"Why am I, Ahlam, considered to be a terrorist when I am part of a movement for freedom and liberation?" she asked during a March 2019 interview with Al Jazeera. You can almost hear the indignation in her voice, the self-importance that she, of such great warrior achievement, should be put down as a mere "terrorist." She continues to insist, as she did in 2006, "I am not sorry for what I did."[15]

Not sorry. Like Bouyeri, she does not feel their pain.

Nor are al-Tamimi and Bouyeri alone. Timothy McVeigh, as noted previously, told biographers he had "no sympathy" for the people of Oklahoma

City. Dylann Roof told his psychiatrist that he was "like a Palestinian . . . after killing nine people." According to the psychiatrist's report, "He said the Palestinian would not be upset or have any regret because he would have successfully done what he had tried to do."[16] And Brenton Harrison Tarrant, who filmed himself for a Facebook audience as he gunned down and killed forty-nine people in a mosque in Christchurch, New Zealand, in March 2019, published a manifesto before the attack, along with a Q&A interview with himself.

"Do you feel any remorse for the attack?" he asks himself.

"No," he answers. "I only wish I could have killed more invaders, and more traitors as well."[17]

To feel remorse is more than mere regret. Notes George Simon, an expert on domestic abuse, "Feelings of regret have nothing to do with perceived moral rightness or wrongness. . . . Remorse is the experience of deep anguish over something you've done that has created a bad circumstance or caused injury to others (whether that injury was intended or unintended)."[18]

But someone who has numbed himself to all feeling, or for whom such sentiments as remorse and empathy feel effeminate—and therefore disgraceful—sorrow, empathy, and remorse become impossible. And for a narcissist, for whom others exist merely as objects to serve his grandiose ego, the notion is almost laughable. How should he feel empathy for something he cannot comprehend as having any real existence or feeling?

"In my experience," writes James Gilligan, "the men who had been most rejected and humiliated and abused, and were therefore most lacking in self-love, behaved as if they could not emotionally afford to love others, as if they needed to conserve whatever limited amounts of love they were capable of for themselves. For that reason and others, it was hardly surprising to find that the most frequently and extremely violent men appeared to be remarkably incapable of love for, or empathy with, other people: after all, how else could they have hurt them with so little inhibition? What was equally striking was the complete lack of feelings of guilt and remorse for the pain and loss they had inflicted on others."[19]

And so he dehumanizes others—not only for himself but also, if he has taken up the mantle of leadership, for the cause. Hitler's brilliantly evil propagandist Joseph Goebbels called Jews "rats," which, like all vermin, had to be exterminated for the health of the people. White supremacists in America applaud as Donald Trump similarly calls immigrants "animals, not people" and warns that they are "infesting" American soil. At best they are too inferior, too repulsive, to be concerned about how they feel.[20]

Still, nothing could be quite so dehumanizing as the Islamic *burqa* or *niqab*—garments that cover a woman's entire body, including—and most importantly—her face. She becomes no longer a person, not even a living being with laughter and smiles and a wiggling of her nose. You do not see her lips part in disbelief, or press together in a kiss. You may see her tears form in her eyes, but you do not see them fall, the dampness they leave along her cheek.

Empathy for her would be like empathy for a brick.

Even a cockroach has a face.

But not a woman.

Was this, too, a part of why Ariel Castro covered his victims with motorcycle helmets—to make them faceless, and so, not real?

* * *

There is hard science behind this. In 2013, using magnetic resonance imaging to scan the brains of thirty-four people, half of whom had been previously diagnosed with narcissistic personality disorder, researchers in Berlin found that the ability to exhibit empathy is directly connected to the volume of gray matter in the brain—not just in healthy people but in narcissists. Pathological narcissists were found to have less gray matter in the left anterior insula, which is believed to play a critical role in emotional awareness and empathy.[21]

Other scientists at the Max Planck Institute have now actually located an area of the brain—the right supramarginal gyrus—that distinguishes our emotions from those of others—essentially an empathy center. When neurons in the right supramarginal gyrus are disrupted, or when it has difficulty functioning, subjects in numerous studies appeared unable to experience other people's emotions; rather they were more likely to project their own onto the other person. According to a statement from the Institute, when one partner in a study experienced positive stimuli and the other unpleasant ones, "their capacity for empathy suddenly plummeted. The participants' own emotions distorted their assessment of the other person's feelings. The participants who were feeling good themselves assessed their partners' negative experiences as less severe than they actually were. In contrast, those who had just had an unpleasant experience assessed their partners' good experiences less positively."[22] In other words, someone feeling particularly validated, holy, victorious, or powerful, will most likely not be able to relate to—empathize with—the pain of his victims.

* * *

Despite all this, some contend that empathy also has a dark side. According to Indiana University at Bloomington professor Fritz Breithaupt, author of *The Dark Sides of Empathy*, "sometimes we commit atrocities not out of a failure or empathy, but rather as a direct consequence of successful, even overly-successful, empathy."[23] In an April 2019 interview with NPR, Breithaupt suggested, therefore, that in his view "a lot of terrorists may not lack empathy. Rather, they see some plight of a group they identify with—they see them suffering and see it as something horrible and that becomes more extreme and activates them to become active terrorists."[24]

Others, such as reporter Eliana Aponte, argue that "the outrage that comes from empathy drives some of our more powerful punitive desires," noting that "when making the case for air strikes in Syria, [then-president] Obama spoke movingly about the horrors inflicted by Assad and his soldiers, including their use of chemical warfare."[25]

That view, however, neglects the importance of honor or shame in motivating terrorism. Moreover, raising empathy to drive support for a war is hardly equivalent; war is not terrorism, and is—hopefully—always a last resort, aimed by governments at governments, not by non-state actors against people; and rarely, if ever, do those on opposing sides of a war—particularly those from non-honor-based communities—celebrate the deaths on the other. This cannot be said to be true of terror attacks, as those watching Palestinians dancing in the streets after 9/11, or who have read online messages of support for Scott Paul Bierle, who killed two women at a yoga studio in Tallahassee, Florida, in November 2018—he's "a hero," some said[26]—can attest.

More, Aponte and those in her camp ignore the crucial egocentric viewpoint of narcissistic rage: a threat to the white race is a threat to me, to my power; insulting Mohammed is insulting me, my faith, my god; attacking Muslims is an attack on the *ummah*, the Muslim community across the world. In Islam an oft-quoted hadith states, "The attitude of the believer and feeling of brotherhood to one another is like that of a single body. When one member of the body is hurt, it will have an effect to the whole body. Each one of you has a responsibility and each one is responsible towards those under your responsibility."

Empathy for those like us is not, therefore, relevant when quantifying the true capacity for empathy (as opposed to Dylann Roof's assertion that "you don't feel sorry for people you don't identify with"). True empathy, rather, allows us to feel for the Other, for those of a different tribe, family, gender, religion, race.

At the same time, perhaps, empathy does carry a darker side. Perhaps it is precisely because we have empathy—too much empathy, even—that we stay, that we appease, that we allow the violence to continue. We try to understand the abuser's point of view, the grievances of the terrorists, to feel what they must feel as deeply as they do to make them violent. We berate ourselves, not them. I probably shouldn't have pointed out he'd balanced the checkbook wrong this month, we think—it must have hurt his pride. Or: We probably shouldn't have gone ahead and published those Mohammed cartoons, produced that film about Muslim women, published that book by Salman Rushdie.

And the terror continues.

CHAPTER 5

THE ABUSER

I actually wasn't remotely interested in Boris when we met. He wasn't at all my type, and we hadn't much in common: I was Joni Mitchell, the Band, Fleetwood Mac. He was Alice Cooper, the Bee Gees, Jethro Tull. I was embroidered Indian blouses and long, flowing skirts. He was tight nylon shirts opened halfway down his chest. He took Spanish. I took French. He was into motorcycles and football; I was about poetry and dance. We hung out in different groups, and though we knew each other's friends, we didn't really like them.

But he had a car and was always willing to drive me home, saving me a long walk and a sixty-minute ride on the New York subways of the 1970s. Plus he had good pot.

We became friends.

Still, even as he pursued me, I couldn't get past the differences. Or the shirts.

And then the fire happened.

We had spent the evening at his parents' house, hanging out, as you do at seventeen, listening to the Eagles, one of the few bands we could agree on. His parents were away. It was nearly Christmas, and cold, and somewhere around midnight the doorman rang from downstairs. There was a fire in the building, he said. We should get out of the apartment.

In the lobby Boris tried to find his grandmother, who lived in the same building. She was not among the residents pacing in pajamas, or dressed in evening gowns just home from a night out. Had the doorman spoken to her? He had not. But the firemen were on the scene, he said, and Boris should stay where he was.

"Not a chance," he snapped back, and pulled my arm, running up the stairs to wake Nana and help her to leave the building.

In that moment, he became a hero.

For the first time, that night I let him kiss me when he put me in a taxi home.

What I didn't understand until decades later was that the whole thing had been a performance just for me. The fire had been real enough; but the man who ran to rescue his grandmother from the possibly burning building was also, I later learned (because he boasted of it to me) the same man who had once dangled his own mother by her belt from the window of their high-rise apartment.

For an abuser both of these make sense. They are the two sides of his patriarchal machismo: the chivalrous savior and the man who takes no nonsense from his women.

Or, for that matter, anybody else.

Boris didn't learn that by himself. Like all boys, he modeled his manhood on the manhood of his father. "Very young boys are not demonstrably prone to aggression against girls," notes *Sex and World Peace* author Valerie Hudson, who has pioneered research on the relationships between family abuse, misogyny, and cultural violence. "It takes active modeling, reinforcement, and rewarding of gendered violence to make it appear functional to boys. . . . Sons' imitations of their fathers' aggression towards their mothers may be the first step in perpetuating patterns of violence against women across generations."[1]

And indeed it wasn't just my boyfriend who felt his father's fury. The dark glasses his mother wore every day, I learned years later, were not to keep the sun from being in her eyes but to keep her eyes from being in the sun, where everyone could see them. Like me, even in summer, she always wore long sleeves. One learns so many ways to hide the bruises.

In addition, experts have observed that seeing their mother being abused (and especially if she is verbally abused) frequently makes boys lose respect for her. They prefer to identify with the stronger, more powerful party; and even if that person also belittles him, he can—and does—reassure himself with the thought that at least he is not as bad a person as his mother obviously is. In this he finds a place for superiority. Coupled with the shame inflicted on him by the abuse he, too, endures, it becomes a toxic—even deadly—mix.

That shame is dark, and large, and overwhelming. The battered child cannot escape his own humiliation; he is helpless against his more powerful father, beaten down not just with punches (or worse) but with the demeaning words spit in his direction: he is a screwup, a wimp, a loser. He is a wuss, a pussy, which is to say, a girl. What could be worse than this?

Even when there are no words, he is consumed by the logic of his plight: if he is being punished, he must have done something wrong; and if his father punishes him so often—or punishes when he hasn't, in fact, done anything wrong at all—then what is bad isn't his behavior. It's himself.

And from that shame erupts a violence of his own.

"The more a person is shamed by others, from childhood by parents or peers who ridicule or reject him," writes James Gilligan, "the more he is likely to feel chronically shamed, and hypersensitive to feelings and experiences of being shamed, sometimes to the point of feeling that others are treating him with contempt or disdain even when they are not. For such people, and they are the rule among the violent, even a minor sign of real or imagined disrespect can trigger a homicidal reaction."[2] Elsewhere he adds, "The most effective way, and often the only way, to provoke someone to become violent is to insult him."[3]

But there are other forces at work. The shamed child becomes the adult who cannot tolerate his own failings, his own mistakes. To acknowledge any fallibility of his own, in fact, becomes so emotionally intolerable that he projects those perceived faults onto everybody else: as John Douglas, a former FBI profiler, has noted, because of their own feelings of inadequacy, "these men attempt to diminish their low self-esteem by blaming others for their own real or imagined shortcomings, which were often caused . . . by the way they were treated by overly-authoritarian fathers."[4] He didn't get fired because he slacked off at the office; he got fired because his boss is an asshole. He didn't forget to bring home the milk—he chose not to do it to teach his wife a lesson: get it yourself, as a wife should. (Or as Rick once said when I'd asked him to pick up tomatoes on his way home, "Get your own fucking tomatoes. That's not my role.") He didn't fall, you tripped him. And now you're going to pay.

Besides, he is a man. He is superior. He learned that from his father.

Not surprisingly then, it is widely accepted that, as Rachel Louise Snyder, author of *No Visible Bruises*, puts it, "Narcissism is one of the key components of an abuser. . . . Generally speaking, [abusers] are about power and control over one person or the people in their family. . . . And so the narcissism plays out in the idea that they are owed something, in the idea that they are entitled to their authority, that their partners have to be subservient to them."[5]

But acting on that desire for power and control involves more than just narcissism. The violence also comes, as Gilligan observes, "when the individual has been socialized into the male gender role that, in our patriarchal culture, means he has been taught that there are many circumstances and situations in which one has to be violent in order to maintain one's masculinity or sense of masculine sexual identity and adequacy, and in which a nonviolent man would be seen as impotent and emasculated, a coward, wimp, eunuch, boy, homosexual, or woman, a man who has 'no balls.'"[6] In a patriarchy, he says, violence is often honored. Nonviolence is shamed. It is this, in part (but in no way exclusively), that accounts for why abused boys tend more often to become overtly violent than do abused girls.

But not every abused child becomes a violent criminal, of course, and even fewer become terrorists. And being battered is not, in itself, enough to make a child into a narcissist, let alone a pathologically afflicted one. Rather, narcissism expert Otto Kernberg and others believe there must also be a source of admiration and praise—usually excessive—that counters the shaming and humiliation. (Some in fact theorize that it is the over-abundance of praise that causes narcissism most of all.)

Boris and Rick both had this in spades: Boris's father was a renowned surgeon with a thriving practice. The family lived in one of the most coveted neighborhoods of Manhattan and traveled in the highest social circles. At our elite school, Boris excelled in sports, and as the adopted eldest son, enjoyed the adoration of a mother who had feared she might never have a child. He was her gift, her joy, and, she must have hoped, the source of love and tenderness her brutal husband no longer gave her.

Rick, for his part, extraordinarily handsome as a child and young man, was the smartest of his mother's sons, the one most likely to make some-thing of himself in a family where neither parent had attended college. His good looks—piercing green eyes; thick, sideswept blond hair; rock star build—got him dates with the Park Avenue girls, trophies among the street kids he grew up with, and with them, a glimpse into a world few of his friends back in the Bronx could ever dream of. Ashamed of his own lower-working-class background, he prided himself on his ability to seduce women from the world that he aspired to. Their attention soothed the wounds meted out by his abusive and angry stepfather, and the pain of his own social space. He was, in essence, the John Travolta character of *Saturday Night Fever* made real.

Or consider Charlie Sheen, whose father, Martin, was notorious for his drunken rages and abuse of his older sons. At the same time, Charlie was not only a child of a celebrated actor; by age eight he was appearing in films himself (albeit as an extra), including in the momentous *Apoca-lypse Now*. At nineteen he became a star in his own right, playing against Patrick Swayze in *Red Dawn*. But none of that stopped the rages, or Charlie's sense of being not quite the actor that his father is, never quite the man. Torn between greatness and inferiority, he has spent a lifetime rampaging against any threat to his authority and fame, any challenge to his manhood and his honor.

And Omar Mateen, the Pulse nightclub shooter with a history of domestic battery, grew up with a father who openly discussed his support for the Taliban in videos posted online. (By the time of the Pulse shooting, he was already declaring himself president of Afghanistan and the leader of the "transitional revolutionary government of Afghanistan," a movement he established for the purpose of unseating the country's current government.) As the only son among four children in a family of Afghan immigrants, the *New York Times* reported, Omar "enjoyed male privilege"[7]—though it is hard to imagine quite what that meant in a family where his mother was arrested at least once for violently attacking his father.[8]

These things matter. In explaining the dynamics of Muslim families, Yasmine tells me, "From the minute a boy is born, he is a prince. He can do no wrong, he is never asked to apologize. Everything he does is perfect and wonderful and amazing." By contrast, she says, the daughter carries the family honor "so you are constantly being told don't laugh like that, don't talk like that, don't sit like that, whereas a boy, just because of the existence of the fact he has a penis, is the pinnacle of the family."[9]

And yet "published evidence suggests that physical, sexual, and emotional violence against adolescents is widespread in the Arab region," the Center for Research on Population and Health at the American University of Beirut reports.[10] Much of that abuse, particularly sexual abuse, is perpetrated against young boys, although the report's authors also note that "in many studies, prevalence rates exceeded other regional global estimates, including rates of violent discipline, fighting, and intimate partner violence against adolescent girls." (It should be noted that child marriage is not uncommon in the region.) Moreover, in nine of twelve Arab countries, "rates of physical punishment in the past month were higher than UNICEF's global estimate of 50 percent, and in ten of 12 countries, rates of psychological aggression were higher than the global estimate of 70 percent."[11] And in a 2015 study of sixteen thousand students in Saudi Arabia, 65 percent were found to have suffered psychological abuse, 40 percent had experienced physical abuse, and 10 percent had endured sexual abuse.[12]

Notably, corporal punishment is consistently higher in the honor-based culture of the American South than elsewhere in the country, according to a 2014 Five-Thirty-Eight report, which found that "people in the South have been about 17 percentage points more likely to agree with spanking than people in the Northeast."[13] Studies have consistently shown that children who are subjected to corporal punishment are more likely to abuse their own children, as well as their partners.[14]

Here is where the threads of shame and honor, narcissism and violence and terror twist until they form a pattern once again. A study performed by the National Consortium for the Study of Terrorism and Responses to Terrorism noted that of the violent extremists interviewed, 45 percent had been the victims of childhood physical abuse; 21 percent reported experiencing childhood sexual abuse; and 46 percent reported having been neglected.[15] As Valerie Hudson notes, "studies have shown that if domestic violence is normal in family conflict resolution in a society, then that society is more likely to rely on violent conflict resolution and to be involved in militarism and war than are societies with lower levels of family violence."[16]

Add to this Gilligan's assertion that insult can be enough to provoke violence, and in the center of a culture where honor is all, violence becomes not just likely, but inevitable. It is hard, in fact, to envision a more toxic recipe: the "prince" son who is at once adored and abused, is predisposed to developing a narcissistic personality; as a narcissist, he feels no empathy, making his abuse of others, a behavior he learns from example, that much more probable—especially if it confers on him a manliness, a confirmation of his power, and more importantly, his honor. And with the abusive structure in the home and the (cultural) oppression of women (who threaten his honor, who indeed control it, who must be kept in line lest they destroy it), violence in the form of warfare becomes virtually ineludible. Or put another way, family abuse—including verbal abuse—especially alongside a glorified patriarchal, machismo ethic, offers a breeding ground for terrorism. Add honor culture and a cause, and the terrorist is made.

And while this may not be true of every child growing up in such an environment, it is true of virtually every terrorist; indeed, terrorism expert Jessica Stern, author of *Terror in the Name of God: Why Religious Militants Kill*, has written that terrorists she has met almost universally "start out feeling humiliated, enraged that they are viewed by some 'Other' as second class. They take on new identities as martyrs on behalf of a purported spiritual cause."[17]

Suddenly the violence of Palestinian suicide bombers, the *Charlie Hebdo* killings, even the destruction of 9/11, seem so inevitable it is almost surprising they didn't happen sooner and more often. Why didn't we see?

* * *

There is another element to all of this that seems worthwhile noting: in almost every case of violent abuse and terrorism I have studied, where a father was not abusive to his son, he was in one way or another absent. Death, divorce, work-related travel, or emotional distance is ubiquitous in these men's lives. Boris, as mentioned earlier, was adopted. Rick's father and mother divorced while Rick was still a small child; he came to refer to his stepfather as his father, though he never called him "Dad" (was he ashamed not to have a father at home?). Osama bin Laden was ten when his father was killed. Breivik's parents divorced while Anders was barely a year old; as described before, his father cut all contact with him after Anders was repeatedly arrested for graffiti—arguably itself a profoundly narcissistic act, a way of being seen, being known, of having an ID: this is me, this is my name. Anders was fifteen at the time. The father of James Fields, the white nationalist who killed activist Heather Heyer in Charlottesville, Virginia, died before James was born, as did the father of Saddam Hussein. (Compounding the damage, Hussein's mother, according to counterterror expert and political psychologist Jerrold Post, was too depressed to handle the child and gave him to her brother until Saddam was three.[18]) Red Army Faction leader Andreas Baader's father was taken prisoner when fighting against the Russians in 1945; Andreas was only two.

(Subsequently he was raised in a household of women—his mother and aunts—who refused to discipline him, rather fawning over him as the one male in the family. His teachers have been quoted as saying that "he had the traits of a spoiled child: talented but lazy and often rebellious."[19]) In a twist, it was Oklahoma bomber Timothy McVeigh's mother who picked up and left, abandoning Timothy, his sister, and their father. Timothy was just ten years old.

Similar situations have played out among the Moroccan (and other) immigrant groups in Europe. Also as previously noted, when Hans Werdmölder traced the violence of young men of Moroccan backgrounds in the Netherlands—a group disproportionately represented both in violent crime and among Dutch ISIS members—he determined much of that activity could be attributed to being separated from their fathers. Many of Europe's Muslim men now in their twenties, thirties, or forties are the sons of immigrant workers whose fathers left them behind, usually with their mothers, in their home country for the first few years while the men got settled abroad. With the father absent the boy became the man of the house, charged with establishing law and order. And yet he was a child, often subjected to the demands, rules, and discipline of his mother—a woman. The experience, for many of these youth, was humiliating.

Worse still was the occasional visit from the father, who then took over the domain. No longer did the son rule the house, the family. He had gone from king to serf.

For many the experience of degradation became more than they could bear.

Alternatively, writes Dennis Balcolm, a family therapist based near Boston, "Abandoned sons can have sustained damage to their sense of worth and self-esteem. The son may acquire a sense of self as the kind of person who is abandoned and the son of a father who would abandon." Such abandonment, he says, "can lead to experiences and feelings of shame and stigma."[20] Indeed when journalist Jason Yates Sexton's father and mother separated, he writes in *The Man They Wanted Me to Be*, "the pain of being abandoned lingered and hurt me in ways I couldn't begin to understand.

I couldn't help but wonder what was so wrong with me that my own father didn't want to have a relationship. There must have been something defective, something that wasn't quite right that kept him away."[21]

In the face of that fear of abandonment, is it any wonder these men seek control, especially of the people to whom they are most vulnerable? If his honor is at the mercy of his wife or daughter; if his identity as a man is tied into being a husband (or "having" a woman); if he *has something to lose*, his best self-protection is control. Dominance. And rule.

Take, for instance, former British hip-hop artist Abdel Bary (aka. L Jinny), who left the UK to join the Islamic State. The son of Adel Abdul Bary, a lieutenant to Osama bin Laden and key plotter of the 1998 bombings of U.S. embassies in Africa, "L Jinny" posted a rap to YouTube about his father's arrest: "Give me the pride and the honour like my father, I swear the day they came and took my dad, I could have killed a cop or two, Imagine then I was only six, picture what I'd do now with a loaded stick. Like boom bang fine, I'm wishing you were dead, violate my brothers and I'm filling you with lead."[22]

Months later Bary, calling himself "Abu Kalashnikov," posted a photo of himself on Twitter, carrying a severed head.

* * *

There is a certain auto-eroticism to this kind of violence, braced in its costume of power. The abuser, like the terrorist, reconfirms his perfection by punishing, and by reshaping (or reconfirming) the hierarchy. Osama bin Laden caused the most powerful nation on earth to tremble; and fear, in the patriarchal mind, is humiliation. No real man is afraid, because the real man has the power. ("If people fear what you may do," writes former terrorist Maajid Nawaz, who now oversees Quilliam, a counter-extremism think tank, "if they fear the masses you may incite, they listen to you before you do it. What they really respect is your propensity to hurt them. The more you can hurt them, the more they respect you."[23])

That respect is power, and that power, says Shannon Martinez, can be addictive. "It's like your physical appearance or the words you're saying cause fear, and that fear feels a whole lot like power."[24] It becomes intoxicating; as Anne Manne writes, the violence they commit becomes "the ultimate high."[25]

And so it is, too, for the abuser as he beats his wife, his child: his fear—of losing her, of losing control of her (she may leave, she may betray him sexually, she might threaten his honor by looking at a boy or leaving the house alone)—retreats, submits, under the supremacy of his brute force. Just as she does.

Until, of course, it returns again.

That supremacy of power, and the longing to have it, is what makes for the box office success of films like *Rambo* and *Commando*. It is not just that the hero fights for the cause of the good, this chivalrous, brave man prepared to kill for justice; it is that he conquers evil with big, phallic guns and the virility of his raw and pulsating muscle.

The winner, after all, is the one who "beats" everybody else.

And because he cannot feel your pain, the beatings never stop.

CHAPTER 6

THE ABUSED

It is summer, and evening, and we are walking on the beach, alone.
The waves shift, cool beneath our feet, then drift out again. The wind
is soft, but it is August now, and the nights are growing cool. In just
three weeks I will be going off to college in Ohio. My best friends will
be in Upstate New York and Washington. Boris will be staying in New
York City. Here, now, facing the vastness of the ocean, everything seems
suddenly so far away.

"It will be so hard to leave," I say, a whisper in the wind.

A fist to my side.

Another to my core.

I fall into the sand, curled onto my knees, my hands instinctively
covering my head.

And wait.

Then I hear him walk away.

* * *

This is how it happens: without warning, beyond reason. I know just that I have said something wrong, done something wrong, and there is nothing I can do to make it right again. There is only a fear that grows so deep I can live with it only if I can make it go away. It is a fear shared by the victims of domestic violence everywhere, a fear that follows us no matter where we run, rising and falling with the events of the day, looming over us, a black shroud that threatens to wrap itself around us until we can no longer breathe. It is the fear that keeps our shoulders hunched as we try to become invisible, recoil from the blows, verbal or physical, we know will come.

It is that fear that gripped New York City in the days after 9/11, Paris after Bataclan. It is terror. And it is real.

To fully understand the making of a terrorist, to fully recognize what terror does to its victims and the societies it hits, means understanding what happens when violence and condemnation, anger and insult and uncertainty define your daily life, when nowhere is safe, not even home.

Part of how it works, part of how it contorts the way you think, whether it is terrorism in the family or terror on the streets, is the not-knowing, the unpredictability, so that what you thought was safe (restaurants and rock concerts, rather than airplanes; visiting a friend; going off to college) no longer is.

And because it makes no sense, you twist your mind any way you can until it does.

The trajectory is complex and gradual, a fall like Alice down the rabbit hole into a different reality, something distant and intangible and strange. We begin to blame ourselves, because we are told we are to blame, even if we don't entirely believe it. Then we condemn ourselves for not believing it, as if this, too, is part of our sinfulness, our inability to understand right from wrong, another blemish to be condemned.

We are so mixed up.

Eventually the confusion, the sense of helplessness and hopelessness and worthlessness, becomes who we know ourselves to be—even as we know, at the same time, that it is not.

This is gaslighting.

America's National Domestic Violence Hotline (NDVH) traces the term "gaslighting" to the 1938 play, *Gas Light*, in which a husband attempts to drive his wife crazy by dimming the lights (which were powered by gas) in their home. When his wife points it out, he denies that the light has changed. Gaslighting, according to the NDVH, "is an extremely effective form of emotional abuse that causes a victim to question their own feelings, instincts, and sanity."[1] People who are victims of gaslighting tend to second-guess themselves, apologize constantly, and question their own value—or the values that they stand for.

The victims, though, are not always people. Sometimes the victim is an entire culture.

And they too often do not see it until it already is too late.

* * *

News report: *New York Times*, August 20, 2001. "Karen Lee Ziner, a reporter for the *Providence Journal*, was removed from coverage of a domestic abuse case after the victim complained."[2]

The real story isn't about the reporter. The real story is about the wife who was beaten with a hammer and, according to initial police reports, found naked on the floor of her apartment. Karen Ziner reported this before a second journalist described the victim as "half-clothed." And so the victim complained, arguing that she wasn't naked.

Like that's what really matters.

This is what happens to us. We don't even understand the horror, the abuse, that we are victim to.

This woman has been beaten by her husband with a hammer and she is upset that a reporter described her as being naked.

The first time Boris hit me, it was February. What I felt was as much the sting of the slap as the shock of it. By August his beatings rarely made me cry. I simply didn't feel it anymore: it was just the sound, the crack of bone to bone, the crash of my shoulder against the bureau in the hall, the clap of his palm against my skin. I no longer waited for the beatings to end.

I waited for the silence.

But pain and shame and shock often go together, as anyone who has ever seen a child cry after taking a harmless tumble knows; and when the shock was no longer there, neither was the pain. The truth is, if I had stayed longer, I, too, could have been this Rhode Island woman. I, too, might have perceived being described as being naked as something more terrible than being beaten by my husband with a hammer.

Yet whom is she protecting? Her abuser? She does not deny the beatings—or the choice of weapon. What she argues is her state of dress—or undress. "He may be bad enough to beat me, but he would never be so bad as to leave me naked," she is saying; or maybe, "I am in bad enough shape to be hit, but I don't go around the house nude." As if this were worse. But for her, at this point, it is.

All proportion, all sense of right and wrong and pain and humiliation are in chaos, as if something had exploded in her head and all the contents shattered, smashed into fragments like dishes on the hardwood floor.

What she is protecting is the fantasy.

* * *

That fantasy: that he is good; the hope: that it will end; the disbelief: that it is real—these are the forces that keep us sane as much as they keep us trapped. But if we are adults, if we have been beaten by partners and not by parents or guardians, we have (usually) a second self that saves us: the memory, however faint, of who we used to be. Because somewhere in the depths of our consciousness remains an understanding of the senselessness of what has become our world, because we know it makes no sense, we who are more fortunate manage to grasp hold of the edge and pull ourselves back to solid ground. A moment comes when reality slashes through the dream, an instant when we plunge out from the fog, and there is no going back. After all the forgivenesses and all the self-doubt, after all the confusion and all the hopes and all the nostalgic memories, what is emerges in sharp and clear relief, like the optical illusion where you see the young girl and not the witch, or the building in front and not behind. Some of us stay anyway, for fear, for lack of an escape route, or until we can get away. But we know. And we are done.

* * *

For others, especially children, it works differently. "While the self-esteem of adults who have attained internalized sources of pride can survive the withdrawal of love from others up to a point," writes Gilligan, "it appears to be difficult if not impossible for a child to gain the capacity for self-love without first having been loved by at least one parent or parent-substitute. And when the self is not loved, by itself or by another, it dies."[3]

As described earlier, children who live with violence at home, and especially those who are abused themselves, develop an existential sense of humiliation and shame, which they manage only by shaming and humiliating others through violence of their own. For boys, if their sense of power and manhood has been broken by a parent, they will rebuild it with the building tools that make a man: muscle, domination, and a demand—under threat, if necessary—for the respect they're due.

But here is their dilemma, based, in a sense, in a fantasy as entrapping as the one that keeps abused women in the grips of their abusers: What can a child do with his anger and disempowerment? When you cannot take revenge against the one who has caused your pain—the cost will be too great, either physically (he'll hit you harder) or psychically (you will need to confront the agonizing emotions raised by a mother or father's abuse)—you displace the rage. You find someone else to blame, someone else you can hit or hate, instead.

As Christian Picciolini blamed the Jews.

As 9/11 plotter Zacarias Moussaoui, whose father regularly beat his mother and sisters, and who spent much of his childhood in orphanages, despised the West.[4]

As Shannon Martinez hated everyone after she was raped.

Indeed the UNICEF report "Behind Closed Doors" observes, "Many studies have noted that children from violent homes exhibit signs of more aggressive behavior such as ~~bullying, and are up to three times more likely~~ ~~to be involved in fighting."~~[5]

Like Mubin Shaikh.

The wall behind his desk in Mubin's study is crowded with certificates, commendations, and awards: Special Operations Command. Canadian Forces Military Intelligence. Criminal Intelligence Analysis. Canadian Security Intelligence Service Pillar Society.

In an indirect but significant way, every one of them has been a product of his own childhood traumas—beatings from his father, at home; whippings at the madrassa he attended in Toronto from the age of five, where, he tells me, the imam "would make us go out and find the stick that he would beat us with, and if your stick wasn't thick enough, he would get one five times thicker because you were being a smartass"; the years of sexual abuse he endured at the hands of an uncle; and the impotence that consumed him when he learned another uncle had also sexually assaulted his younger sister. "I can think back now, and I'm 12 years old and I remember having an argument with my mother," he recalls. "'How come you aren't doing anything about this?' I remember developing this feeling of powerlessness and helplessness."[6]

He decided to start studying martial arts. "I know that's why I did that, to feel no longer powerless," he says. This was followed by joining the army cadets "to become stronger and more powerful." He knew, he says, that "because of what happened to me and to my sister, no one was going to defend and protect us, so I would be the defender and protector."

It was a short step from there to where he soon found himself, as the "protector and defender" of the faith. He radicalized. On a trip to Quetta in 1995, he connected with the Taliban and decided to join their violent jihad.

"You develop this militant identity," he says. "It's not a passive, 'I'm a defender of my people'; it's a very active and aggressive identity of defending and protecting." Warrior-like. Even in his extremist years, he says, "I could feel I was stronger. I discovered this is how you make sense of it, this is how you empower yourself. I deliberately put into my mind that I was going to be someone that you did not fuck around with."

Yet something else happens to these child victims of abuse. Even as they defiantly commit to attaining power, even as they raise their fists or wave their jihadist flags, the shame engulfs them, washing over them like a wave that pulls back out into the tide, taking all their value along with it; and they are left there, naked, worthless, and alone.

Some turn that feeling of worthlessness inward, falling into self-destructive patterns of self-harm, or alcohol and drug abuse.[7] Simply put: they flee instead of fight. Or as Sandra Bloom puts it, they "try to dance with death through risk-taking, playing Russian Roulette games with their own bodies."[8]

When Mubin Shaikh and I discuss the abuse he endured as a child, he shows me the back of his left hand.

Small scars form random patterns across the skin.

"Cigarette burns," he tells me. "I did them to myself."

And it's not just those abused by parents. It can happen to all of us. It happened to me.

At first I was lucky; the college I left Boris for was small, intensely intimate, and rigorous. The dorm I lived in was filled with fellow hippies playing the Grateful Dead and Joni Mitchell on guitar, and friendships were fierce and strong. Academically, I soared. There was value again. Gradually I healed.

But not completely.

Haunting me, still, was the sense of my imperfection: I had not been a good enough girlfriend—I left Boris when he had begged me not to, instead of standing by my man. I had argued with him too much. A good woman is quiet, is grateful, is soft and pretty and understanding, and I was none of that. (This, notably, is also the vision of womanhood that helped lure so many Western girls to Syria and the Islamic State.)

On top of that, I had wanted to be a writer. But I wasn't actually writing. I was no longer sure I could.

So I took control of what I could, took power, as it were, over myself. I could make myself prettier. I could be thinner, and somehow this would, I knew, make me more lovable, a better woman than I'd been.

It took awhile, and several failed fad diets, but two years after gradu-ation I found the key to thin: cocaine. ~~You could do coke and not even think of eating. And you could write!~~ You could stay up late and write all night, and wasn't that anyway how it was supposed to be? Like Kerouac?

Over the course of the next year, I went from doing a quarter gram twice a week to a gram (and sometimes more) a day. My weight dropped from 110 to 103 to 97. I bought new jeans. I stopped going to the gym—who needed it?

And best of all: I escaped the memories.

Eventually I ran out of money. I'd had enough of it all anyway, by then—the sleepless nights, the panicked phone calls to my dealer when I was running out, all of it. I was done.

Also, I met a man.

He was European and handsome, an artist who had shown work at my mother's gallery in Soho. He was talented and elegant and smart, and I could not quite believe that he was interested in me. Our life became a whirlwind of travel between New York and Europe—Paris, Milan, Flor-ence, Basel, Nice. I was wildly in love.

And then on a visit to his family's home, I uncovered a photograph of the only other woman he had loved. A straw hat rested on her long blond hair, shielding her from the sun. Red lipstick outlined her mouth. But what I noticed most was: she was thinner than I was.

Over the next year my weight dropped from 110 back to 97 again. Then 95. Then 90. Then below. If he was ever going to love me as he had once loved her, I was going to have to be thin and thinner. I was going to have to be better, prettier, than I was, a far more perfect woman, because what I was, I knew (even if he hadn't figured it out just yet), wasn't good enough. And this was all I had the power to change.

Other women have told me stories just like this. Like Melissa, after she met the man who changed her life.

For them, too, it was perfect at first. He brought her flowers. He made her dinner. They went out to clubs, to visit friends. She could barely believe her happiness when he proposed.

On the day they left for their honeymoon, a friend promised to come by to bring the photos he had taken of the wedding. Though there was plenty of time before departure, her new husband was getting edgy.

"Relax," Melissa said. "We're fine."

But Andrew would not relax. He paced. He grew annoyed. Melissa, upstairs packing and excited about the romantic trip ahead of them, was undeterred. "Really, Andrew," she admonished him. "Calm down."

"I was in the hall," she recalls, "and suddenly he was hitting me on the back of my head. I completely collapsed from the shock. The next thing I knew he was kicking me in the back, in my legs, and then he went back and finished packing." Their friend arrived moments later. Melissa pretended everything was fine. "I mean, we were just married."[9]

Within months the attacks worsened. On a night shortly after the birth of their child, her husband requested she make french fries for dinner. Son on hip, Melissa ventured to the kitchen to prepare them, heating the oil, peeling the brown knobs of roots, slicing and slipping the raw potato into a bowl to slide into the pan. With the oil still on the fire and baby crying, Melissa returned to the living room and began to nurse him on the couch.

"I smell something burning," Andrew said, zapping the TV remote. He did not move.

Neither did Melissa.

"Would you check?" she said. "I really can't get up." The baby nursed.

Her husband rose from his place and walked calmly to the kitchen. Then he grabbed the handle of the pan, lifted it from the stove, and threw it, full of burning oil, at Melissa and their infant son.

When I meet her two years later, a year after their divorce, Melissa admits to me that she is now recovering from bulimia—an aftereffect of the time that she was married. She also cuts, she says, showing me the scars, but she is getting better. "It's not easy," she admits, "but I am coming to feel that I have a future with new things and without violence."

* * *

Not so, though, for all women and girls abused by fathers or mothers or husbands. When Anat Berko spent five years interviewing Palestinian women serving sentences for terrorism in Israel, she was taken by the number of them who had actively chosen to become suicide bombers, rather than to continue their lives at home. One woman told her, "Those girls don't think they will go to jail, they think they will die. They think death is better than living the way they do."[10] Another whom she calls Jemilla explained, "The men want to carry out attacks, they make the decision and do it. There are girls who didn't make that decision. They only wanted to get away from their families. They were unlucky—people didn't treat them nicely, maybe they were beaten at home. That is why some of the girls carried out attacks. Their mother and father and brothers beat them; maybe they made a mistake like improper sex conduct. The father yells at the mother and calls her names, and the mother wants to do the same, so she takes it out on the girl. Who can she yell at? Her husband? He's Allah at home! So she yells at her daughter and calls her names and the daughter runs away from home and carries out terrorist attacks."[11]

It's the perfect solution, really: destruction of others and destruction of self, together in a gesture that promises to give them honor, even fame. It is vengeance, making a heroine of someone they all said was worthless. But it is also an escape, finally, from her own torment and shame.

Still, not all women suicide bombers are motivated by abuse in the home; in her extraordinary portrait of female terrorists, *Invisible Martyrs*, Farhana Qazi, the former U.S. Counterterrorism Center agent, notes that during the 2003 U.S. war in Iraq, many women "protested the loss of their husbands, homes, and honor. Mothers felt the need to avenge the loss of their sons." One woman told her, "I lost my children and husband, and have no reason to be in this world anymore."[12]

Yet other women, like the mother Jemilla describes, follow the pattern outlined in the UNICEF report, of bullying and aggression. In the flourishing days of the Islamic State, for instance, many women also took on the role not of terrorists, but of disciplinarians, joining the Al-Khansaa and Umm al-Rayan brigades that ensured all women in the Caliphate obeyed laws prohibiting them from appearing in public without a male guardian, requiring them to wear full cover (*nikab*), and otherwise adhered to sharia laws. But their discipline was frequently as violent as the terrorists', according to multiple reports. One woman told NBC News reporters that "the female morality police favored a torture tool known as 'the biter'— metal prongs designed to clip chunks of flesh as punishment for women who violated strict ISIS dress codes."[13]

Here, too, they found a way to redeem themselves, taking on roles to protect the honor of the community as a way of gaining honor themselves; note Ryan Brown and Kiersten Baughman, "Men in honor cultures strive to build and defend reputations for strength, bravery, and an intolerance for disrespect. Women in honor cultures typically strive to build and protect reputations for loyalty and sexual purity. To the extent that men and women live up to these cultural expectations, they have honor. If they ever fail to do so, however, they experience the stain of dishonor, which can be difficult (if not impossible) to expunge."[14]

"Intolerance for disrespect." "The stain of dishonor."

This was what I hadn't understood that night with Boris on the beach. It is why what seemed senseless to me made perfect sense to him. It is why Andrew, for whom being asked to help with the cooking was an assault on his role as husband, came so close to burning his wife and child.

There is another part of that story of the evening on the beach. After I regain my breath, I walk down the shoreline to where Boris has left the car. He is there, in the driver's seat, waiting. He offers to drive me to the train back to New York. I'm not certain. I am so confused. And then, "Will you marry me?" he says.

And I say yes, even though I know that I don't mean it, because what else can I do?

What I understand later is this: Boris had begged me not to go. And I defied him.

It is that defiance—that insistence on one's own integrity and values, one's own life, that a narcissist finds so threatening: your life should not matter more than his. He is, after all, the man.

For a man in a patriarchal sphere, a man who views his world through honor-tinted lenses, my defiance was tantamount to an attack. As Dov Cohen explains it to me, "I am a man. I have a job to do. That is, my job is to take care of my family, my job is to protect my honor. I am also in charge of keeping people I'm responsible for in line, and I'm entitled to a certain amount of deference for that. So when you do things that challenge my legitimate authority, you're asking for it."[15]

In many ways this idea, this vision of the world, is much of why the West still struggles to understand the violent fury of the Middle East.

Because just as men in Saudi Arabia and Afghanistan and elsewhere oppress women, fearful they will lose their honor; just as the Taliban shot Malala Yousafzai in Swat Valley because she dared to get an education—opening her up to ideas of freedom, and possibility, and reason—just as Christian Picciolini and Shannon Martinez sought to destroy immigrants and gays who threatened their privilege and prestige; just as Rick would frequently phone the homes of friends I'd gone to visit, making sure that I was really there; so, too, Boris faced the realization that he could lose control of me. The power.

Interestingly it was the same for Christian Picciolini. At seventeen, realizing his girlfriend was about to leave for college, he, like Boris, panicked. "All her reassurances that college wouldn't change her love for me hadn't ever stopped the fear that she'd fall for somebody else and leave me. At the very least, if she attended college she would live in a world I was not part of," he writes in *Romantic Violence*. "Abandoning me. Like my parents had." And so, he decided, "There was only one solution. I had to keep her here. I had to propose to her. It wasn't enough to tell each other we would be together forever. It had to be official. She had to say yes, she must marry me. . . . I wanted her here with me. What she thought she wanted was secondary. And we'd be together. That's what she needed most, right? I knew what was best for both of us. I was the strong one. I was the leader. It was my destiny."[16]

It's all in there: his need to control his woman. His fear of abandonment, having felt abandoned by his parents. He would lead. He knew better than anyone, was the stronger one, was the chosen one. "It was my destiny."

"God put me in your life for a reason," Rick would often say to me.

"Who decides who lives and who dies?" a policeman asked Anders Breivik after his arrest.

"I do," Breivik said.[17]

And yet there are those for whom suffering from violence does not lead to abuse, or terror—like Yasmine Mohammed, whose stepfather whipped the soles of her feet until they bled and blistered. And when, after her first marriage, Yasmine finally removed her *hijab* in public, her mother threatened to kill her. Now she works to protect others from enduring this same horror, even in the face of threats to her life from the Arab world, where the punishment for apostasy is death.[18]

Psychoanalyst and terrorism expert Jerrold M. Post suggests that people like Yasmine, like Mubin Shaikh and Shannon Martinez, could perhaps also be called narcissists—people who, like jihadist and white supremacist leaders, see themselves as the saviors of their people. (Perhaps I fall into that category as well. Maybe all journalists do.) Says Post in *Narcissism and Politics: Dreams of Glory*, "At the healthy end of the narcissistic spectrum are those bright, creative, and driven individuals who, from early on, are reaching for the stars. Ambitious and self-confident, whether in science, art and literature, or political leadership, they believe they have something special to contribute, and they pursue those lofty goals throughout their lives. Without reaching for the stars, their dreams of glory will not be achieved. . . . In the ranks of political leaders, healthy narcissists pursuing dreams of glory have been associated with towering triumphs that have positively transformed history."[19]

Shaikh concedes that this may be what has also motivated him to go from cozying up to the Taliban in the mid- to late 1990s to his work now performing interventions and counseling with radicals and working with counterterrorism forces around the world. And it may well also explain the work of others, like Picciolini and Maajid Nawaz, founder of the British counterterrorism think tank Quilliam, who both saw themselves as saviors then and, arguably, still do, albeit in a healthier way today. ("Hitler. Julius Fucking Caesar. Me. The new holy trinity," writes Picciolini of his neo-Nazi days. "Jesus Christ had nothing on me."[20])

What makes the difference?

Much can be ascribed to culture and the possibilities that surround you—whether it's the family or the community at large. In a stable, secure culture, there is less to fear. Where there is support and empathy, there is less to prove. Where violence is not glorified, it is less likely to be part of how one lives and who one ultimately becomes.

But if, as I've described, the culture is one that demeans (through corporal punishment, emotional or sexual abuse, and discrimination); when manhood is defined by aggression, violence and control; when threats to one's control (manhood) demand defending, and violence is the best or only way to regain it; when failing to be violent is seen in fact as a failure to uphold honor, manhood, value—if this is all one knows, then this is the person, the values, the life, that define and determine who one becomes.

Even then, sometimes, there's an out. Ayaan Hirsi Ali, the Somali-born activist who escaped an arranged marriage and went on to become a leading figure in the fight for women's rights in the Muslim world, once told me that it was the storybooks she read, hidden inside the pages of her Koran, that saved her. "We had to go to Koran school, twice a day, Saturday and Sunday," she recounted. "We had to read the Koran every moment that we had free, just recite the Koran, in Arabic, which is *not* my language, which I *do* not understand, just be religious and read the Koran, my mother would insistently say, we heard it until we were blue in the face. But it isn't this which helped me become who I am. It was all the hidden moments that we used to steal from my mother and tell her we were reading the Koran, and in the folds of the Koran we were reading Oliver Twist."[21] From here she learned of worlds and values entirely unlike her own, and imagined places and games and ideas she would never have dreamed of.

It wasn't much different for Yasmine Mohammed. Though she lived a world away in Canada, she faced the same religious despotism at home that Hirsi Ali had in Africa—as, too, did her cousin Aisha, growing up in New York. "Aisha always says that our mothers' mistake was that there was a television in the house," she says, laughing. "The 80s were all about family sit-coms: 'Growing Pains.' 'The Cosby Show.' So you're watching these shows about these families and you know for a certain degree that it's Hollywood, but you also know that these families are significantly different than your own. And so I watched TV and knew it didn't have to be like that. You could fight back. Even 'Little Mermaid'—I was in grade nine when 'Little Mermaid' came out and she's defying her father, and I was like, *whoa*. These things could happen and there would still be a happy ending. You do not get these messages in the Arab world."[22]

But the truth is, even for those who do, it isn't always a happy ending.

CHAPTER 7

TERROR, HONOR, VIOLENCE

Khalida Brohi was about thirteen when her favorite cousin disappeared.

"Has she been married off?" she wondered, but none of her relatives would say.

And then she learned: her dear cousin Khadija, age fourteen, had walked five miles with her uncle, the family patriarch, to stand at her own grave. And then he strangled her to death.

Khadija had known that this was coming. Promised to a cousin in marriage, she had instead fallen in love with another boy. Her uncle had no choice: she had sullied the family honor.[1]

Nowhere do honor, patriarchy, violence, and terror come together more vividly and more dangerously than in the phenomenon of honor killings. And nowhere is narcissism more deadly.

Honor killings, and honor violence in general, are not unique to any religion or cultural group, though Dr. Phyllis Chesler, author of "World-wide Trends in Honor Killings," the definitive study on the subject, has found that "ninety-one percent of the honor killings committed on five continents, including the West, were committed by Muslims."[2] Although the UN estimates that five thousand women are killed for honor every year, experts have long considered that estimate ridiculously low: in fact, Brohi claims "about 1000 women are killed each year in Pakistan in the name of honor. And these are just the reported cases."[3] European countries like the UK, Germany, and the Netherlands have all estimated that approximately two honor killings occur within their borders every month.

And these are just the murders. They do not include violence such as the burning and stabbing of Aiya Altameemi in Arizona, or the acid attacks that destroy the lives of girls like Iranian Ameneh Bahrami, who was blinded when a classmate threw acid in her face; she had rebuffed his proposal of marriage.[4]

The stories are horrific. They tell of fathers, even mothers, killing daughters; brothers killing sisters; uncles killing nieces; husbands killing wives. They are the tales of people like Wafik Abu Abseh in Jordan, who bashed his sister in the head with a rock in 1998. "We do not consider this murder," he later told the *New York Times*. "It was like cutting off a finger."[5] Abseh's mother, brother, and sisters "nodded in agreement" as he spoke.

Or there is the story of sixteen-year-old Aqsa Parvez in Ontario, who argued regularly with her father, Mohammed, a Pakistani immigrant, about wearing her *hijab*. Often she would put it on when leaving the house for school, then remove it once she arrived. But the fact was, she just didn't want to wear it. Period. She wanted the freedom all her friends had, to feel the wind blow through her hair. And so on the morning of December 10, 2007, Mohammed Parvez strangled her to death.

Here, too, the family understood what he had done—and supported his decision. In an interview with police, Aqsa's mother broke down. "Oh, my Aqsa, you should have listened," she reportedly cried. "Everyone tried to make you understand. Everyone begged you, but you did not listen."[6] At the trial Mohammed Parvez himself explained his actions, certain they were justified: "This is my insult. My community will say you have not been able to control your daughter. This is my insult. She is making me naked."[7]

Then there is the story of Mohammed Shafia, an immigrant from Afghanistan living in Montreal, who discovered two of his daughters, ages seventeen and nineteen, were dating boys. So he killed them both, along with another daughter, age thirteen, and the first of his two wives in a polygamous marriage. Officials found the four drowned in their car, a black Nissan Sentra, on June 30, 2009. Mohammed had used his own Lexus to ram the Sentra into the water.[8]

But Mohammed Shafia didn't act alone. His son, Hamed, and his other wife conspired with him and were also convicted of the murders. During their trial the jury heard recordings of Mohammad Shafia discussing the killings afterward in their home. "May the devil shit on their graves," he said. "Is that what a daughter should be?" And later, "I say to myself, 'you did well.' Were they to come to life, I would do it again . . . they betrayed Islam. They betrayed our religion. They betrayed everything."[9]

And there was the Afghan woman Navisseh, and her ten-year-old daughter, Arezoe, found dead in their flat in Maastricht, the Netherlands, in 2003. None of their friends and neighbors were surprised by Navisseh's death. She walked around in Western clothing. She was divorced and looking for another man. It was scandalous. "She knew how Afghan men are," one neighbor told a reporter. "First she wears a burqa in Afghanistan and now here she walks around in such free, Western dress!" Another said simply: "They had only themselves to blame. They violated their culture and their honor." One man who lived nearby explained that he, too, had worked for years to bring his wife to Holland from Afghanistan. "If she should now say, 'you hit me, you're a bad man, I don't want you anymore, I am leaving,' do you think that would be easy for me?" he asked. "Do you think I would accept that after a divorce, she would then go with other men? I brought her here for a better life. . . . She should look after the children and the household. Do you think I could stand to see her with another man? What should I do? . . . What can I tell my children, that I have no honor? How could I ever look others in the eye? . . . I didn't bring my wife here to divorce me. That was not the idea. So I would kill her." His son, asked by the reporter for his opinion, said simply, "I think it's right."[10]

Such honor killings do not just happen in the Middle East or Canada or Europe. They happen in the United States as well. In 2008 eighteen-year-old Anina Said and her sister Sarah, seventeen, were shot and killed by their father in Texas for their "Western" behavior; their mother assisted in the murder. In February 2009, Buffalo, New York, resident Muzzamil Hassan admitted to beheading his wife. Twenty-year-old Iraqi-born Noor Al Maleki, then living in Arizona, was killed by a father infuriated by her "un-Islamic behavior." Fauz Mohammed was nineteen when she was stabbed by her brother and father in Henrietta, New York, for her "immodest dress." And there was Hatice Peltek, a Turkish immigrant living in Rochester, New York, who was bludgeoned to death by her husband in 2004 after being raped by his brother.[11]

All of these girls, these women, were guilty of a single crime: they had forsaken the family honor. More specifically they had forsaken the honor of the man who essentially owned them—their fathers, their husbands.

According to the *New York Times'* Douglas Jehl, "More than pride, more than honesty, more than anything a man might do, female chastity is seen in the Arab world as an indelible line, the boundary between respect and shame. An unchaste woman, it is sometimes said, is worse than a murderer, affecting not just one victim, but her family and her tribe. It is an unforgiving logic, and its product, for centuries and now, has been murder—the killings of girls and women by their relatives, to cleanse honor that has been soiled."[12]

Serap Cileli, a Turkish-German woman who herself escaped one arranged marriage before being forced into another, is more explicit: "In many families, boys grow up as first-class citizens, and girls are second-class citizens," she told an interviewer in 2006. "Boys see their fathers hitting their mothers and learn to abuse their wives. Daughters are seen as a burden and as a possible source of social shame. . . . The concept of honor is attached to the physical purity of the woman, and that's why only her blood can cleanse the shame her actions bring on a family."[13]

Only her blood. This is why the bloodied sheets of Muslim brides are sometimes hung outside the window, proof of the new wife's virginity paraded as a flag of family honor. Perhaps, then, it would be more accurate to say that honor lies in the blood of a woman, and not just between her legs. She must bleed to prove her honor, and bleed again to reclaim it for the family. As do, say, the girls who become suicide bombers after their honor has been sullied by divorce or rape. How better to redeem themselves and their fathers?

So ingrained is this into the culture of many Islamic-majority countries that in several, men receive little or no punishment. Until 2016, for instance, those who committed honor killings in Pakistan could avoid punishment by paying "blood money" to survivors; current law now requires a twenty-five-year minimum sentence, though this is not always enforced. In Iran, according to a 2015 Amnesty International report, "Under the Penal Code, men who assault or even kill their wives are excluded from the punishments ordinarily applied to such crimes if they prove that they did so while their wife was involved in an act of adultery (Article 630). Fathers or paternal grandfathers who kill their children or grandchildren are not subject to proportional punishments (Article 301) which may exacerbate the risk of 'honor crimes' against girls and women."[14] What's more, "A father can only be sentenced to three to ten years' imprisonment for killing his child." According to the Iran Human Rights Documentation Centre, "In practice this gives fathers legal immunity if they kill their children and opens the door to more honor killings without any effective and deterrent punishment. In cases where another family member kills a girl or woman in the family, Islamic Shari'a gives the victim's next of kin (*awliya-al-dam*) the right to determine whether the condemned should be sentenced to death or be forgiven."[15]

The honor culture of the American South isn't always much better. As Richard Nisbett and Dov Cohen note, until 1974, "Texas law held that if a man found his wife and her lover in a 'compromising position' and killed them, there was no crime—only a 'justifiable homicide.'"[16]

Meantime, as governments begin to crack down on honor killings, and as diaspora communities find their traditions at odds with Western laws, a new phenomenon is emerging: honor suicides. In some instances these "suicides" are in fact homicides, disguised by family members in order to avoid legal penalties. Girls are said to have "jumped" from windows, "drowned themselves," swallowed poison "accidentally." But as a Finnish Immigration Service report observes, "Women are also sometimes pressured into committing suicide so that no one will be punished for their deaths. More than half of the honor killings of women that came to the attention of the UN Special Rapporteur on Violence against Women were made to look like suicides by self-immolation."[17]

In Turkey the phenomenon is especially dire, particularly in the conservative Eastern and Kurdish regions. Take, for instance, the 2006 *New York Times* story of seventeen-year-old Derya, ordered to commit suicide by her uncle. In a text message he told her, "You have blackened our name. Kill yourself and clean our shame or we will kill you first." She wouldn't have been the first: her aunt, the *Times* reports, was killed by her grandfather for having liked a boy, and Derya's sin was the same.[18]

More messages followed: from her brothers, from her other uncles, from her father. So she tried drowning herself in the Tigris River. The effort failed. She tried slashing her wrists but survived that, too. At the time of the *Times* story, she was living in a shelter, hiding from her family.

Other girls are not so lucky. In efforts to save their sons and fathers from punishing jail terms, more and more families are turning to forced suicide rather than outright murder. "Women's groups here say the evidence suggests that a growing number of girls considered to be dishonored are being locked in a room for days with rat poison, a pistol or a rope, and told by their families that the only thing resting between their disgrace and redemption is death," the *Times* reported.

And once they have died, Khalida Brohi explains, their clothes are burned. Any photographs of them are thrown away. They are entirely erased.

For honor.

* * *

An artist I know spent his time in jail surreptitiously creating art. He fashioned a knife from the inside of a battery and the label of antiperspirant, and used it to carve the faces out of six hundred stolen playing cards—mostly the jacks, the kings, the queens. He gathered soap, and pressed newspaper images of mug shots onto each, and placed them where the faces of the cards had been. He sketched portraits of fellow inmates to survive.

"I made them human again," he said.[19]

When you give someone a face, you give them a soul. A heart. A being. This is why advertisers animate things like hamburger buns or put smiles on balloons.

This is what fundamentalist Muslim men steal from Muslim women. Faceless in their *niqabs*, hidden behind their veils, they have no being. Faceless, they become objects without meaning, beings without a soul.

* * *

It isn't always women, however. In 2009 a group of Muslim boys in East London stabbed a young non-Muslim man before forcing him to drink sulfuric acid. Then they poured more acid over his face and body and beat him on the head with bricks. His crime: being accused of having a relationship with a married Pakistani Muslim woman. Both he and she denied that they were lovers.[20]

I want to be clear. This is not the same as domestic violence. Arguments that honor violence is a form of domestic abuse ignore the full hideousness of these crimes, which carry a seal of approval from the family and community at large. While, by contrast, in what you might call "ordinary" domestic violence—brothers almost never kill their sisters, mothers rarely kill their daughters, cousins do not generally kill cousins, or uncles their nephews and nieces—honor killings are, as Phyllis Chesler says, a form of "family conspiracy . . . one backed up by parents, grandparents, sisters, brothers, aunts, and uncles."[21]

Here is the twist: she will die for *their* honor.

And not by her own choice.

You might say, even, that in Western domestic abuse, the abuser is the "lone wolf" terrorist. But in matters of honor violence, families become, in essence, a terrorist group.

Moreover some of those who beat their daughters, or burn their faces to disfigure them, or shoot them as they sleep, do so reluctantly, pressured by tradition, communities, and families. Occasionally a relative may be flown over from abroad to handle the situation, or the women and girls sent away—a kind of preplanning and deliberation that very rarely, if ever, plays a role in domestic abuse. Girls living in the West may be told they are going on vacation—and then are brought by their fathers to a country where honor killings are better tolerated, and laws kinder to the killer.

This, for instance, was what happened to eighteen-year-old Zarife G. (her last name has never been made public), a Dutch-Turkish girl who had long tussled with her strict father. Though Zarife was considered a "proper Muslim girl" by her teachers, who later observed that she wore her head scarf every day, her father was mistrustful, accusing her of spending time with men.[22] Fearful of his violent rages, in January 2003 Zarife escaped to a shelter. But as often happens, her father tracked her down, promised to respect her choices, and in August took her with him on a trip to Turkey.

She never returned.

It was only when she didn't show up at school in September that alarms began to ring. But it was already too late.

Worst of all, there is nowhere for these women to run.

When Nicole Simpson finally freed herself from O.J., her parents never threatened to kill her if she did not return. When I left Boris, I could take refuge with my family. When I left Rick, I did the same; and though he stalked me for years afterward, no one would have considered handing me back to him like a lost glove. Friends rallied to protect me. No one, and certainly not my mother and father, would have locked me in a room and forced me to choose between returning to him and death. For those facing honor killings, for girls like Khadija, there is no sanctuary.

Some, if they are lucky, manage to escape. I have seen them, these girls, desperate to live a normal life in European cities, yet daring to live outdoors only behind a mask, their hair tucked into a wig, and trusting no one with their real names, their stories. For a time the Dutch government took to housing women threatened by honor violence in prisons; it was the only place that was considered safe enough. Meanwhile the men and women, the husbands and fathers and brothers and mothers who sought to murder them, walked free.

Yet they, too, are terrorists. They, too, are seeking to force change. They, too, respond to humiliation with violence aimed at intimidating others, as the Taliban who shot Malala Yousafzai in Pakistan were sending a message to every other Muslim girl seeking an education, as the killers of *Charlie Hebdo* editors sent a message to others who considered publishing "insults" to their prophet. ("One has only to kill a few girls and women to keep the others in line," says Chesler.[23])

And like terrorists, they become heroes: the husbands, the fathers, the sons, the brothers, the mothers, who burn wives and daughters and sisters with acid, or bludgeon them with stones. While the girls suffer torture at their hands, the torturer is lauded. Where there are legal penalties, the community protects him. Nobody will tell. No one even whispers—except to one another. And there, among each other, they congratulate him, they praise him, for doing what was right.

Because, as with terrorism, the phenomenon of honor violence creates and establishes an ethic in which failure to capitulate to the patriarchal order (or god), is a form of profound dishonor; and dishonor is punishable by death.

* * *

But as noted earlier, honor violence does not only exist in Muslim and Hindu communities, in regions that seem alien, unlike us. In only slightly altered form, it still exists in the American South and other havens of white supremacy. While in Turkey or Saudi Arabia or Pakistan, women are killed and beaten for their (alleged) sexual impropriety, among white supremacists it is not the women who are to blame, who deserve death for any imagined impropriety. If the man she is accused of being with is black (or another minority), it is understood that he has taken a white woman's honor. He has filthied her, disgraced her, and so he has taken not just *her* honor but her man's—be that her father or her husband. And here, too, there is but one answer, one possible resolution: the menfolk must have their revenge. (They, after all, are the ones sworn to fight for her honor.) This is what *To Kill a Mockingbird* was all about. It was why Dylann Roof shouted, as he fired his Glock .45 at the worshippers at Mother Emanuel African Methodist Episcopal Church in Charleston, South Carolina, "Y'all are raping our white women."

"Raping our white women." Who hold a man's honor between their legs. White honor. His honor.

For men like Dylann Roof and Mohammed Parvez, as for men in all honor cultures, "honor" is determined by his strength, his power, his ability to refuse humiliation and to take revenge where needed. Ultimately it is about how the community perceives him. Ultimately, in the inherent narcissism of honor culture, it's all about how he looks.

And your life will never matter half so much as that.

CHAPTER 8

THE WOMEN

There was a party that night, and everyone who was anyone would be there. But there would be boys and alcohol, and even at fourteen, Shannon was wise enough in the ways of the world to know her parents would never let her go.

So she lied and said that she was going to visit a friend.

The party was full. The rooms were hot. Everyone *was* there, and there were boys and alcohol, and Shannon drank and danced. Punk was her thing, and the music pounded, and soon the room began to spin, and still she went on dancing.

And then the fun stopped.

The night that Shannon Foley Martinez was raped by boys she wasn't supposed to have been with at a party she wasn't supposed to attend changed her life forever. It wasn't just the rape. It wasn't just the shame that consumed her, as it does so many victims of sexual assault, or her guilt for being where her parents would have told her not to go, and it wasn't even the anger—at the boys; at the parents she couldn't confide in, knowing they would be more dismayed with her for being at the party than they were concerned about what she'd endured; and at herself, as most rape victims are, for having placed herself in that situation. It was more the depth and power of emotions she had no name for, had never learned to feel.

"I was raised that you could only have a small amount of emotion on the spectrum," the former white supremacist tells me now. "You could be sad, but you couldn't be despondent. You could be happy, but you couldn't be like rockets."[1] Today, decades later, she keeps a list of emotions on her kitchen counter "because I don't know them." And without understanding those emotions, she says, "how are you going to access them at all—particularly the vulnerability required to process through the deep dark? It's almost impossible to do when you don't have support and don't already feel safe."

And it is this, she says, that is so much of what turns people toward violence and hate. "When there is abuse being perpetrated onto you, when you are stripped of your fight response, one of the ways we heal from that experience is by touching into anger."

And that anger becomes empowering.

This is the paradigm, too, that sets so many extremists and abusers on their path. As philosopher Eric Hoffer observed, "When, for whatever reason, self-esteem is unattainable, the autonomous individual becomes a highly explosive entity."[2]

For women, especially those in honor-based societies whose rights and opportunities are too often crushed, the broken self crippled by abuse and helplessness can, with the coaxing of her anger, set off just such an inferno. And it is just that kind of coaxing that explains the women who, like Martinez or Safaa Boular and the Palestinian bombers, seek out a sisterhood in a larger movement and an outlet for their rage. As Hoffer puts it, "A mass movement . . . appeals not to those intent on bolstering and advancing a cherished self, but to those who crave to be rid of an unwanted self."[3]

Women have a particularly complex relationship with extremism, thanks in part to the complexity of their roles in both honor and non-honor (or "dignity") cultures, and the societal traditions patriarchal systems impose. If twenty-first-century men grapple with what it means to be a "real man" in the #MeToo age, women since the dawn of civilization have been called on to fit into one of two essential ideals, both seductively romantic: she is either the Cinderella princess bride, a Rapunzel trapped high in a tower, waiting to be rescued by a man on a white steed; or she is Minerva, Athena, the warrior goddess, compassionate virgin, patron of heroic endeavor. In America she is a steel magnolia or a gentle Southern belle; in the Middle East she is either a lioness, guardian of her man and of her children; or she is the pure and modest servant of her father or her husband. Equally in Pakistan, Khalida Brohi explains,

> Many . . . times I'd heard women talking to one another after meeting with abuse or mistreatment from men: "Adi [sister], it's our fate." "Ama [Mother], it's our fate." "Women are made to go through such trials. Have patience [sabr]. Remember, Allah loves patient people."
> Sabr. Patience. Women used the word generously with one another. Sabr is a jewel for a woman. A woman who doesn't speak about her own mistreatment meets with good fortune in the end. . . . Too many women in Pakistan were programmed to believe that they should accept everything that happened to them as their fate. They had been taught and encouraged to practice sabr in the face of all misfortune and abuse, no matter how intense or horrible. They accepted violent, unethical behavior in men because they believed they should. Women encouraged one another to keep silent when they were mistreated, to keep waiting, to be patient, in the belief that one day things would be fine.[4]

If this is the identity that so many women learn to fill, no wonder others, such as the Palestinian suicide bombers Anat interviewed (and many of the Western girls who joined the Islamic State), see extremism as a gateway to freedom—from the men who abuse and rape them or from a Western culture that no longer feels like theirs. For all the ISIS brides, girls eagerly in search of husbands and chivalrous knights and households with picket fences, chasing after the seductive suitors who recruit them on the internet, there are also girls like Alabama-born Hoda Muthana, whose abusive mother and strict father filled her days with fear: that her husband would be chosen for her, that she would be shipped abroad. Even as she radicalized, Hoda knew she wanted to determine her own destiny; making *hijrah*, or the journey to the Islamic State, would serve the purpose of hurting her parents—a gesture of her anger at them—while giving her both freedom and a chance to devote herself entirely to her faith.[5]

"For the girls, joining ISIS is a way to emancipate yourself from parents and from the Western society that has let you down," Sasha Havilicek, chief executive of the British Institute for Strategic Dialogue, told the *New York Times* in 2015.[6] For some it is, too, a way to escape from abuse and a culture filled with narcissistic rage, while gaining purity and redemption. For women it is often (though not always) this, more than pathological narcissism, that leads them to terrorism.

Though Hoda, the daughter of a Yemeni diplomat to the United States, was born Muslim, her family was not particularly devout. Their focus was on tradition more than scripture, leaving Hoda to seek information online as she began turning more and more to religion. And that is precisely where the danger for so many of these women lies.

"There is this assumption, when a woman joins a terror organization, that she is automatically a victim and has been pulled in against her will," Yasmine tells me. "Although that's true in some situations, it's important not to assume that for all women, because they are just as susceptible to the brainwashing as men are. Boys are pulled in by all the promises of virgins and guns, and girls are told different things: they're told a man will take care of you, you will have lots of babies—and when they say this, they hit on the population of women who want that. They'll say, 'oh, they'll have other wives, and you'll get to be best friends.'"[7] For girls like Hoda who feel estranged from others around them, who no longer feel connected to their friends and classmates, there is an enormous appeal in this: they are being promised a world where everyone is just like them.

The majority of Western women who joined the Islamic State, according to the BBC, are converts.[8] And of the Dutch converts who joined the Islamic State, 61 percent were women, a figure that seems to be consistent with other countries as well.[9] Like Hoda they sought knowledge about Islam not so much through local mosques and imams, but on the internet. Their searches landed them, as it did Hoda, in chat groups, on websites thick with information (or propaganda) about the "true" Islam and the responsibilities of good Muslims.

And all the while, Mubin Shaikh says, recruiters remain on the lookout, especially on dating sites and places like Facebook, where vulnerable, heartbroken women are easily attracted and seduced. "They see who makes these comments," he explains, "and then they go on and talk to them. It's the same as child sex predators."[10] They make promises, create daydreams of the big house she will have, the husband who is a brave and handsome fighter. Someone will send her photos of the beautiful jewelry he will send her for her wedding night. "They tell them they will live like a queen," Mubin says.

Laura Passoni, for instance, a Belgian convert who joined ISIS and then managed to return to Europe, had just broken up with a boyfriend when she got caught up in the spell of an ISIS recruiter. He tempted her with visions of life in a luxurious villa and the horses she would own. In a video she made after her repatriation to Belgium, Passoni says, "He sold me a dream I would have everything I wanted in Syria."[11]

What draws them? What brings these women into Islam at all, let alone to terrorism?

Experts like Anne Speckhard, coauthor with Mubin Shaikh of *Undercover Jihadi: Inside the Toronto 18* and director of the International Center for the Study of Violent Extremism, say that many find a form of safety in a culture where women are covered and, as they understand it, protected. (Many women say they found comfort in a religion and community where women are not sexualized.) Carla Rus, a psychiatrist who specializes in working with Muslim girls and young women, explains it is the promise of structure, coupled with adolescent rebelliousness, that often starts them on their journey.[12] They no longer have to question what they will wear each day, or whether something is either not sexy enough or too sexy to wear, or fear being viewed as a sexual object: the *burqa* and *niqab* take care of all that. They no longer have to find an order to their days, or consider whether they will have a career or stay at home with their children. They will spend their days at prayer. It is set out for them.

"People choose order over chaos," Afshin Ellian, an Iranian-born counterterrorism expert and professor of jurisprudence at Leiden University, tells me. "They will elect a government that creates order every time, that builds stability where there was none."[13] I think of Mussolini's proverbial trains and know that this is true. It is why, too, Palestinians voted for Hamas. It is maybe even why I stayed with Rick: there were rules. As much as I might feel threatened, they also protected me. It was only when the rules became indefinite, when what had been allowed no longer was, or was unpredictable, so that the curtain that should have been kept open on Monday afternoon should have been kept closed on Tuesday, that life became unbearable.

Chaos had returned.

Once they convert, these women, like the men, adopt the honor codes of Muslim culture. And as they spend more time in the community, online propagandists and local radicals bombard them with messages about the Muslims being killed, the "genocide" being perpetrated in Israel, the American slaughter of Muslim women and children in Iraq and Afghanistan. Added to this is the social alienation they frequently experience, the problems of bigotry—and there is plenty of bigotry—in the West. Muslims in Europe tend to have a more difficult time getting job interviews, their CVs tossed into the trash simply on the basis of their names.[14] More, women—given that they are burdened with the public demonstration of their faith by way of dress—may be harassed for wearing *hijabs* or other Islamic dress on the streets of Paris or London or Amsterdam or Detroit. And in the face of this shame and degradation, the women, no less than the men, seek revenge. Or freedom. Or both.

Obviously not all female converts radicalize, any more than all abusers become terrorists. As Bart Schuurman, coauthor of "Converts and

Islamist Terrorism," a policy brief produced by the International Centre for Counter-Terrorism in The Hague, once told me, "We don't want all converts to be seen as a terror threat. . . . Conversion itself should not be seen as a risk factor for violence."[15]

At the same time, the number who do become extremist radicals is notable, and was so even before the rise (and recruitment efforts) of the Islamic State in 2014. There was, for instance, the Irish-born Samantha Lewthwaite, now known as the "white widow" and believed to have masterminded the 2013 terrorist attacks in Nairobi that killed seventy-two people, including several children, at a popular shopping mall. (Lewthwaite is also the widow of Germaine Lindsay, one of the suicide bombers involved in the July 7, 2005, attacks throughout London.) Jamie-Paulin Ramirez and Colleen La Rose, also known as "Jihad Jane," are both American converts convicted in 2010 of plotting to murder Swedish cartoonist Lars Viks, who had drawn an image of the Prophet Mohammed as a dog. There was also the Canadian Amanda Korody, who with John Stewart Nuttail was convicted of "facilitating a terrorist activity" for their failed attempt to blow up the British Columbia legislature on Canada Day in 2012.

But just as not all female converts radicalize, those who do share much with those born into the faith. Writing in *Invisible Martyrs*, Farhana Qazi explains the salient triggers she found in almost every case of Pakistani extremists. "Some viewed violence as a weapon of choice," she writes. "[They] joined extremist groups to give purpose to their lives and effect change: to rewrite the future, to say *I am* within the boundaries set by men, to cleanse an unwanted past, to fall into favor with God, to cast away something broken or bruised or scraped, to push beyond the limits of their gender, to find a like-minded lover, or to experience the connection that a woman feels when she joins a sisterhood."[16]

All of this rises from the traumas of life in fundamentalist, patriarchal Muslim families, says Qazi, among girls "hunted like animals in the wilderness for so-called honor crimes," girls whose lives are "dictated by a patriarchy of irrational and ignorant men, many of whom support the radical interpretation of Islam—the barbarism, the beastly action and a culture of humiliation and shame narrated by violent extremists."[17] Consequently, she says, Muslim girls coming out of fundamentalist households may, as Hoda did, search out a life and community that will allow them to escape their families. "Violent extremism [becomes] their new tribe, offering females a group to be a part of." Along the way, they hope, they may even gain redemption—or honor.

Few have recognized this better than the Islamic State, which actively used women to recruit other women online, with enthusiastic Twitter and Tumblr accounts that gushed about the joys of life and sisterhood in the Caliphate. To read these accounts, and the questions other wannabe girl jihadists have asked about life in the Islamic State, is to realize just how young and naive so many of these girls are. There are questions about whether to bring a hair dryer and curling iron. There are questions about whether there will be chocolate.

British *muhajirah* Aqsa Mahmood, who calls herself Umm Layth, for instance, often described a utopian community filled with brotherly and sisterly love, and the promise of a greater future where everyone is the same—ironically, essentially no different than the ethnostate vision of the alt-right in places like the United States. Others wrote of Nutella pancakes and romantic walks in idyllic landscapes at sunset. They posted videos of picnics with their husbands and their friends. And in a reach to those who might have hesitated to make *hijrah*, Umm Layth cooed, "The families you get in exchange for leaving the ones behind are like the pearl in comparison to the shell you threw away into the foam of the sea which is the *ummah*."

Above all, these women, both those posting during the height of the Caliphate's power and others who continue to spread the word for jihad in the name of groups like al Qaeda, emphasize the mother-wife-female role expected under sharia and in the Islamic State. At the same time, they succeed in widening their recruitment reach by appealing to those who prefer to see themselves with greater power, or—true to the lioness and steel magnolia archetype—what the International Centre for Counter-Terrorism calls "the last line of the Caliphate's defense—the final spiritual and physical defender of the home and family."[18]

"Sisters our role is more important than any other, and even the brothers know they are not as capable and as strong as a woman is created to be," Umm Layth wrote. "We are created to be mothers and wives—as much as the western society has warped your views on this with a hidden feminist mentality."[19] And in an article published by al Qaeda's Arabian Peninsula Women's Information Bureau in August 2004, "Umm Badr" cajoled, "My noble sisters . . . the woman in the family is a mother, wife, sister, and daughter. In society she is an educator, propagator and preacher of Islam, and a female jihad warrior. Just as she defends her family from any possible aggression, she defends society from destructive thoughts and from ideological and moral deterioration, and she is the soldier who bears his pack and weapon on his back in preparation for the military offensive . . . the Muslim woman is a female jihad warrior always and everywhere. She is a female jihad warrior who wages jihad by means of funding jihad; she wages jihad by means of waiting for her jihad warrior husband . . . she wages jihad when she shows patience and fortitude with her husband who is waging jihad for the sake of Allah. . . ."[20]

The jihadist woman, in other words, is loving and strong, capable and kind, devoted and gentle and brave. She is everything every young girl has ever imagined herself to be.

* * *

"To give purpose to their lives," says Farhana Qazi, "to say *I am* . . . to cleanse an unwanted past, to push beyond the limits of their gender."[21]

This isn't just the women in Pakistan Qazi spoke with. It is also Shannon Martinez.

And it is alt-right leader Lana Lokteff, a kind of Gloria Steinem for the antifeminist white-power movement who appeals to women to be the "lionesses and shield maidens and Valkyries" who support men in their fight to create a white ethnostate in the United States.[22] Indeed her call for a sisterhood of white women to support their white men by being "good wives" and producing babies echoes ISIS propaganda so closely that it is almost difficult to tell them apart. Speaking at the "Identitarian Ideas IX" conference in 2017, for instance, Lokteff, an attractive blonde with a surprisingly young, almost childish voice, declared, "Women are the key to the future of European countries. Not only as life-givers, but as the force that inspires men. . . . There are three important things for a woman, and they're ingrained into our psyche. And no matter how hard you try, they will never be removed. Beauty, family, home. Women want to be beautiful, attract the best mate possible, and be protected and provided for until death. . . . We value the beauty of Western civilization and the refined human form. European men built civilization and facilitated beauty in all its forms. It's the ultimate romantic gesture to European women. They built our civilization to enable the home and the family, and to protect women." Declaring the nation "your tribe" and "extended family" (think of the Muslim *ummah* and the online communities that so seduce young Muslim girls), she then asserted, "Women have a special power to inspire and motivate men. To give them a reason to fight. The woman makes the man."[23]

It's not just Lokteff, of course. When white supremacist group Vanguard America initiated their "women's division" in 2017, for instance, they promoted it on Twitter: "The woman has her own battlefield. With every child that she brings into the world, she fights her battle for the nation. Strong nations grow from strong families."[24]

And so, as journalist Seyward Darby described it in a landmark article about the women of the alt-right, "By supporting the alt-right, they stand shoulder to shoulder with men who think that female independence has undermined Western civilization. . . . They describe the alt-right as a refuge where white women can embrace their femininity and their racial heritage without shame."[25]

The parallels between Lokteff's speech and the directives of ISIS and al Qaeda are telling. Just as jihadist and white supremacist men often radicalize in response to past shaming, abuse, and a need for power or "honor," so, too, do female jihadists and white supremacist women travel very much the same paths as one another. And so, too, just as it does for girls born and raised in Muslim homes—young women like San Bernardino killer Tashfeen Malik, for instance—or converts who have endured abusive homes or extreme bullying, radicalization often mobilizes in white Christian women the kind of violent rage that set Shannon Martinez on her path to white supremacism. It is a rhetoric that promises power and control while also promising security, that blends the "Wonder Woman" mystique with Rapunzel and Scheherazade.

And how better to seduce women like Shannon Foley Martinez; women like Safaa Boular and Hoda Muthana; women who feel degraded, damaged, hurt; women who, for several possible reasons, cannot access, cannot even name what it is they feel? If you cannot know what you feel, you do not know what you want. And so someone stronger, someone you believe is wiser, tells you. This is how the propaganda works, and the brother-sisterhood. Something resonates, and you take it.

("No one else will ever love you," the batterer says, or: "You only want that because your friends tell you so. That's what you get for hanging around with those people." And because you have come to loathe yourself now, too, because you no longer trust your own desires, you believe him. How do you know what is real, anymore, or what is right?)

Then there are the times, both for Muslim and white radical women, that it all comes together, when they fall in love with someone already radicalized. Speaking of the women of the Dutch Hofstadgroep, the terror cell responsible for the 2004 murder of Theo van Gogh, Carla Rus told me, "Sometimes they are just so crazy about the boy that they start reading the material. She becomes part of the group in order to conform and to win his praise, and then because she becomes afraid of being dropped, either by the group or by him, she begins to pick up the norms and values of that subculture."[26]

The same can be true, of course, for non-Muslim young women as well. Love, longing, desire, confusion have no religion, no geography, no race.

From here, Shannon Martinez believes, a cycle forms and takes on a life of its own. Seeing yourself already as damaged, she says, you decide,

"I'm going to be a better Nazi, or a better girlfriend, or a better jihadist."[27] And so you find yourself in a world of violence, in a place that doesn't redeem you after all, a place that doesn't bring your selfhood back, but funnels you even deeper into the suck. "Part of the mechanism, the amplification of radicalization," she says, "is that there was this process by which I felt ever decreasingly important. My self-worth and sense of individual value plummeted. And at the same time that was happening, I felt that I had more value in terms of the movement. While I felt more worthless, I was more valuable. That mechanism is why people are willing to blow themselves up and kill other people—as you are stripped more and more of your individuation, you see no personal value, but what you see in terms of the contribution you can make to the community." And so the cycle continues.

The tragic irony of that cycle is the unrelenting search for honor and reward, for meaning, for purpose, for importance—or as Qazi puts it, the ability to say "*I am*." In a patriarchal world, East or West, the role of the woman is tied to the man: his honor is between her legs, is in her blood; she is the carrier, the "reason." The role, the purpose, the meaning, of women in the alt-right is to support their men, just as it is the role, the purpose, the meaning, of Muslim women to support their jihadist husbands, and to raise jihadist sons.

There is no "I am."

* * *

For those on the alt-right, the neo-Nazi groups and followers of extremist leaders like Richard Spencer, the creator of the term "alt-right" who says he seeks a "peaceful"[28] ethnic cleansing of non-whites from North America, what's at stake is the future domination of whites, and specifically white men. Unlike the leaders of ISIS and al Qaeda, the goal isn't to conquer the world and transform it into a global caliphate, but to hold on to power in a world that is increasingly diverse, and when the white population will soon become a minority. The primary job of women, then, is to populate the world with more white babies and then to raise their sons to demand the same of their own wives in the future. They should raise their sons and daughters to understand the primacy of the white race, and their daughters, in raising their own children, to do the same. They should bring other women into the fold, and yet do so quietly, with oh-so-feminine voices and genteel speech.

But white supremacist groups face an inherent problem: most white supremacist men revile women as much as Lokteff believes they long for them. Breivik blamed the world's ills on the rise of feminism and on the feminization of men. Conflicted by his near-sexual relationship with and utter dependence on his mother, and her tendency to verbally abuse him throughout his childhood, he came, in a way, to personify the relationship that male white supremacists, in their demand for the conquest of the world by white men, have with white women overall. This they share, too, with the women-hating so-called incels, the "involuntarily celibate" men who blame women for their own sexual and romantic failures—men like Scott Paul Beierle, for instance, who shot up a Tallahassee yoga studio in November 2018.

For such men there is one driving force: to overcome the vulnerability of sexual longing, the vulnerability of their need for love and above all, to distinguish themselves from the weakness and inferiority that is women, they assert the maleness, the patriarchal machismo, of their manhood.

They will not be shamed by their loss of status as the "rulers of the world," these white men who hold the power. Not by non-whites. Not by women. Not by anyone. They brandish their swords.

Which is why it was no surprise to many when Richard Spencer's now ex-wife accused him of threatening to kill her, or when she testified under oath that he had held her by the neck and jaw while she was four months pregnant, or that he had once dragged her down the stairs.[29] And why it is also no surprise that some wings of America's white supremacist movement now call for what they term "white sharia," which they describe as a violent patriarchy. Accordingly Andrew Anglin, who ran the neo-Nazi DailyStormer.com from 2013 to 2018, has said that the womb of white women "belongs to the males of society."[30]

(It is perhaps also worth noting that Nicole Brown Simpson's sister testified in the O.J. Simpson trial that while out to dinner in 1987, "O.J. grabbed Nicole's crotch and said, 'This is where babies come from and this belongs to me.'"[31])

And yet as Robin Morgan so eloquently observes in *The Demon Lover*, there is at the same time for many women an allure to men who stand against a perceived enemy, who make you feel safe. And as every abused woman, every abused child, knows, this is the trick he plays: he is the gallant knight who saves you from the evil villain, and you are so frightened and confused and relieved and unsure that you forget entirely that he was the villain, too.

* * *

This is not to say that Lokteff's husband, the Swedish-born Hendrik Palmgren, has ever abused her. There is no apparent public record either way. But it explains the sense of threat, in part by women who have been raised in abusive homes (in America, domestic violence rates are highest in the South, and official rates of domestic homicide and rape by white males are more likely in honor states[32]), a sense that adds kindle to the fire of white supremacy—there is danger everywhere, and you don't know where or when. It drives the fear that if Muslim men are flying airplanes into buildings and shooting up restaurants in Paris, all Muslim men could be dangerous; if black men are robbing banks, all black men could be dangerous; if Donald Trump tells you that Mexico is only sending their rapists to America, all Mexican men could dangerous. Danger is everywhere.

But the white men, your white men, will protect you.

And the women in these groups? They can regain their honor and their own empowerment by helping to make their men stronger.

Terrorized, traumatized, they are looking to feel safe—the women on the right, the women of Islamism. These are the ties that bind them.

CHAPTER 9

THE TIES THAT BIND

Yasmine and I chat on Skype, relaxed in the warmth of a July afternoon. Growing up, she tells me, she was constantly terrified of ending up in hell. Yet even as she feared it, silently she rebelled against the idea. "I knew what was expected of me, but inside I was always resisting it," she says, "hoping and wishing one day I would be free. Unlike these women of ISIS. Because if you let go and just submit as you are supposed to, which I couldn't, if you submit you will get pulled into that so deep that you will no longer know the difference between up and down and right and wrong. Your humanity has left, you are pulled under."

"Like an abuse victim," I say.

"Yes," says Yasmine, "because right and wrong are dictated to you and contradict what you feel."

"So if you don't do the things that go against your instincts, you'll be punished in hell, and if I didn't do what Rick said, even if it was against my instincts, he would beat the hell out of me."

Right, says Yasmine. "Basically that's the parallel."[1]

Here again, the threads cross and tie, linking the abused and the terrorized, the abusers and the terrorists, into the webs and patterns that they weave.

In the end it is all the same. Insult a pathological narcissist and they will hit you harder. In the churches and the synagogues, in the mosques and in the concert halls, the restaurants, the schools, in the living rooms and the bedrooms, in the streets.

* * *

In the months after 9/11 Americans searched their culture, their politics, their country, themselves. Headlines filled the covers of magazines with questions like "Why Do They Hate Us?" while pundits debated the ways America should change, must change, to stop the violence, the hate. And so, to stop the fear.

But the fear didn't stop. We added security to airplanes, and they attacked us on the streets.

We kept the curtains open, or we closed them.

This tendency to blame ourselves unites the victims of terror and abuse in countless ways, all of which do little or nothing to solve the problems, and certainly nothing to stop the violence. If it is about who we are, it is also about who they are: malignant narcissists whose need for honor translates into power, violence, and death.

But mostly we don't see that.

For the victims of abuse, as for the victims of terror, what we lack most is what abusers and terrorists have far too much of: the absolute conviction of being right. We turn in, believing the accusations even when they make no sense (and the more so when they do). We blame the victim all the more when that victim is ourself.

This is when the shame comes.

And the cycle goes on.

Among the known responses to abuse is a state of hyper-vigilance: for years after my relationship with Boris ended, I could not bear to feel a body come too close. Strangers on the street who brushed me as they passed set my heart pounding so hard I had to stop and catch my breath. I could not walk easily in crowds. In the months after 9/11 a friend told me that when planes flew low over lower Manhattan, brokers would remind one another to charge their phones. In Washington DC, the crafters of American military policy focused on executing "pre-emptive strikes."

More recently, in the face of high rates of violent crime in American black communities, white police have begun shooting unarmed black men for questionable reasons; think, for instance, of Samuel DuBose, an unarmed black man fatally shot by a policeman in 2015 for driving with a suspended license, and Philando Castile, a school cafeteria worker killed in 2016 by an officer who thought he "matched the description of a suspect in a robbery days earlier."[2] Think of former Dallas police officer Amber Guyger, who fatally shot twenty-six-year-old Botham Jean when she walked into *his* apartment, thinking (she claimed) it was her own.

And there is this, as well: the closed eyes, the denial, the refusal to see, to believe. We who ogle at car accidents on the highway cannot watch the beheading videos ISIS puts on the internet and the media broadcasts on prime-time news. Women who get involved with men they know have abused other women convince themselves "it won't happen to me." In the months after 9/11 Europeans insisted "it won't happen here." Then it did: In London. In Madrid. In Amsterdam. And more.

* * *

The journalist kneels in the desert. The masked assassin stands above him: his executioner. The knife is small. This knife is the one he will use to slice the head from the body. These are the journalist's last minutes. This is how it ends. He is an American and a Jew. We turn our heads away. In this last act, he, Steven Soltoff, has been the journalist he strove in life to be: he told a story. He showed the world the truths we would never otherwise have known. And he made them do it for him, by their own evil, by their own egos, by their own barbaric, primitive minds and what they comprehend of power.

We didn't want to see.

It was more than our minds and our humanity could imagine possible, or wanted to.

We see the lover, not the man whose hand crashes against our cheek.

We turn away. We deny. We excuse. We forgive. We forget. Over and over again.

Or we resign ourselves. We stay. We accept this new world, this life, and adapt—or do our best to adapt—in order to accommodate what is. We do not ask him to check dinner cooking on the stove. We do not sketch images of Mohammed. We accept the marriages arranged for us. We keep our faces covered, or our hair. We keep the curtains drawn.

It makes no difference.

* * *

In 2006 Muslims rioted across the world, from Paris to Pakistan, from Copenhagen to Zanzibar. They threatened to bomb consulates, set fire to the embassies. They called for various beheadings. The protests and the anger ran for years. The reason for their fury? Cartoons. And then in Paris in 2015 two members of al Qaeda killed for them.

But the cartoons were an excuse, a target for an endless, bottomless, enormous rage.

Yet it was the European media, the American government, the public—who apologized. We should not, they said, have published jokes that so offended you. We should not have written words with which you disagree.

But there were no apologies, however, from most Muslim communities across the globe. Nor from the Middle Eastern media. From them came neither atonement nor remorse. It was an instant lesson in tyranny, in terror: even when what you have done wrong is virtually inconsequential compared to the response, you apologize. Even when you've done nothing wrong at all.

"My feet are cold," I say, laughingly placing one toe against his leg. I think that he will start and then laugh with me. He does not.

"Fucking bitch," he hisses, and then his voice grows stronger. "What the fuck do you think you're doing?"

And I tell him I am sorry, afraid that he will hit me next. The ceiling lowers. The walls narrow. Shadows fall. I grow afraid even to touch him, longing for his touch, for his forgiveness, for his pardon. Touch me and tell me I am still okay, I am not to be put out with the trash, you do not hate me; touch me and tell me I am not a despicable, worthless person. I'll do whatever it is you ask.

Terror. This is how it works.

* * *

It is, of course, not quite the same for women as for an entire country—at least not for women in the West spared the traditions of honor violence: there are places they can run, laws and communities to protect them. In a world of terrorism, where terror raises its head now on every continent, there is nowhere to go.

"Each day," Robin Morgan writes, "we act out a series of small, multiple trusts. We trust that with a turn of the wrist on the cold-water faucet, hot water won't scald us. We trust that the motorist bearing down on the crosswalk will observe the same traffic-light change as the pedestrian stepping off the curb. We trust the key that fit the lock this morning will still fit the lock tonight. We trust that when we bare our teeth at strangers, they will understand it as a smile."[3]

This is it, too. We trust that when we open the curtains we will not get punched. We trust that when we kiss our fiancé hello he will not hurl us across the room. We trust that when we leave for work in the morning no one will blow the building up for Allah.

* * *

In Paris these days the gendarmes no longer walk the boulevards. After 9/11 an attack that kills one hundred thirty people in stadiums and restaurants doesn't seem so serious. Terrorist stabbings at European train stations no longer command the headlines. We grow annoyed by things like taking off our shoes at airports. We resist the archiving of metadata from our phones.

He will be better. He won't do it again. It wasn't really all that bad.

In what is known as the "cycle of violence," psychologists have identified three main phases: the "tension building phase," the "violent episode phase," and the "remorseful, honeymoon phase." In the first phase the victim responds to obvious tensions in her partner (or the child to his parents) with submissive acquiescence, afraid of an impending eruption, the explosion set off by a button she cannot see or sense until it is too late. He is suspicious of the things she says and does. Or she is not giving him his due. She is not giving him the respect that he deserves. That he demands.

"You are afraid of true intimacy," Rick would tell me. "You are afraid to let yourself go, to trust completely."

He was right, and I knew it. I did not trust completely. We were arguing about my bank card. He had already stolen more than a thousand dollars from me, cashing a check he was supposed to apply to a security deposit on an apartment and spending it on himself instead. "If you can't trust me with your bank account, then you don't really trust me." It was a profound insult, he said. How could I? How dare I?

I gave him the card.

It, too, made no difference.

It was years before I understood that I was not to blame, that there was not something wrong with me, that I was not the wrong one, the damaged one.

And therein lies another link still. Indeed if any single question binds the victims of abuse and the targets of terrorist attacks, it is this: What did we do wrong? And for both, the answer eventually is clear: we said no.

This is the pattern. It is always the same. The demands grow larger. The rules grow tighter. Already half defeated, she gives in more and more. Each time there is a small reward: a kiss, a kindness, a day without bruises. But it is not enough; eventually the demands come that she cannot accept, or the expectations are unspoken: she "should have known," he says. Or: he'd warned her once before, why couldn't she remember?

This is when the violence breaks open. France refuses to revoke its *burqa* ban, concerned for public safety and the secular principles of its republic. American troops remain in Afghanistan and Iraq. Black people still vote, and Hispanics are still coming over the border, and women are still holding corporate positions that should belong to men. Something must be done.

"Somebody had to do something," said Dylann Roof in his taped confession.[4]

And then the calm begins, the "remorseful, honeymoon phase." He's so sorry. But if she only hadn't. . . . If the laws were only different. . . . She gave him no other choice. . . . Yes, she says. It was probably her fault, she says. Maybe we should reconsider, the prime minister suggests. She forgives him. They embrace. They put it all behind them.

Eventually the gendarmes no longer walk the streets.

* * *

When I review these ideas with Shannon Martinez, she smiles. Radicalization works the same way, she tells me: the seduction phase, isolation, the violence, shame. When she sends me a graphic of her version of the cycle, I am startled by how well it describes the true cycle of domestic abuse—far better in fact than the standard model, the pattern of tension, violence, honeymoon.[5]

In Martinez's pattern there are four, not three, phases: seduction, alienation, intensity, and increased dependence through acts of violence or threats of violence that reinforce the idea that you are "damaged goods." "As personal worth and value decrease, allegiance to the movement increases," she explains. "I no longer have value, but I can at least find value in what I give to the movement."[6] For an abuse victim, that value comes in what she gives to the relationship, what the child gives to the parents, the child who tries, ever harder, for his father's elusive approval.

Still, I think there's even more than this, captured in the hunger and despair of narcissistic need. The belief in your own superiority, held alongside a sense of shame, increases the need to show—to broadcast—your real worth, your real and indisputable power: Hitting harder. Killing more. Inspiring more fear.

"Somebody asked me once what I wanted to be when I grew up," Christian Picciolini writes in *Romantic Violence*. "I told them at ten I wanted to be a doctor; at twelve, a detective, an explorer, a spy; but by fourteen, I wanted to rule the world. I might have been half-joking about it then, but I was serious now. I'd had a taste of power and loved everything about it. Acceptance. Freedom. Fear. Respect. Control."[7] Elsewhere he recalls gaining notoriety with his buddy Al Kubiac as "the two toughest motherfuckers around Blue Island. . . . For the first time, I felt completely in control of my own life. I'd yearned for so long to fit in with my peers and now they'd begun to vie for my attention. The ones that had once ignored me now revered me."[8]

And so the seduction phase begins again.

* * *

Joining a cult, I learn, is also like being beaten, a slow process based on isolation and conformity and trust. Not surprisingly it also parallels completely the process of radicalization. "It's better this way," the members say. "It's normal," Boris said. "It's your fault," Rick told me. "It's the real Islam," say the recruiters for jihad. And you believe it. Even when I asked others which was true, my idea or his, and they said mine, I still wasn't sure. He was so convincing.

"If ten people stand in a room and tell you line A is longer than line B when in fact it isn't, you will eventually say so, too," psychiatrist Carla Rus tells me.[9] Sixty percent do. More than half. "They will go against what they see with their own eyes." And if they are isolated, if their only input is from the people in the room, there is no reevaluation, no adjustment, and it becomes the norm. Torture also happens like this, she says, through the obedience to authority. People can be convinced anything is good. If he cries and screams he's likely to talk, soldiers may be told, and if he talks we can save thousands of lives, and besides, if you don't we'll give you a dishonorable discharge, because this is what we're here to do: save lives. And so they do it.

And this, Carla says, is why blonde women blow themselves up for Allah.

* * *

I remember the exact moment I fell in love with him, at an Irish bar on Lexington Avenue in 1979. He was a high school dropout. I was a college sophomore home for Thanksgiving break. It was less than a year after I had escaped from Boris. It was twenty years before our own romance would actually begin.

I remember what we were wearing: Rick: tight blue jeans, neatly pressed; hiking boots; a dark red shirt, velour, with a zipper at the throat, open to show a boyish neck; me: a dark red V-neck sweater I'd traded my friend Tori for, a long Indian-print skirt, and cowboy boots.

I remember what we drank: Heineken (him); a glass of Soave Bolla for me. I remember there was sawdust on the floor. Our table was the kind you have to put a matchbook under to keep it steady, but we didn't.

And I remember what he said, looking at me from across that swerving table: "Who hit you?"

And that was when I fell in love with him.

I had never told him what had happened, about the sizzling July nights clutching at the corners of Boris's studio apartment, waiting for the next hit, and the next one, and all of them, so it would finally be over. I hadn't told him of the bruises I hid beneath long sleeves on simmering August days, or the lies I told of falling down the stairs or walking into a grand piano we didn't even really own.

But he was street smart and noticed the details. Maybe he had recognized the way I drew away from him when he gestured too close to my face. Maybe he had seen a scar, still visible months later, beneath my eye.

But because he knew, because he understood, he became my knight in urban armor. "You don't need to be afraid," he said. He would teach me how not to be afraid. He would teach me how to trust again. And I believed him. He'd grown up among the gangs. He knew how to fight the bad guys.

But what it took me decades more to see was that I felt safe with him *because* he knew how to be violent. What is a knight but a warrior?

Somewhere hidden in the fairy tales that shape our cultural identities— and for many of us, our own—the melding of romance with warfare, heroism, and violence, the lover and the sword—are the notions we translate into our societies and our governments: the armies they command to keep us safe and the programs with which they show (or convince) us of their care, like welfare systems and environmental laws.

This is the muscle beneath the patriarchal systems of the world—from sharia-based cultures to our own. Of course my knight could protect me.

It is true I fell in love with him mostly because of his insightfulness. But it was that hero's swagger that seduced me in the end. I could not foresee the violence that swagger carried at its side.

And yet, I know now that in so many ways, it should have been clear, in the way that Tamerlan Tsarnaev's descent into terrorism should have been clear.

I remember when he asked me who had hit me, I didn't answer him. I remember that I knew he didn't need me to reply. I remember that I asked a question of my own: How did he know?

And he told me, slowly, unwinding the narrative with a storyteller's skill: He was out of control in high school. His mother sent him to his aunt to live. He could burn his restless energy in the mountains. He would be away from the gangs of New York City. And his aunt ruled with an iron hand.

He knew because he had felt that iron hand.

Until he had had enough; and one day he pulled her gun out from the closet and waited for her to come home.

"I just wanted her to tell me why," he says. I am staring, my glass of wine now sweating in the overheated bar. "Why the beatings with the belt? Why the nights locked in my room? Why?"

He held the gun pointed at her for hours.

Then he turned it on himself.

And put it down again.

He knew. For this I trusted him. And he kept his word; over the next few years he pulled me from the mire of my fear.

Eventually we lost touch; and then nearly two decades later, he phoned. He was back in New York after years away, he said. He'd come back because he needed a new start. He needed a new start, he said, because he had spent a year in prison.

"What happened?" I said.

"For domestic violence," he said.

Surely something had gone wrong. Not this man. It was impossible. It was a mistake. It was, after all, the height of the O.J. Simpson case. Police were overreacting, I said. It was her fault, he said. She kicked him in the groin. He hit her back. Then the police came. He should not have been arrested.

I believed him.

My friends and family didn't. A woman I met online with contacts in law enforcement in the very county where he'd been incarcerated offered to pull his file. I declined. He had rights to privacy. It would be wrong for me to violate them.

It was years after we'd separated that I learned the truth: the fight had not, as he had told me, involved car keys, but it did include him slamming the woman unconscious, dragging her naked by her hair through their apartment, and violently resisting arrest.

Boris, too, had torn into other women before, women that I knew. No one told me, and it never occurred to me to ask. No one taught us, when they used a teddy bear to show us how to put on a sanitary napkin in sixth-grade sex-ed class, that we should find out these things and what to do when it happens anyway.

And so we do not know, any of us, to pay attention to things like the fact that 44 percent of white supremacists report being abused as children, 21 percent endured sexual abuse, and 46 percent report childhood neglect.[10] Or that Omar Mateen, the Pulse nightclub attacker, allegedly abused, even tortured, his ex-wife; that Tamerlan Tsarnaev was arrested for beating an ex-girlfriend; that San Bernardino shooter Syed Farook was raised in an abusive home; that Mohammed Lahouiaej-Bouhel, who rammed a truck through a crowd of revelers on Bastille Day in Nice in 2016, also beat his wife.[11]

Anyway, we don't really want to know those things. They are personal, private.

Like the archiving of metadata, or the monitoring of mosques, or background checks on guns, we decline to dig into others' affairs. We are not supposed to peer into keyholes. We are not supposed to rummage in other people's drawers. It's bad manners. We wouldn't want them rummaging in ours.

And so we don't.

* * *

But abuse isn't always physical; and terrorism is not always violent. Emotional abuse, experts agree, can be more damaging than the punches and the stabbings and the blood: it can change a victim's very image of herself, build—or destroy—a child's character. Tell a child often enough that he is worthless, and he will believe it. Tell a woman she is hideous and unlovable, isolate her at home, and she will eventually believe that, too. No matter what she sees when she looks in the mirror. "They don't love you; they feel *sorry* for you," he'll say, and that kind of makes sense, after a while. Or maybe it's just that nothing makes sense. Nothing.

Similarly, through what some call "stealth jihad," many radical Muslim communities are working to reconfigure the very nature of Western culture, placing limitations on free expression through political means, as, say, through criminalization of some forms of speech, particularly blasphemy. But their tactics are often insidious. In Maajid Nawaz's memoir of his days as a Muslim terrorist in the 1990s, *Radical: My Journey Out of Islamist Extremism*, he describes the primary strategy of Islamist groups he belonged to in the UK: gaslighting. "We disguised our political demands behind religion and multiculturalism," he recalls, "and deliberately labeled any objection to our demands as racism. . . . It is no wonder then that the authorities were unprepared to deal with politicized religion as ideological agitation; they felt racist if they tried to stop us." This, he explains, was deliberate. "Islamism demanded no less of a root-and-branch overhaul of society. But because it was cloaked in religious garb, no one quite knew what to do with it, and people were desperate not to offend."[12]

White supremacist groups, too, seek to change the nature of European and American culture, from calls to "build that wall" to efforts to reverse civil rights for the LGBTQ community and the U.S. Supreme Court decision for *Roe v Wade*. And not unlike the Islamists, they use religion to couch their claims: It is "against their faith" to serve a homosexual couple. It is "against their faith" to allow other women to have abortions. The forces of evil are everywhere. "Jews are the children of Satan (John 8:44)," Robert Bowers, who shot up a Pittsburgh synagogue on October 27, 2018, killing eleven people at prayer, posted online. "The Lord Jesus Christ [has] come in the flesh."[13]

But in truth, it's also more.

"The uniting philosophy in these cases," writes Jared Yates Sexton in *The Man They Wanted Me to Be*, "isn't religious, but patriarchal. Just as McVeigh envisioned a federal government emasculating the sovereignty of men, school shooter Dimitrios Pagourtzis saw his advances being rejected by a female classmate as a nullification of his masculine sovereignty, leading him to kill ten in the Friday, May 18, 2018 high school shooting in Santa Fe, Texas. Again, as men are taught that emotions are for women and the only acceptable means of communication is anger, their aggrieved entitlement is routinely finding an outlet in senseless violence."[14]

Put another way: it is narcissistic rage, fueled by a patriarchal demand, a pounding and fearful yearning, for power and control. These men are seeking, demanding, acquiescence and attention. They believe that they and their significance is all that matters, that the world should run according to their order. And so they dictate. They beat. They shoot. They bomb. They do not care. Their rages overtake them, overtake us, overtake entire countries to destroy all that stands directly in their way: America. Europe. Women. The woman. The immigrants, the blacks, the Jews, the wife, the child. When David Luckenbill, an expert in violent crime, studied the confrontations between victims and their killers, James Gilligan points out, he found that "the opening move that started this process was some behavior by the victim that the perpetrator interpreted as insulting or disparaging to him and that would cause him to 'lose face' if he 'backed down' rather than responding with violence even when the victim was only a child who refused to stop crying when ordered to."[15]

"Even when the victim was only a child who refused to stop crying when ordered to."

And so, like the abused women, like the boys beaten by their teachers and their fathers and their imams, we, all of us, our communities and governments, make the choice to fight or to flee, as much in the face of terrorist attacks as in the face of threats to what we believe to be our privilege, our right, our honor. Some of us, wrapped in fear and darkness, shrink back, become invisible, surrender. We submit. We stop publishing the cartoons. We withdraw our troops from Baghdad. We debate what "freedom" means. If he doesn't want us visiting our family, we will no longer see them. When he asks us to leave our jobs and stay at home, we do. When Muslim communities decried an art exhibition of nudes painted in Arabic script in June 2019, the Saatchi Gallery in London covered up the works with sheets. When Muslim radicals threatened the Deutsch Oper in Berlin in 2006, it canceled its performance of Mozart's *Idomeneo*, which would have included a scene depicting the severed head of the Prophet Mohammad.

Or else we burn the mosques down, or the synagogues; we pack explosives stuffed with hardware in a Karrimor sport backpack and take it with us to an Ariana Grande concert, or we drive a van into a crowd.

We are either angry or afraid.

No. We are afraid.

* * *

And there's more. The most dangerous moment for a woman in an abusive relationship is when she takes action—the moment that she leaves.[16] And the acts most likely to engender an attack by terrorists in the West? The moments Western governments, too, take action to protect themselves, conducting military attacks on Muslim-majority countries, or instituting laws that Islamists consider "insulting" or "disrespectful," such as France's *burqa* ban. There is, too, the victim-blaming: "America had it coming," some said after 9/11; and in the hours after Bouyeri stabbed and shot Theo van Gogh to death on the streets of Amsterdam, scores of Dutch Muslims collectively celebrated online, sharing messages like "the pig is dead," while the far left muttered that "well, he had provoked it."[17] It was an echo of the words women hear so often: "What did she do to deserve it?" and "Then why didn't she leave?"

And so we come together, the terrorist and the terrorized. We are the child who wouldn't stop crying, even when ordered to stop.

CHAPTER 10

PEACE AT HOME, PEACE IN THE WORLD

Over drinks at Brasserie Beymen in Istanbul, my friend Asli explains to me how it is that Recep Tayyip Erdogan has managed to hold such power, to endear himself to the majority for so long, and how dictators in general rule the Middle East.

"In our tradition," she says, "the father beats, then gives. First he hits you, then he offers you candy and gifts. This is what the people are used to, so they feel comfortable with Erdogan, with a man who says first 'I take away your freedom' and then 'but I will console you with a sack of coal.' And they are grateful."[1]

This is where the abuser and the terrorist become one. He hits you then consoles you. He takes you to dinner. The beatings stop. The bombings end.

Until the next one.

I cannot help remembering, as Asli speaks, the words of modern Turkey's founder, Kemal Ataturk: "*Yurtta sulh, cihanda sulh*"—peace at home, peace in the world.

Or terror.

"First he hits you, then he offers you candy and gifts." It is the paradigm of the abuser. It is also the paradigm of the families and cultures that build pathological narcissism in their children—as, say, Breivik's mother did, and Tamerlan Tsarnaev's parents, or O.J. Simpson's, and so on.

For all of Ataturk's Westernizing reforms, most of those who have supported Erdogan remain conservative, defined more by their devotion to Islam and their country's Ottoman past than to the modern secularization of the republic. In Erdogan they see what America's conservative Evangelicals and white supremacists see in Donald Trump: make Turkey great again. They seek a return to a world where they, and not the secular liberals, wield the power. They want a world with an order that they understand, is predictable, and even a world where, as the Palestinian terrorist "Jemilla" told Anat Berko, the husband is Allah in the home. Everything has a place. Patriarchy reigns. And with it, a culture of honor.

But where there is an honor culture, there is also a culture of violence. Endless wars ravage the honor-based tribal cultures of Africa, incite the perpetual warfare between Sunni and Shiite States of the Middle East, and bolster the efforts by Salafist militants to install a global caliphate, with the entire world under their iron rule.

So, too, as Ryan Brown and Kiersten Baughman found, is "coercive violence against women . . . more likely within a culture of honor" in the United States. In a series of studies, the two determined that "white men in honor states committed rape and murdered their female partners (or former partners) at higher rates than did white men in non-honor states."[2] In another study Brown further found a link between honor cultures and the prevalence of school shootings—explaining why, at the time of the study (2009), "culture of honor states had more than twice as many school shootings per capita as non-culture-of-honor states."[3] In fact, as distinct from other violent crimes, which "typically show stronger and more consistent associations with temperature, rurality, and environmental-insecurity measures," Brown notes, school violence stands apart. "That the culture of honor appears to be such a robust predictor of school violence supports the hypothesis that school violence might be partially a product of long-term or recent experiences of social marginalization, humiliation, rejection or bullying, all of which represent honor threats with special significance to people (particularly males) living in culture-of-honor states."

It doesn't end there. In yet a third study, Brown and others found that ideologies of male honor in the United States linked directly to "militant responses to terrorism." Subjects in this study were asked to respond to a hypothetical attack on the Statue of Liberty. As Brown and his colleagues note, members of honor cultures tend to experience "relatively more shame in response to imagining themselves as disgraceful members of their families, and the extent to which they experienced this emotional reaction more than their [non-honor-culture] counterparts was accounted for by their greater concern with family honor."[4] "In light of this emphasis," they write, "it is not surprising that reputational threats in the form of insults carry special weight in cultures of honor and elicit a variety of negative reactions . . . not the least of which is violence, especially among males . . . [who tend to experience] a concern with men's reputation for toughness, fearlessness, and aggressiveness in the face of provocation."[5] Further they cite Pulitzer prize–winning historian David Hackett Fischer, who "noted that honor in the historical southern U.S. 'meant a pride of manhood in masculine courage, physical strength, and warrior virtue.'"[6] (The inclusion of "warrior virtue" here is particularly striking.)

That same sensitivity, which the study's authors describe as "the importance of reputation maintenance," was reflected in the attitudes of subjects from honor states toward the fictional attack. Both white men and white women consistently supported violent retaliation for terrorist attacks. "Masculine honor ideology in the U.S. could contribute to militant responses to terrorism for at least two reasons," the authors explain. "First, protection of family and possessions is closely associated with masculine honor. Therefore, endorsing actions intended to safeguard one's homeland from threats would be expected of people who value the honor ethic among men. Second, it has been well established that U.S. men who are concerned with masculine honor tend to respond to personal insults with aggression. . . . Construing acts of terrorism as *national* insults . . . suggests that people influenced by this ideology will respond similarly to terrorist threats because doing so reflects an unwillingness to be disrespected or intimidated, whether at the personal or national level. Likewise, to the extent that honor cultures coincide with cultural collectivism . . . and the merging of the personal and the collective within the individual self-concept, national insults might be experienced like the personal insults that are so inflammatory to culture-of-honor men."[7]

From the home to the streets. And the patterns grow more intricate: the father who beats then gives, the father who brutalizes or abandons while the mother worships and adores, develops a child hungry for honor, starving for respect and recognition, aching for vengeance and power; and the child now grown whose need for honor and sensitivity to insult (because so much is at stake, because he has already been so profoundly insulted and is therefore so weak) urge him to take action (physical strength, warrior virtue). And in that physical strength, that warrior virtue, those stars in the patriarchal sky, is the seizing of power, too, over women. Who must be controlled. Who must be owned, lest anyone take them away—or worse.

Women, after all, pose a particularly dire threat to these men. Women alone have the power to dishonor, to betray, not just through sexuality but by the breaking of hearts. Is it, after all, really adultery men fear, those men who insist that their honor lies between a woman's legs, or is it being replaced by someone she loves more, the fear that haunts every man embattled by self-hatred and his endless valiant efforts to defend against it? More, women, empowered, could rob him of his own superior position—which is why girls may not attend school in rural Pakistan and Taliban-ruled Afghanistan, just as black slaves in America were not allowed to learn to read. And above all, as Khalida Brohi wrote, "Even if I have nothing, I should have honor."[8]

* * *

But not every assault on a man's honor comes from the father who beats him, the woman who betrays him, the terrorists who attack his homeland. In the honor-based families of the Middle East, the assault may originate (as discussed earlier) in the mere existence of a more powerful West and the degradation of the once-magnificent Islamic world; or it may come from the sacrilege of other Muslims who fail to submit appropriately to their beliefs of a "pure" and correct Islam. Equally in the honor-based families of Muslim immigrants in the West, these slights come, too, in the form of discrimination—be it real, imagined, or self-imposed. The son of Moroccan immigrants to Europe whose parents are illiterate (or do not speak the language) may struggle through school, unable to ask his mother or father to help him with his lessons. When he fails, his father accuses him of "dishonoring the family." His teachers embarrass him before the class. His fury burns. When he is unable to find a job—either because he has flunked out of school, or left early rather than endure the shame, or because his CV is tossed out unread on the basis of his Muslim-sounding name—the shame and anger boil harder.

He seeks revenge. It is here he might, as it were, explode, the proverbial ticking time bomb.

Literally.

Or he aches, alienated and lost. He seeks belonging and finds it in the mosque, a mosque too often presided over by radical imams, too often frequented by recruiters for ISIS and al Qaeda, men—even women—who promise what he yearns for: brotherhood, power, prestige. He learns again the lessons he learned raised in an honor-based home, an honor-based community: Honor isn't earned. It is given. Or, if necessary, taken.

* * *

I know it's coming from the moment that I wake: Saturday. He will shower and go for a walk somewhere. I will work out to a video while he is gone. By the time I am showered and dressed, he will have returned and undressed. He will be lying on the bed, naked in the ceaseless sun, bare in the bare light, waiting. I will pretend that I don't notice. I will avoid the bedroom entirely and hope he falls asleep. He won't. The weight of his waiting will overload the room, seep past the bedroom door into the living room, over the coffee table covered with the newspaper I am pretending now to read, pretending not to notice the leadenness of his silence, his wordless demands as he waits for me. In my bedroom. In my bed. Waiting not to make love to me, but for me to service him. Saturday. This is the routine. It is what he expects, having worked all week, having tried (usually without success) not to scream or threaten me. Do it now and I'll be good all this week, he will say. From my bedroom. From my bed.

It is so cold as I cross the living room and enter the bedroom door.

* * *

Not surprisingly cultures that oppress women and glorify violence as a means to honor tend also to be authoritarian—think of Saudi Arabia, Iran, Yemen, Afghanistan, and indeed the authoritarian government of Erdogan, who audibly bemoans feminism ("You cannot make men and women equal," he has said, "that is against creation.") and calls on women to birth at least three children.[9] In fact M. Steven Fish, professor of comparative politics at the University of California at Berkeley, argues that Muslim countries tend to be authoritarian largely *because* of "the subordination of women."[10]

If indeed misogyny and authoritarianism are linked, could that explain the support Donald Trump has gained as president from right-wing nationalist and supremacist groups—populations who also view women as baby vessels and consider, as Breivik did, that the emancipation of women has been the downfall of Western civilization? With the right and power of women to choose their own lives—including (and especially) whether or not to bear children—these men argue that whites are becoming a global minority in large part because white women are not giving birth. (Although, as Michelle Goldberg has noted in the *Daily Beast*, actually the opposite is true: as she observes, "In modern, industrialized countries, feminism is correlated to higher birthrates."[11])

Hence despite its demonization of Muslims—especially fundamentalist Muslims—the ideologies of the alt-right and white supremacists in general have more in common with Islamism than they do with the democratic cultures they claim that they are fighting to protect. Both, after all, assume supremacy. Both see taking part in that fight as a matter of male duty and honor. Both idealize strength and machismo, finding valor in violence and war. And both, as Goldberg suggests, take misogynistic views of women.

Accordingly these are unmistakably true as well of Trump, a man who has boasted of a manhood so great and powerful that women "let" him grab them by their genitals; whose first wife stated under oath that he had beaten and sexually molested her;[12] who prefers the company of dictators like Vladimir Putin and North Korea's Kim Jong Un to democratic leaders such as France's Emmanuel Macron and Angela Merkel of Germany.

This is, too, the man who reportedly rejected his former wife Ivana's suggestion to paint a fresco of cherubs on the ceiling of their living room in Trump Tower; in its place he installed a painting of warriors on horseback.[13] "When I come home and dinner's not ready," he once said, "I go through the roof."[14] And despite the so-called Goldwater Rule (which says that a person cannot be given a mental health diagnosis without being examined personally), thirty-seven mental health experts have informally declared Trump a pathological narcissist, publishing their findings as *The Dangerous Case of Donald Trump: 37 Psychiatrists and Mental Health Experts Assess a President.*[15]

Trump's idealization of violence ("In the old days, they'd have taken him out on a stretcher," he waxed nostalgically at a February 2016 rally when security officers ushered a protester from the crowd; and the following month: "We had some people, some rough guys like we have right in here. And they started punching back. It was a beautiful thing.") speaks to the hearts of macho white nationalists, as does his demonization of Hispanics and Muslim immigrants. Violence makes the man. The man wears the pants in the family. He would never push a pram. A man is only a man if he can crush everybody else.

It is the voice of the white supremacist, of the Muslim father demanding honor, of Rick's words echoing across my memory.

"Hail, Trump!" alt-right leader Richard Spencer shouted to his audience at a conference in Washington DC shortly after Trump was elected. The group responded with Nazi-style salutes.

And no wonder. These members of white supremacist groups, like Muslim extremists, carry that patriarchal view into bodies they frequently (over)train at the gym (pipe bomber Cesar Sayoc, Christchurch shooter Brenton Tarrant) and exercise in the boxing ring (Tamerlan Tsarnaev). In Breivik's world the multiculturalization of the West was emasculating its (white) male population, while women dared to consider themselves men's equals. Violent incels—involuntarily celibate men, or men who have trouble attracting women—decry the power of women to say "no."

And so now some call for a "white sharia."

A meme of the alt-right, "white sharia" refers to a future system in which white men become the apex of all power and women are relegated to the positions they hold under true sharia law, with no rights of their own, subject to male guardianship. They would be forbidden to leave the house without a man, denied the right to divorce, earn an income, or vote; as one white supremacist blogger put it, "If men are to lead the nation, how can we expect them to lead if they can't lead in their own homes?"[16]

Iraq War veteran Sacco Vandal, a former Marine, created the white sharia concept in 2016, according to the Southern Poverty Law Center.[17] Vandal, who together with his twin brother, Matthew, changed his last name from Wurgler in 2005, coauthored the "American Militant Nationalist Manifesto" in 2015. (Matthew also changed his first name to Vanzetti. Get it?) "We cannot allow the feminists, foreigners, traitors and villains to conspire any longer!" they write. "Let us kick out all the illegal immigrants. Let us send the ungrateful Muslims back to the Third World hole we rescued them from. And while we are at it, let us send the feminists back with them." Elsewhere Sacco has stated, "We have to strip females of suffrage and most if not all political, legal, and economic power. Our men need harems, and the members of those harems need to be baby factories."[18]

The link is clear. The Anti-Defamation League (ADL), in its landmark 2018 report on misogyny and white supremacy, explains, "Just as white supremacists, anti-Semites, and Islamophobes have been undeniably emboldened by the Trump administration's rhetoric and policies, it seems clear that misogynist extremists feel validated and empowered by the ascendance of a man who they believe views women through the same reductive lens: as sex objects without agency and humanity, as faithful but lesser helpmeets [*sic*], or as harpies coming to steal their power."[19]

I've seen it happen.

We met, that first time, on the street: our eyes locked across the avenue. Then we continued on our way. Later, when I walked back home again, he was there, too, striding toward me.

"So," he said. "What's your name anyway?"

Some thirty-five years later, and over a decade after our relationship had ended, I found Rick again, on the same street corner where we'd first met. He looked pretty much the same, though age and too much alcohol had left their traces in the creases beneath his eyes, the roughness of his skin. I told him I had seen his posts on Facebook: racist screeds that had disgusted me, mentions of "1488," a code common among white supremacists. ("Fourteen" refers to the "fourteen words" the ADL calls "the most popular white supremacist slogan in the world": *We must secure the existence of our people and a future for white children.* "Eighty-eight" stands for the words "*Heil Hitler,*" the letter "H" being the eighth letter of the alphabet.) I knew better than to address racism directly. We had fought enough in the past about what I thought even then were signs of his racist views. I told him it was anti-Semitic. He laughed.

"There's a race war in America," he told me. "You'd better get prepared."

Being "prepared" had become a big issue for him. Like many other white supremacists, he had also previously been deeply involved in the prepper movement, which seeks to "prepare" for the inevitability of doomsday by loading up with survival rations (dehydrated beef, peanut butter, water purifiers), weapons, and other gear, while practicing "survival skills" that will allow them not only to survive a nuclear or otherworldly disaster but—in keeping with the proper image of the warrior-knight—to save women and children left stranded and helpless around them. Not surprisingly, as the Southern Poverty Law Center has noted, "Besides spreading fear and paranoia and preparing for the end times, the Prepper Movement provides a gateway to more radical ideologies and extremist movements, such as militia groups, white supremacists, and sovereign citizens."[20]

In Rick's case, it clearly had.

And so had the misogyny that comes with it, an expansion of his past violence against women and his belief that he "deserved" to be serviced by women at his command and his desire. On his (now deleted) Facebook page, he had written:

> "Happy Friday Virginia, no I mean vagina's. [*sic*] Vagina is the most dangerous weapon on earth that tastes good and is actually good for you just as long as you buy it flowers every Friday. Watch what happens when you miss two Fridays in a row."

Shortly after, he began filling his page with images of guns, explanations of which gun was best for which purpose, adoring reviews of AK-47s, and complaints about the "chimps" and "amigos" who were ruining his life, showing up everywhere he was with their animalistic behavior, sub-human, he said, all of them racist, and "I want Trump deporting Mexicans." Praising Donald Trump, he insisted that Democrats were blind but that he, with his brave survivor skills and superior understanding, would save them. "No man gets left behind on my watch," he often wrote. Not quite a year later, he extended his greetings to "Brothers and sisters resisting the downsizing, outsourcing of our gene pool, and the annihilation of our European ancestry."

* * *

The misogyny of the white supremacist movement has largely kept women on the sidelines, reduced to their role as "trad wives" (traditional wives) supporting their husbands, just as ISIS women support theirs. But that is changing, thanks in part to women like Lana Lokteff and other outspoken far-right figures such as Wolfie James (who authored the "Seven Reasons Alt-Right Men Are the Hottest" post) and Canadian nationalist Lauren Southern, famed for claiming "Allah is a gay god."[21] Though like their

Islamist counterparts these women are seen primarily as vessels for the baby-making that presumably will save the white race from being over-taken by non-whites, they themselves believe that they can play a larger role, helping to encourage more women into the fold and softening the edges to the general public.

Still, they are a minority, and many male members of the movement oppose their activism. While historically women were active in the KKK during the 1920s, for instance, their role has dwindled since. Accord-ing to the ADL, "Richard Spencer told *Newsweek* he's not sure women should have the right to vote. Matt Forney [once] wrote, 'As men, it is our responsibility to bring girls back to their proper place. To lead them into their natural roles as wives and mothers. We men do not choose or reward girls for their clown college degrees, their meaningless cubicle jobs, or their supposed "intelligence." We reward them for their willingness to please us and make us happy, and in doing so make themselves happy. No amount of phony education or career "success" will scratch that deep itch in a girl's soul: the desire to serve a man.'"[22]

Not surprisingly, then, women have been largely barred from the "Daily Stormer," the far right's most prominent website. And recalling her years as a white supremacist, Shannon Martinez remembers that while "there's lots of lip service given about being the 'sacred vessel' of the white male, and even though there were ten men in my house, I had to cook and clean and not ever contradict the men."[23]

That emphasis on keeping the women in the home also, of course, serves the purpose of keeping her away from outside influences and other—especially non-white—men. While outwardly expressing concerns "their women" might be raped by Mexicans, the larger issue seems to be preventing them from forming relationships with non-whites—not much unlike the concerns fundamentalist Muslim fathers have about their daughters dating non-Muslims. Neo-Nazi Andrew Anglin, for instance, once posted on "Daily Stormer" that "the White European female's craving for Black Dick threatens to collapse civilization itself."[24] That this underscores Anglin's own feelings of (masculine) inferiority only heightens the connections here to narcissistic rage, fueled by the narcissistic injury of black male desirability: women might want them more than they want us, and how can that be when we are so obviously the superior race?

Consequently if they are going to save their women—and thereby the white race—white men must take up arms. They must fight for the security and preservation of their people like the knights they were meant to be. Not for nothing did Breivik refer to himself as a member of the medieval Knights Templar.

Indeed the passion white supremacists have shown for medieval history (an age of princesses and knights, heroes and villains, ravishing whores and devoted virgins) is notable. Christchurch shooter Brenton Tarrant also described himself as a member of the Templar order. Former white nationalist Derek Black enjoyed medieval reenactment as a child, and posted medieval crests on "Stormfront," the neo-Nazi site his father owned and he helped manage.[25] Others herald the Middle Ages as an enviable moment when all of Europe was white (it wasn't). Again, by romanticizing their violence, these men throw their shoulders back, announcing their manliness, their greatness; they are the chosen ones, chosen to lead the white race to victory; they are vanquishers of evil, heroes for all time.

And just as Palestinian mothers celebrate the martyrdom of their suicide bomber sons, fellow members of white supremacist chat groups like "8chan" reportedly hail white terrorist killers as "saints." Speaking on CNN's *Anderson Cooper 360* in the aftermath of white supremacist Patrick Crusius's shooting at a Walmart in El Paso, Texas, on August 4, 2019, reporter Sara Sidner described "8chan" posters, "When you go onto these sites as you go down the rabbit hole with who have gotten on there and are talking, as soon as something like this happens and the shooter is white and the target is black or brown people, they light up with glee. They are often praising the suspected shooter, they are often deifying the suspected shooter, they are calling that person a saint, there is this sense that this person is doing right by the white race."[26]

Not surprisingly women are viciously disparaged on "4chan" and "8chan" sites. Someone posting as "Anonymous" gloated on May 15, 2019, "Alabama bans abortions without exceptions. We are taking back control of their uterus', boys, and its glorious! The South will riiise again!" [*sic*].

"The South will rise again." Honor will be restored.

* * *

So much in the childhoods of the abusers and terrorists I have known and studied has been the same. So much of what they have done with those childhoods has been based on restoring honor stolen from them by parents or their communities. So much ties them together, the violence in their homes, the violence they mete out into the world. But just as not every child whose soul is battered becomes a narcissist or an abuser, not every narcissistic abuser becomes a terrorist. Why? And what makes some people radical and others go so far as to commit terrorist attacks?

The core answer comes from James Gilligan, who believes that "while shame is a necessary condition for the causation of violence, it is not a sufficient condition. In that sense, shame bears much the same relation to the causation of violence that the tubercle bacillus does to the etiology of tuberculosis. (That is, only a minority of those exposed to the bacillus come down with the disease, and yet no one develops the disease unless they have been exposed to the bacillus.)"[27]

Or put it this way: not everyone who is abused becomes an abuser, and not every abused child who is at the same time glorified becomes a narcissist, and not every narcissistic abused child becomes either an abuser or a terrorist; but there have been few, if any terrorists not also saddled with a history of pathological narcissism and abuse.

From there I have become convinced that, above all, the difference between the one who terrorizes in the home and the one who extends his terrorism to the streets can be marked largely in the depth of their desire, the magnitude of their narcissistic vision of themselves—that insatiable hunger to matter—and the cause they make the center of their lives, the cause that will lead them to realize their greatest narcissistic dreams, the heart not just of who they are but of their magnificence.

If this could be put in mere mathematical terms, and not just human ones, you might say that cultures (including family cultures) that breed narcissism breed abuse. Cultures (including family cultures) that breed abuse breed narcissism. Terrorism is the result of narcissism plus abuse plus X (a cause).

"From as early as I can recall," Picciolini writes, "I wanted to be the game-winning athlete who was carried off the field on my team's shoulders after hitting an upper deck grand slam to win the championship series in the bottom of the ninth inning; to be the hero who tackled the gun-toting hijacker; to have a national holiday named after me for my contributions to the human race. I didn't always care how I achieved greatness, but that hunger for glory was what made me tick."[28]

The step from here to terrorism is often merely circumstance. Opportunity, for one: Shannon Martinez got to know the skinheads in her school because they listened to the same music that she did. Recruiters for ISIS scout the mosques and social media. They find you. You find them. A match is made. Purpose is discovered.

"Passionate hatred can give meaning and purpose to an empty life," writes philosopher Eric Hoffer. "Thus people haunted by the purposelessness of their lives try to find a new content not only by dedicating themselves to a holy cause, but also by nursing a fanatical grievance. A mass movement offers them unlimited opportunities for both."[29]

I'm not sure, however, that one need feel "purposeless" to be enchanted by a cause; to the contrary, a sense of purpose without specific direction can be exactly what it takes to find a place in a world that offers "glory" and the sense of what Picciolini describes as a "valiant mission."[30] And so the opportunity—finding the Islamist groups in your neighborhood who support your anger at the white Brits who call you "Paki" or the white Dutch who call you a "cunt Moroccan";[31] finding the biker white dudes who offer you the privilege and adrenaline rush of joining them in their attacks on Spanish-owned bodegas down the block—leads young men (and sometimes women) into the black halls of ideologies of their cause: conquest. And you can only succeed in conquering something if you can be made to hate it enough that you are willing to do anything to destroy it. Anything.

Destruction requires violence. Builders sledgehammer walls and dynamite entire apartment blocks. In March 2001 the Taliban used a truckload of dynamite to demolish the 1,700-year-old sandstone sculptures of Buddha in the Kush mountains. Traitors are shot in back alleyways. Evidence is burned or broken or shattered. Regimes are toppled in war.

Children who witness violence at home, Valerie Hudson and her colleagues determined, are the ones most likely to perform that kind of violence—not just of objects and monuments, and not just interpersonally, but intergroup. "Those children found to be most violent are sons of abusers, following in their fathers' footsteps by becoming violent in the same types of conflicts that trigger their fathers' violence. . . . Studies have shown that if domestic violence is normal in family conflict resolution in a society, then that society is more likely to rely on violent conflict resolution and to be involved in militarism and war than are societies with lower levels of family violence," they write in *Sex and World Peace*.[32] Citing M. Stephen Fish, they add that "the oppression of females . . . provides the template for other types of oppression."[33]

In other words, as noted earlier, in families where women and children are abused, where there is violence in the home, those same children are more inclined to use violence, particularly against women, particularly in the home, but anywhere there is conflict. And this is all the more true if that violence is sanctioned by their communities, the cultures of honor that surround them. Or as domestic violence expert Janey Stephenson puts it, "The men who massacre the public are the same men who butcher women privately in their own homes. The same principles of power, control, fear and violence apply."[34]

Which is why, in the words of Robin Morgan, "for the street violence to end, the domestic violence at its root must end."[35]

Peace at home. Peace in the world.

CHAPTER 11

CULTURE OF TERRORISM

As I write, in August of 2019, America reels in the aftermath of another terrorist attack and a mass shooting no one can quite explain. In El Paso, Texas, where a terrorist shot up a crowded Walmart leaving twenty-two dead and twenty-four injured on a Saturday afternoon, people now tell each other to "be safe out there," just as New Yorkers did in the weeks after 9/11.[1] We hugged everyone: Bus drivers. Checkout clerks. Policemen.

Especially policemen.

In Dayton, Ohio, where a shooter whose motives remain at this moment unclear but who was known to have kept a "kill list," a heart-shaped billboard covers the window of the bar where twenty-four-year-old Connor Betts killed his sister and eight others. "Dayton Strong," it reads, amid a background of red and blue hearts. Flowers and candles left by Dayton residents cover the sidewalk below, as they did the doorways of New York firehouses and apartment buildings in September 2001.

Now it happens all over again; but this time neither killer was a Muslim and they weren't from far-off lands. In Dayton, Betts had a history of misogynistic behavior and an obsession with violence; though he seems to have celebrated the El Paso attack, he identified himself on Twitter as a "leftist" and had indicated support for Antifa, the far-left anti-fascist group.[2] In El Paso the terrorist is Patrick Crusius, a twenty-one-year-old white Trump fan, furious about the impending Hispanic "invasion" and potential "race mixing" that threaten to destroy America—and, by extension, threaten to destroy him. On the "8chan" message board where he posted an anti-immigrant screed before the shooting, members later praised him in words reminiscent of the messages that often appear on Twitter and other social media sites after an Islamist terrorist attack: "Hail all our men of action and martyrs," one person wrote.[3] Others, the *Wall Street Journal* reported, "mocked him for failing to kill more people, or for targeting Hispanics instead of Jews."[4]

Four days later, Donald Trump did what presidents are meant to do at times like this. He flew to El Paso to meet with survivors in the hospitals where they were being treated.

Most refused to see him.

Recognizing that the president was likely to lose a grand photo op, his handlers rushed into action. A two-month-old baby had been orphaned in the attack when his parents covered his body to protect him. After being hospitalized for two days, the infant had been released the day before Trump's arrival.

Calls were made. Cars were dispatched. The child was brought back to the hospital and placed in the arms of the first lady, who smiled at the snapping shutters of the nation's photojournalists. Her husband, the president of the United States of America, gave a thumbs-up. He looked good now, he must have thought then, presidential, compassionate, with his pretty wife and the poor sad little baby. What a photo this would be.[5]

But even this wasn't quite good enough. Failing to receive the praise he had hoped for for the visit, according to the *Washington Post*, "President Trump grew angry with aides in Air Force One on Wednesday for failing to allow cameras to record his visits to [all] the hospitals treating the victims . . . complaining that he was not receiving credit for the trips and his foes were dominating television news."[6]

America had reached the apex of narcissism and a terror all its own.

In fact the United States is facing an epidemic of narcissism, according to Jean Twenge, PhD, author of several studies on contemporary narcissism and the books *Generation Me* and the appropriately titled *The Narcissism Epidemic*. Twenge, along with coauthor W. Keith Campbell, PhD, has identified a rise in narcissistic personalities among those born between 1982 and 1999, whom she calls "Generation Me," and those born between 1999 and 2012, whom, in a clever play on words, she refers to as "i-Gen." This is the generation who spent their days in kindergarten singing songs like "I am special, I am special, Look at me, Look at me" (to the tune of "Frere Jacques") and who, as she notes in *The Narcissism Epidemic*, in high school, "pummel classmates and then seek attention for their violence by posting YouTube videos of the beatings."[7] They are the ones who "don't have to join groups or talk of journeys because they're already there. They don't need to 'polish' the self, as [Thomas] Wolfe said, because they take for granted that it's already shiny."[8]

Consequently, this, then, is also the generation of young men so "special" that when girls do not accept their proposals for a date, they consider themselves perfectly within their rights to promote violence against them.

Twenge's observations are not merely anecdotal. Her student Brittany Gentile discovered, while pursuing her master's thesis, that "among 28,918 college students, the average GenMe college student in 2008 had higher self-esteem than 63 percent of GenX students in 1988."[9] In additional studies Gentile found that "both high school and college students are . . . more likely to believe they're superior to their peers. . . . Fifty-eight percent thought they were above average in intellectual self-confidence, compared to only 39 percent in 1966—even though students in the 1960s earned higher SAT scores." Moreover "GenMe high school students were also more likely to see themselves as above average: 65 percent of 2012 students believed they were above average in intelligence, compared to 57 percent in 1976. The number who described themselves as 'far above average' in intelligence nearly doubled. Sixty-one percent believed they were above average in school ability, up from 56 percent in 1976. Yet on objective tests such as the National Assessment of Educational Progress, 12th-graders scored about the same in the 1970s and 2000s."[10] Further, in *The Narcissism Epidemic*, Twenge and Campbell note that "in data from 37,000 college students, narcissistic personality traits rose just as fast as obesity from the 1980s to the present, with the shift especially pronounced for women. The rise in narcissism is accelerating, with scores rising faster in the 2000s than in previous decades. By 2006, one out of four college students agreed with the majority of items on a standard measure of narcissistic traits."[11] This explains why, as Jerrold Post writes, "college students' scores on the Narcissism Personality Inventory rose twice as fast in the years from 2002 to 2007 as in the decades between 1982 and 2006."[12] And so on.

The birth of social media has further exacerbated the problem. Social media has bred a generation for whom self-worth is based in no small measure on Facebook and Instagram "likes," the numbers of "friends" and "followers" one has, and other forms of scorekeeping. Girls often as young as eight spend hours each day watching (or creating) YouTube videos about makeup and lessons on being more beautiful. They post their ubiquitous selfies—the beating heart of the narcissism epidemic—"Look at me! Look at me!"—and wait for the compliments to flow in. So dependent do they become on those flattering words ("So pretty!" "Beautiful you!" "Hot!") that when they do not come, or there are not enough of them, they become depressed, sometimes clinically.

As a natural outcome of this, they become hypersensitive to criticism. Not enough "likes" is an affront. Not enough praise is an insult. To be insulted is to be victimized. It is shaming. And so often, it demands revenge.

That victimhood does not just manifest itself in an inadequate number of compliments. In a hypersensitive generation, mere disagreement is frequently enough. Opposing viewpoints, particularly those they feel deny social justice (as they themselves define it), are met with censorship, violence, or both. White supremacist groups insist that whites are now facing discrimination, not just "genocide," complaining that they are punished for promoting and defending pride in their own race while black activists are supported for doing the same; or that, in the face of affirmative action efforts, they are inherently at a disadvantage when applying to jobs and schools.

For their part, i-Gens, especially those leaning to the far left, insist that they are being forced to tolerate what they view as hate speech, particularly on campuses (since theirs is the current college-age generation). Minutes before a planned appearance by white nationalist Milo Yiannopolis at the University of California at Berkeley in February 2017, members of Antifa and other left-wing activists ignited fires, threw rocks at police officers, and broke store windows in downtown Berkeley, causing the school to cancel the event. When controversial *Bell Curve* author Charles Murray, famed for his theory that white men are genetically more intelligent than minorities,[13] was to speak at Middlebury College in Vermont, students—some of them masked—physically attacked him, as well as his discussion partner, a left-wing professor by the name of Alison Stanger.

Many of the shooters we are witnessing in America today—school shooters and terrorists and others—follow that same "victimization" ethic, born of the hypersensitivity to criticism that (pathological) narcissism inevitably brings. Notably, too, the members of GenMe and i-Gen are more inclined to blame others for their own failings—as narcissists tend to do. (While Twenge and Campbell [and I] do not mean to suggest that GenMe and i-Gen are filled with pathological narcissism, studies show they are generations—and consequently a culture—in which pathological narcissistic traits do exist on a more subdued scale, increasing the likelihood with which pathological narcissism will occur within the population overall, just as, say, murderous violence is more likely to occur in cultures where general violence becomes the norm. Indeed, note Twenge and Campbell, "Narcissistic Personality Disorder [NPD], the more severe, clinically diagnosed version of the trait, is also far more common than once thought. Nearly 1 out of 10 Americans in their twenties and 1 out of 16 of those of all ages, has experienced the symptoms of NPD."[14])

And so the rage that follows insult, the blaming of others, the insistence on special privilege, the fear of "disrespect," colors the victim culture of these narcissistic youths. Hence, not surprisingly, in an interview for *Time* magazine, Jason Manning and Bradley Campbell, authors of *The Rise of Victimhood Culture: Microaggressions, Safe Spaces, and the New Culture Wars*, note similarities between victim and honor cultures as communities of "high sensitivity to slight, such that verbal offenses or even disagreements merit a serious response."[15]

Indeed "victimhood culture," or what I call "victim chic," is in many ways endemic to shame/honor cultures; think of the CIA's description of Arabs: "Unable to find themselves at fault . . . they are naturally led to seek the cause of their troubles in outside sources—the will of Allah, the imperialists, Israel, family and personal obligations, and many real wrongs which have been done them. . . . Some of the secondary schools of the Middle Eastern countries schedule athletic contests with one another, and after each game members of the losing team will get together and discuss the event. Not infrequently they conclude that 'the referee was against us' instead of acknowledging their own faulty plays or the other team's superiority."[16]

And it is intrinsic to narcissism.

Journalist Zoe Williams has pointed out another link between victim chic and the childhood of a future narcissist, the one straining between feelings of unimportance and neglect and being the center of the world.[17] It is not unlike the experience of Safaa Boular, the would-be British Museum bomber whose mother abused her until Safaa was diagnosed with diabetes, and then—briefly—treated her "like a little princess." To Williams, social media and smartphones not only form sources of narcissistic validation but act as diversions for mothers who cannot pull themselves away—another way they serve as accessories to the victim trend. "Look at me, Mommy!" the little girl calls out as she swings high in the playground. "Mommy, look!" But Mommy is too busy looking at her phone. "Mm-hmm," she says, but her daughter isn't fooled.

Instead she tries something that she knows will work, because it always does. She cries. She "falls" off the swing, skinning her knees—blood worth the sacrifice, because now Mommy looks. Mommy comes rushing to her aid, and now she is Mommy's entire world.

"I love you," Mommy says.

Lesson learned.

* * *

Central to the "victim" movement is the focus on "microaggressions"—or "the brief and commonplace daily verbal, behavioral, and environmental indignities, whether intentional or unintentional, that communicate hostile, derogatory, or negative racial, gender, and sexual orientation and religious slights and insults to the target person or group," according to Derald Wing Sue, the so-called godfather of the concept.[18]

Alongside its obsession with "intentional and unintentional slights," victimhood culture is one in which people seek "safety." "Trigger warnings" have become omnipresent on college campuses, where students demand to be alerted in advance to anything that might "trigger" memories, fears, or emotional distress relating to things like rape, suicide, or racism. *Romeo and Juliet*? Trigger warning: it depicts suicide. Ovid's *Metamorphoses*? According to students at Columbia University, "These texts, wrought with histories and narratives of exclusion and oppression, can be difficult to read and discuss as a survivor, a person of color, or a student from a low income background"[19]—this despite the fact that millions of others across the world have read these same texts over the course of the past two thousand years without experiencing massive psychological or emotional harm.

But the narcissist is especially sensitive. And so triggers like these or microaggressions, such as the time a college food service at Oberlin College in Ohio served sushi with reportedly undercooked rice to its students, are unacceptable insults, assaults against the honor and very identity of those who consider themselves the targets.[20] Besides, triggers make them "uncomfortable," and discomfort is in itself an assault, demanding a "who do you think you are?" (or "Do you know who I am?") response. Inflicting discomfort, assaulting with insult, however slight, and even if unintended, shows a lack of respect. And to be disrespected—"dissed"—calls for action. Think of the Mohammed cartoons again, the honor killings across Muslim communities, job losses in American honor states, the demoralization of calls for Confederacy monuments to be taken down. Think of the insult of the woman who leaves her abusive husband, who asks him to help make dinner, who looks at another man—or seems to, who left the curtains open so the neighbors could look in. Even if she didn't intend to. And so on.

And indeed these self-proclaimed victims, particularly those on the far left, have begun to insist that "words are violence" that should be met with violence. In a Brookings Institute survey from 2017, as many as 51 percent of American college students supported the kinds of violent behaviors that took place at Berkeley and Middlebury, and nearly 20 percent agreed that violence is an appropriate response to words they find offensive or viewpoints they oppose.[21]

Accordingly, alongside this comes a parallel, if paradoxical trend: victimhood as power. The more I can declare my hurt, the insult done me, the more I can make others do my bidding—which, most often, involves some form of personal validation. To be a victim is to hold the strings—which is why reporter Conor Friedersdorf pointed out in the *Atlantic* that "students do research to demonstrate that their group is treated worse than a different group."[22] In other words, the worse off you are, the better. Indeed, noted author Bradley Campbell, "Today victimhood takes on a certain status, honor, or dignity."[23] Victim chic.

And if being a victim is honorable, holds status, the more you insult me, the better I am. What's more, because I am so "special," you have no right to insult me—but I have every right to exert violence against you for doing so.

Most members of (left-wing) victim culture, as Campbell and Manning note, do not, however, respond with outward violence as occurred at Berkeley and elsewhere. Instead they run to Mommy—or, on campuses, to the administration. However, "if the authorities' response is insufficient," Campbell and Manning write, "they too, are offenders, and students appeal to still higher authorities to dismiss these oppressors, or to the public to shame them. Students thus take to social media, stage demonstrations, or starve themselves. Their cause is just, their plight is severe, and others must help."[24] This becomes more than simply another means of handling—or retaliating against—the offense. It is another way to claim their honor. If it is not violent, it is no less aggressive; they are only getting others to do the dirty work.

Plus there's a bonus: the victims are now the center of attention, with others rallying around them. They are the subjects of school newspaper articles and maybe even local news. They are a movement. They are heroes.

It is a twisted logic.

But here we are again.

* * *

Here's the thing about being a victim: it gives you license to act out. Sociologist Mitch Berbier determined that among white supremacists, victimhood is "carefully crafted" within the movement.[25] Reporting on Berbier's work, Joshua Roberts of Reuters observed, "Victimhood, it seemed, is how the groups assured themselves they weren't being racist—the excuse being that hey, they're suffering, too."[26] Hence just as for the i-Geners facing a world where microaggressions fly like bullets across the battlefield of their lives, for members of the alt-right, KKK, and other supremacist groups, that "suffering" is omnipresent: threats to their very survival are everywhere, and growing more dire by the day.

"It's war," Rick told me.

"We were heroes trying to save people," Picciolini writes of his early days in the movement. "Patriots. Why the hell couldn't anybody understand that?"[27]

"They are the instigators, not me," El Paso terrorist Crusius wrote on "8chan." "I am simply defending my country from cultural and ethnic replacement brought on by an invasion. . . . I am honored to head the fight to reclaim my country from destruction."[28]

Whether or not the rise of non-Western immigration to Europe and the United States constituted, as political scientist Samuel Huntington famously called it, a "clash of civilizations," it has unmistakably created a clash of identities. If "you will not replace us" is the anthem of right-wing extremists, an influx of immigrants and the failure of the multiculturist experiment have provided them the stage on which to sing it. Where far-left sympathizers argued that "America's oil greed" made the United States deserving of the massacre on 9/11, or that Theo van Gogh's references to Muslims as "goat-fuckers" made him a fair target for his assassin,[29] right-wing extremists—and even some centrists—have, since that time, expressed discomfort with the willingness of European schools to excuse Muslim girls from class trips or other events that would have them be "too close" to boys, or with changes in dress codes aimed at satisfying the conservatism of Muslim immigrants, or with the decisions by corporations (who never worried in the past about offending Jews) to cancel Christmas parties for fear of offending Muslim co-workers. *Is* their culture, they wonder, in fact being replaced?

That threat felt by non-Muslims—not just of the danger of terrorism but of demands on their cultural heritage and tradition—is largely what has given rise to Europe's expanding right-wing populism, just as it did in America.

Meantime, extremist Muslims shout "Islamophobia" at every perceived slight, such as when a teen was barred from an amusement park ride in Rye, New York, in 2011 because she refused to remove her *hijab*—even though scarves, like hats, were prohibited for safety reasons.[30] Opponents of a proposed mosque near Ground Zero in New York in 2010 were "Islamophobic," even if they supported the building of a mosque on another site instead. Still, right-wing attacks on existing mosques, and verbal abuse against women wearing *hijabs* on the streets of London and Stockholm and Berlin, are all too real.

Once again, we are all afraid.

And if we are all afraid, if we all are under threat, then we are victims of one another.

Which is why victim ideologies now run rampant across social media, skillfully shaped and shot, like arrows, by recruiters who know the vulnerabilities of their targets: twentysomethings mostly, who feel they've been robbed of the chance to demonstrate their greatness to the world, who know that they are special but too much stands in the way (or threatens to in the years ahead), i-Gen kids of all races and faiths whose pain and failures and limitations are clearly someone else's fault: Black people. White people. Muslim people. Jewish people. Non-Muslim people. Hispanic people. Women. Inferior people, all of them, who do not know their place. "The greatest rage—and the greatest danger," writes Jessica Stern, "stems from those who feel they can't keep up—even as they claim to be superior to those who set the pace."[31] The men who marched with torches through Charlottesville, Virginia, in August of 2017 were not racist; they were acting in self-defense, they claimed, "heroes, trying to save people."

So, too, are jihadists—"jihadism," after all, is defined as the struggle against non-believers.[32] Palestinian terrorists argue that they are defending their people from the brutal occupation of Israel. European Muslims continue to express support for the Islamic State and its battle against the Satanic West: indeed, according to Europol, "In 2018, all fatalities from terrorism were the result of jihadist attacks: 13 people lost their lives. In addition, 46 people were injured in jihadist attacks. . . . In 2018, EU Member States reported 16 thwarted jihadist terrorist plots, a fact that indicates both continued high terrorist activity. . . ." Further, they add: "Despite the degradation of IS organizational structures, the group maintains the intent to conduct attacks outside conflict zones, potentially using former members and individuals inspired by propaganda."[33] Consequently, according to an August 2019 report from the Pentagon's Office of Inspector General, ISIS is "solidifying," and with the ongoing help of some three thousand foreign fighters, is continuing to recruit support via social media and among the seventy-three thousand displaced Iraqis, Syrians, and others housed at Syria's Al Hol refugee camp.[34] European counterterror experts therefore remain alert for future attacks, particularly as ISIS fighters begin returning home or are released from prison.

Simultaneously a growing al Qaeda, quiet during the height of the Islamic State, is now gaining power in the Middle East, Africa, and beyond.

Preying on religious divisions in Yemen's civil war, the terror group has built itself into a threat the U.S. State Department in August 2019 called "as strong as it has ever been" in its defense of the Muslim *ummah* from the infidels of the West.[35]

Much of this comes out of the ISIS playbook. "Using its Arabic magazine, martyrdom videos, poetry and popular songs, Al Qaeda has endeared itself to the local Sunni people and Yemen's powerful Sunni tribal leaders," reported George Mason University's Christian Taylor in July 2019. "It has also ingratiated itself to Yemen's Saudi Arabia–backed militias to battle the Houthi [Shiite] incursion."[36]

Meantime, Britain's security minister has warned that the group is "developing technology to bring down planes and target airports," according to Australia's ABC News in 2019.[37]

Those who bring down planes, like the terrorists who brought down the World Trade Center Towers in New York, will, too, be martyrs, heroes, freedom fighters, warriors defending their victimized people, regaining their honor. But so, too, will be the Western white supremacists who exact their revenge against them—or other Muslims they encounter. For both, this is what they know. This is what they believe. This is what makes them men—they, the brave, the courageous, the great and chosen ones.

And so they battle on, each struggling to terrorize the other, each believing, as I noted in the opening pages of this book, "the weapon is fear; the laurel, power"—or as Donald Trump expressed it to journalist Carl Bernstein in 2016: "Real power . . . is fear."[38]

* * *

If fear is power, it is also what binds the pathological narcissist to his prey—whether the terrorist or the abuser, or even the run-of-the-mill narcissist and the society he lives in. Nothing is more precious than his honor, his position, his eminence; and the greatest fear we have as humans is the loss of what we value most deeply. Because the narcissist's entire value as a human being, his very existence, relies entirely on maintaining his delusion of grandeur and glory, this is what he fights for, and most fiercely.

How he does it, achieving the power and the deference that he seeks, is simple and for him, entirely clear: he will instill fear, too, in others: "I never got so much respect before in my life as I did when I pointed a gun at some dude's face."

* * *

Fear. Like empathy it, too, has a place in the brain. It begins in the amygdala, located in the temporal lobe, triggering stress hormones that contribute to the "fight or flight" response. That information is then communicated to the hippocampus, which helps to identify the threat, enabling us to distinguish between, say, a child with a water pistol and a child carrying a real gun. It may also, researchers have found, contribute to political behavior.

MRI imaging in studies published in 2011 and 2017 found that large gray matter volume in the amygdala corresponded with viewpoints generally held by conservatives, and a preference for the status quo. Liberalism, however, author Ryota Kanai and others found, was "associated with increased gray matter volume in the anterior cingulate cortex."[39] "Conservatives respond to threatening situations with more aggression than do liberals," according to Kanai and his colleagues, while those with more gray matter in the anterior cingulate cortex tend to have "a higher capacity to tolerate uncertainty and conflicts."

Those hypotheses were corroborated in a study by H. Hannah Nam and others, who determined that those with higher volumes of gray matter in the amygdala are generally less inclined to join in political protests, and more likely to support hierarchical social systems.[40] "A system-justifying psychological orientation favors the social, economic, and political status quo, and may promote vigilance to social hierarchy and a preference for ideologies that characterize extant inequality as legitimate and necessary," they write. "Many behavioral studies have shown that system justification accounts for attitudes and behaviors that attribute legitimacy to existing hierarchical social systems, such as stereotyping, conservative and meritocratic ideologies and a reluctance to help those who are disadvantaged.

Moreover, *system justification is theorized to arise from basic psychological needs to manage threat, uncertainty and social relations—three functions that are linked to the amygdala.*"[41]

Further, as Hilary Brueck observed in *Business Insider*, "Threats of terrorism make everyone less liberal"[42]—a trend that researchers determined after 9/11, and as evidenced by the swell of support for military action under President George W. Bush. At the same time, she says, "groundbreaking research that Yale psychologists published in 2017 revealed that helping people imagine they're completely safe from harm can make them (temporarily) hold more liberal views on social issues." By contrast, she reports that, according to Yale psychology professor John Bargh, "research has shown that you can make liberals more conservative by threatening them and making them somewhat afraid."[43]

In other words, feeling you are under threat, or being fearful, can make you more likely to adopt conservative views—and the aggression, support for militancy, and preference for traditional order that come with them. This would seem to be especially true for those particularly susceptible to fear—either because of past trauma, sensitivity to honor/shame concerns, or brain structure (or a combination of these), and so for whom conservative standards of order, patriarchy, hierarchy, and tradition offer consolation and a sense of stability and safety. They are the fortresses against the terror.

Not coincidentally these are just the issues that factor into religious fundamentalism—Islamic, Christian, and others—as well: the assurance of paradise and redemption from hell, the orderliness of prayer, the hierarchy of patriarchy, the promise of protection. In Islam the threat of hell is particularly horrific, warning of "scalding water" to be poured on the bodies of sinners and unbelievers, their skin to be set afire and after being burned, replaced and burned again, and "lashed with rods of iron."[44]

What's more, expressions and feelings of empathy and compassion also vary between liberals and conservatives, again possibly based on gray matter in the brain; strikingly, there is a greater "me" factor when it comes to empathy among conservatives than among liberals. Indeed studies show that while liberals tend to feel empathy for a wide range of people, conservatives tend to be more compassionate when it comes to their own families and inner circles.

This makes sense; those who are more fearful— that is, with more gray matter in the amygdala—will likely be less trusting and feel less connected to an "other," while liberals with larger anterior cingulate cortexes and consequently a higher tolerance for uncertainty (and risk) are inclined to be more open. This would also explain why white ultra-conservatives are more concerned with protecting the white race, and why religious Muslim fundamentalists would fight for the preservation of the *ummah*. Self above all.

In addition the fact that conservatives tend to be intolerant of so-called out-groups may also reflect the fact that they have shown a stronger response to distasteful images (like a man eating worms, one of the illustrations used in the study). After all, as Breuck points out, "If you're more likely to turn away from a foreign pathogen, you're probably also more likely to be averse to unfamiliar groups."[45] And indeed among the ways Donald Trump incites the anger of his far-right followers, is to describe the neighborhoods of blacks and Hispanics as "dirty," "infested," "disgusting"—words that activate the centers of their brains that are sensitive to feelings of revulsion (and fear), the very same centers that make them take on more conservative views. Similarly, radical Islamist recruiters commonly refer to Jews as "apes and pigs" and infidels as "unclean," the "vilest of creatures."[46] As revulsion and fear rise, hate and aggression rise with them.

What is concerning, however, is the profile of those at-risk i-Gen youth whose fearfulness and hypersensitivity lead to an intolerance of a different sort. These are the ones who generally refuse to engage in discussion on social media, preferring to issue ad hominems before blocking anyone with whom they disagree. These are the ones who refuse to listen to speakers whose ideas distress them. As they (and those who follow them) increasingly perceive the world as a battlefield to be navigated, as they lose tolerance for discord, will the narcissistic rage arising from their narcissistic wounds turn them increasingly violent as well?

* * *

There's more: still another thread weaves through the terrorist, the white supremacist, and most domestic abusers—and increasingly among the GenMe and i-Gen youth: a lack of exposure to and involvement in the arts.

This matters.

Salafist Islam prohibits imagery, music, and nonreligious texts. Depicting people is considered blasphemous (hence, in part, the protests against images of Mohammed); one hadith cautions, "He who creates pictures in this world will be ordered to breathe life into them on the Day of Judgment, but he will be unable to do so."[47] Another reads, "Don't you know that angels do not enter a house wherein there are pictures?"[48]

And while Western culture, even among the most conservative Christians and Jews, does not prohibit art, there is a long history of censorship that continues today (including former U.S. Attorney General John Ashcroft's decision to cover up the breasts of Lady Justice in 2002). In addition, in a 2014 Pew study, "solid conservatives" in America ranked "Art and Theater" dead last in a list of nine areas of interest (including health, sports, entertainment, religion, and politics).[49] Needless to say, white supremacists identify most with the "steadfast conservatives" group, a political segment that strongly opposes gay marriage (84 percent) and agrees with the statements "our country has made the changes needed to give blacks equal rights with whites" (81 percent); "society is better off if people make marriage and children a priority" (80 percent); and "immigrants today are a burden on our country because they take our jobs, housing, and health care" (73 percent). (Notably, 53 percent of this group also believes that "Humans and other living things have existed in their present form since the beginning of time"—a view shared by Salafist and other extremist and conservative Muslims.)

It seems, then, no coincidence that while domestic abuse reaches all corners of the world and all levels of the socioeconomic spectrum, in America women are more likely to be killed by their partners in the gun-toting, conservative South—which, significantly, also has the overall lowest literacy rate in the nation (along with California and New York).[50] There is, however, one notable outlier: Alaska—the state that had the highest rate of domestic homicides (men killing women) in 2016, according to the Violence Policy Center, and was ranked forty-ninth out of fifty states in literacy levels in 2015.[51]

By contrast, studies have shown that women with higher levels of education in Saudi Arabia were 7 percent less likely to experience abuse.[52] Conversely, similar studies in Turkey, and anecdotal evidence of Muslim families in the West, suggest rather that higher education for women often leads to them seeking greater independence—making them more vulnerable to abuse by patriarchal fathers and husbands.[53]

Moreover, according to the American Psychological Association, children from families with lower socioeconomic status in the United States (which they define as encompassing "not just income but also educational attainment, financial security, and subjective perceptions of social status and social class") are "two times as likely as their higher [socioeconomic status] peers to have had three or more adverse experiences"[54]—or, that is to say, have experienced three or more incidents of abuse. Even more significantly, a conference held by the Center on Global Counterterrorism Cooperation (CGCC) in 2013 determined that "a quality education in itself can play a critical role in helping young people distance themselves from extremism and resist the 'pull factors' that drive them to recruitment."[55] "Empowering students to think critically teaches them to challenge ideas, construct rational thoughts, and engage in meaningful debate," the CGCC determined. "Schools could also . . . support local and national cultural heritage programs, such as plays, arts, and cultural shows which could help students challenge pre-existing notions and develop their imaginative and strategic capacities."

Yet this is precisely what the narcissists of GenMe, i-Gen, and victim chic—the ones demanding "trigger warnings" and the silencing of controversial speakers—are resisting most vehemently. They aren't "comfortable" with ideas that challenge. They aren't willing to immerse themselves in such glorious pieces of literature as *Macbeth*, or *The Merchant of Venice*, or *Mrs. Dalloway*, or to view paintings of nude women by, say, Rubens or Renoir or the tormented Egon Schiele ("objectifying women's sexuality").[56]

Meantime, schools across America are reducing their funding for art classes and the National Endowment for the Arts (NEA) has seen major budget cuts under the Trump administration (which in 2018 proposed a reduction in NEA funding from $150 million down to $29 million; the National Endowment for the Humanities from $150 million to $42 million; and the Institute of Museum and Library Services from $235 million to a mere $23 million).[57] Not all of these cuts ultimately passed—the fiscal year 2019 Appropriations Bill provided a $155 million budget for the NEA—but Trump's desire to reduce funding so drastically speaks to the value that he and his base accord to the arts. Or don't.

* * *

It didn't start there, though. "Over the last few decades, the proportion of students receiving arts education has shrunk drastically," according to a Brookings Institute report.[58] Yet, the report's authors observe, "we find that a substantial increase in arts educational experiences has remarkable impacts on students' academic, social, and emotional outcomes." In a two-year experiment involving ten thousand third- through eighth-grade students at forty-two elementary and middle schools in Houston, Texas, the report's authors determined that not only did arts education increase writing abilities and produce a 3.6 percentage decrease in "disciplinary infractions," but students who were given arts education showed "an increase of eight percent of a standard deviation in their compassion for others. . . . Students who received more arts education experiences are more interested in how other people feel and more likely to want to help people who are treated badly." In other words, they were more empathic.

These outcomes are not unique. Dozens of studies have shown similar relationships between empathy and arts education, while others have indicated that ending illiteracy can reduce youth violence.[59] This can be explained in any number of ways, including the simple fact that sophistication with language offers an alternative to violence as a means of expression. Equally, opportunities to create have enormous therapeutic benefits, particularly for trauma victims and those who have experienced violence in their past.

What's especially intriguing is the fact that more brain resonance studies have shown that the anterior cingulate cortex—that same part of the brain that is more active among liberals, relating to empathy, greater tolerance for conflict, and "openness"—is also involved in creativity. "The right [anterior cingulate cortex] is one of the core regions of the salience network," according to researchers Baoguo Shi, Xiaoqing Cao, and others.[60] The salience network is one of three areas of the brain (along with the *default mode network* and *executive control network*) most responsible for creative thought.[61]

But such artistic endeavors are frowned on in patriarchal cultures such as the honor societies of the South, where visual art is considered by some as effeminate, sissy, the stuff for women and "fags." Dance is often considered even worse than art, and literature not much better. Boys who read are "nerds" and "weaklings." "At home, from the time I woke up to the time I went to sleep, I was either reading or watching old movies," recalls Jared Yates Sexton in *The Man They Wanted Me to Be*. "I scribbled in notebooks and on receipts at my job as a cashier at Walmart. To my father and the other men in my life it was a weak vocation, something a woman or a gay man might do, an embarrassing pastime I needed to grow out of. There was no room at home or in school for men to be creative or intelligent. Any attempt at either resulted in bullying, excommunication, or constant derision for being a 'fag.'"[62] A thinking, creative man, in other words, is no more than a woman, and a woman is the lowest you can be.

The arts are even more condemned, or at least limited, in most Muslim cultures, especially—as noted—in Salafist societies. In the past few years Iran has imprisoned dozens of musicians, artists, poets, and others, such as musicians Yousef Emadi and Mehdi Rajabian, and Rajabian's brother Hossein, a filmmaker—all of whom have been subjected to torture for "insulting Islamic sanctities" and "illegal audio-visual activities."[63] Hossein Rajabian had produced a film about women's rights; Mehdi Rajabian and Emadi had distributed music abroad that included political subjects before their arrest in 2016. Two years later authorities shut down a production of Shakespeare's *A Midsummer Night's Dream*, arresting the play's director, Maryam Kazemi. According to Radio Free Europe, the arrest followed the release of a trailer for the production, which included scenes with men and women dancing together.[64] The Taliban, who forbid Afghan women to receive an education and have banned music, also famously dynamited the Buddha statues in Bamyan before smashing 2,500-millennia-old Greek, Persian, and other artifacts at the National Museum of Kabul in 2001. The fighters reduced even monumental sculptures to thousands of shards, many "the size of fists or even a coin," according to the Associated Press (AP).[65] "We could not prevent them," conservator Sherazuddin Saifi, told the AP. "They were breaking all the locks, entering each room and smashing all items into pieces."

Fewer opportunities to learn about the arts, to view sculptures or paintings, to listen to music or to read, means fewer opportunities to develop capacities for empathy, fewer opportunities to learn about and find commonalities with foreign cultures and lifestyles, and fewer opportunities for expression. Fewer opportunities to create, along with limited literacy, means an increased chance people will communicate physically, which is to say, using violence.

All in a time when narcissism is on the rise in the West, tolerance is declining worldwide, and violent fanaticism combined with honor culture is expanding in the Middle East, in Europe, and at home in the United States.

The culture of terrorism is right now.

CHAPTER 12

TOWARD A SOLUTION

Jason Walters waits on a bench outside the Hotel des Indes in The Hague. I have never seen him, not even in photographs; but I recognize him immediately nonetheless—large, dark-skinned, thirties. We have agreed to meet here for drinks, Jason and I. Ten years ago, he was a Muslim extremist, one of the most dangerous men in the Netherlands. I am a Jew and an American. Ten years ago, I wrote about Jason Walters. Ten years ago, I would have been exactly the person he would have wanted to kill, and he would have been proud to do it.

I have deliberately not reread what I wrote of Jason before we meet, about his involvement with the Hofstadgroep, the terror cell that included Mohammed Bouyeri, Theo van Gogh's assassin. I have not read the media reports of his arrest, after a fourteen-hour standoff with police, though I remember watching it on national TV. This is a different Jason. He has repudiated not just Islamist extremism but Islam and religion altogether. After nine years in prison he emerged with a college degree in philosophy and now works as a counterterrorism expert for the Dutch government and others. Who he was is part of who he is, but I don't want to know who he is or was from anybody else's words.

I want Jason to tell his story to me himself.

Everything.

He is larger than I expect, and lighter. He wears a woolen cap, the old-fashioned kind, which I decide is the color his hair would be, if the cap didn't cover it so completely.

Over tea, Vedett, and Sauvignon blanc, we talk of pain and harm and fury. We talk of the idea that killing people is for God and so it is okay. We talk of people becoming objects, obstacles to Allah and a better life, not living beings with people to love, with blood that beats and gardens that they tend. You kill them because it makes you a better person. You kill them for the reward. They don't matter. He asks me about living with abuse and I explain to him about it eventually not seeming as bad and he says yes, it's the same about watching beheading videos.

We lock eyes across the table.

In prison everything was so close, he says. Your eyes never had a chance to focus far away. Now he wears glasses. When he first got out he could not estimate distances, how far away a car was, for instance, and whether it was safe or not to cross the street. He was in prison for nine years. He'd had no idea Bouyeri had killed or would kill Van Gogh. He watched the news and with his friends wondered who it could have been. Only late in the day did they put together the fact that Bouyeri, who never left his house but had not been at home when they went to visit him that morning, had, on this one occasion, left his house to kill.

"We made an impact on the history of the jihad movement," he says now. It occurs to me that there is a tinge of pride in his voice. For all his rebirth and reinvention, Jason still has a need to matter. Did they, really? "We were the first to go after someone for blasphemy," he says. The Muslim cartoons followed, and *Charlie Hebdo*. I think they would have happened anyway, but what do I know? He follows the trends from a different side of the line. Where I stand, no one noticed; few people outside the Netherlands remember unless you actively remind them. But perhaps jihadists do. Perhaps it changed the dialogue. He is inside, and I am not.

He gets threats but will not get a bodyguard. "I think there would be an outcry," he says. I don't think so. I think people are grateful for his reinvention, for his coming to our side, and would be happy to protect him, but I get it. He was part of a conspiracy to kill, not just Theo van Gogh but all of us. I sit across from him, a Jewish girl from New York, and he talks about the magnitude of 9/11. "There was before and after," I say. "It was the defining moment for my generation," he says. He is stunned when I tell him I was in New York that day, that I had almost even been at what we now call Ground Zero.

As we leave the Des Indes he receives a message from a woman he knows who is still in Syria. "They are bombing," she says. A woman was just shot and killed on the spot, right next to her, right now. More are dying all around her. They are running. She is so afraid. This is a jihadist, a woman who chose to go to Syria to kill, a woman who likely would have stabbed me in a moment if we'd met. And still my heart breaks as she runs, fearing for her life. I know that fear. Will it change her? Will it make her understand? Or will it only add to her hatred and her fury?

If she survives.

I first learned of Jason's transformation through an interview he gave after his release. He had specifically chosen to speak with Esther Voet, the former director of the Centrum Informatie en Documentatie Israel, Holland's main Jewish rights organization, who had become the editor of the country's Jewish newspaper, *Nieuw Israelietisch Weekblad*. In prison, he told Voet, he'd begun trying to "assimilate science with belief, with the beginning premise that all modern scientific insights could also be found in the Quran. That," he had decided, "would be a great way to win hearts and minds. If you could find Einstein's relativity theory in the Quran, that would be a strong argument that it was given by God."[1]

It didn't work. "The whole thing collided into itself," he recalled to Voet. "But then came a kind of emptiness." If he couldn't prove God after all, what did anything really mean? He decided to study instead, receiving a BA in cultural studies while still serving his sentence. His coursework focused on "literature, cultural history, philosophy and art, with emphasis on the early modern era to the Enlightenment." He discovered philosophy, the area of study he continues to pursue now at Leiden University, working, coincidentally, with the same professors who once mentored Ayaan Hirsi Ali—his onetime sworn enemy whom he had, in his radical days, conspired with his fellow members of the Hofstadgroep to slaughter.

"Plato, Nietzsche, and Heidegger became crucial to the process for where I finally landed," he told Voet. "What I had sought for so long, I found in philosophy. And so then the whole world had to be rediscovered, as if I'd been born again. I'm still doing that."

Along the way something happened. In 2008, while still in prison, Jason watched the film *Schindler's List* when it aired on Dutch TV. "At the end of the film," he recalled, "something in me broke. . . . I was so shaken by that song [at the end of the film] that I burst into tears."[2]

By the end of the evening, when we have both had too much to drink and the late spring sun is setting over the houses of Parliament, Jason Walters, the ex-Muslim ex-terrorist, and I, the Jewish girl from New York's Upper East Side, are friends. I have learned much more of who he is and he, I think, more about the life of someone he once would have violently reviled.

I learn, too, about his brother, Jermaine, also radicalized and a member of the Hofstadgroep, whom Jason had tried to reform but couldn't; Jermaine died a fighter on the battlefields of the Islamic State in 2015, leaving behind a pregnant wife and three small children. "I will never forgive him," Jason says to me.

What I learn, in part, is this: their father, a black American soldier in the U.S. Air Force, left his mother when Jason was ten years old and Jermaine eight. He had raised his boys taking them to church on Sundays, but when he moved to a new village, living among Moroccan families, the boys discovered Islam from their new friends in the neighborhood. Jason converted at age twelve, Jermaine some years later.

And then came 9/11—"the defining moment" for his generation.

When I ask him, weeks later, about his *Schindler's List* epiphany, he pauses.

"It was a very profound, emotional moment," he says slowly. "It just hit me, and I can remember—the world never really was the same afterward. It just changed me. All hatred basically just melted away. I felt so deeply ashamed. It was this confrontation with pure evil, and it functioned also as a mirror in some sense. Because I basically shared this, this is very recognizable, this is the implication of everything you've been standing for."

"Everything you've been standing for was hatred of Jews?"

"No," Jason says. "But Islamic extremism is very genocidal in nature."

I ask him if he saw it that way at the time. "Or did you see yourself as saving the world?"

"Both," he says. "Killing evil is a way of making good prevail."

I smile at him. "I think you are still doing the same thing," I say.

"How come?"

"Because here you are. You're working to remove evil. To save the world as you now understand it. In a certain way you were a freedom fighter then and you're a freedom fighter now."

Jason shakes his head.

"I don't have any illusion of saving the world," he says. "I know I can't save the world. . . . I consider myself more like a therapist of society, confronting society with unmasking self-deceit and lies we tell ourselves to make us feel good."

I don't tell him this, but I still think it's all part of the same thing. He still wants to be a hero. He still believes that he can be the guiding light.

* * *

For Jason and Jermaine Walters, the attacks of 9/11 took on a different import than they did for their Dutch-Moroccan Muslim friends; the brothers, after all, were half American. Their father's homeland had been attacked. While his friends rallied around bin Laden and al Qaeda, Jason, then sixteen, struggled to make sense of it all, to understand what had really happened on that day, and why.

Originally, he explains, it had been the aesthetics that drew him to Islam—the rituals, the submission to God. After 9/11 it became more an intellectual conviction. He was looking for answers, and Islam, he says, became "the paradigm, the entire reality."

"Nine-eleven was a catalyst," he recalls. "It is the kind of event which requires immediate interpretation. It requires meaning. You have to attribute meaning to it, and take a stance. And that's when I started going into the books and following the conversations of extremists, and I quickly became convinced that the extremists had a stronger story, because they have the source texts on their side. Others were cherry-picking their sources all the time. So it was kind of the main step, that the al Qaeda narrative was the right one, because they have the source texts."

"The narrative." If it was the "narrative" of al Qaeda that radicalized Jason Walters, it was equally the narrative of *Schindler's List* that redeemed him. True, *Schindler's List* is not fiction. But it is told as a narrative, a story. It is not a documentary, but a drama, written, acted, and filmed as art, with all the nuances and implications, all the pulling at emotion, that art enfolds and then inspires.

It was much the same for Maajid Nawaz, the British-Pakistani former extremist. Like Jason he found himself adrift while spending time in prison. Like Jason he began to seek new answers. "I devoured the classics," he recalls in *Radical*, but he also delved into Tolkien's *Lord of the Rings*, Orwell's *Animal Farm*, and William Golding's *Lord of the Flies*. "Reading English literature did for me what studying Islamic theology couldn't," he writes. "It forced my mind to grapple with moral dilemmas."[3]

It forced him, in other words, to reason.

But literature did something more. As for Jason after watching *Schindler's List*, a break formed in Nawaz's armor. In prison, Jason told me, he almost never cried. "I thought it made me too weak," he said—not manly, not masculine enough. When the film, as he says, "broke" him, it also broke down his inhumanity. Compassion found its way in.

For Maajid Nawaz, love came with it. When he met Rachel, his second wife, he writes, she "embodied the antithesis of the violence that had once forged me: her comfort in the abstract, among the arts, her subtlety and tenderness being the very traits I needed to rely on to soften my combative instincts, to anchor my weathered soul."[4]

If anything can end the narcissism, the rage, the violence, I am certain it is this: the comfort in the abstract, among the arts, and in the subtle transformative power of literature.

This is not mere wishfulness. In 2013 psychologists David Comer Kidd and Emanuele Castano at New York's New School for Social Research determined that reading literary fiction (as opposed to pop fiction or beachside paperbacks) enhances the capacity for empathy—or what they call "theory of mind."[5] "What great writers do is turn you into the writer," Dr. Kidd told the *Guardian*.[6] "In literary fiction, the incompleteness of the characters turns your mind to trying to understand the minds of others."

What's more, reading the description of a motion seems to stimulate areas of the motor cortex, which governs the body's movements—even in nonfiction.[7] But the effect seems to be especially strong when reading novels. Canadian researchers Keith Oatley and Raymond Mar, for instance, have found that "individuals who frequently read fiction seem to be better able to understand other people, empathize with them, and see the world from their perspective," according to a *New York Times* report on their work.[8] Even more important, the ways fiction can nurture empathy can begin even in the youngest child. According to the *Times*, another study by Dr. Mar "found a similar result in preschool-age children: the more stories they had read to them, the keener their theory of mind."

Years later Oatley further explained his findings in the *Washington Post*: "When we read about other people, we can imagine ourselves into their position, and we can imagine it's like being that person. That enables us to better understand people, better cooperate with them. . . . People who read more fiction were better at empathy and understanding others."[9]

Notably this same effect was also observed when children watched movies—but not when they watched TV.[10] That Jason Walters watched *Schindler's List* on television would, it seems, be beside the point; movies, particularly films with complex narratives, are to television shows what high literature is to the dime-store novel. Quality cinematography, in-depth characters and story lines, powerful acting—these combine in a film like *Schindler's List* in a way that no thirty-minute sitcom or reality TV show quite can.

For those of us already devoted to literature, this comes as little surprise. Poetry seduces us with precisely its capacity to re-create a vivid image, a sensation, a fragrance, in our minds. Take, for instance, T. S. Eliot:

> "You gave me hyacinths first a year ago;
> They called me the hyacinth girl."
> —Yet when we came back, late, from the Hyacinth garden
> Your arms full, and your hair wet, . . .[11]

To read these lines is not just to envision the hyacinths, but to feel them, heavy, purple, wet, the full arms, armfuls of damp blossoms; to breathe in their honeyed, thick perfume, watching, perhaps, as petals tumble to the carpet. And in this abstract experience, this sense of feeling what someone else has felt, could feel, empathy is born.

* * *

Buried within this is the interpretative act, an effort required by literary texts and poems but not so much by popular fiction or nonfiction. Before the advent of America's "Common Core" curriculum, which has, among other things, reduced the emphasis on reading literature or learning about other arts—like painting or dance or music—classrooms echoed with the sounds of voices trying to find the meaning in a story. What does the character represent? Why does she ask her mother this question? If she represents innocence, what about her stepsister? Why does the boy go to London? And so on.

What emerges from this is the understanding that texts—literature— contain metaphors, that what you read does not always mean what it seems to say; and so, accordingly, religious texts, rich in allegory, may not be meant to be taken literally either. Rather they are metaphors in and of themselves. And so one comes to understand, too, that not everything is always what it first appears to be.

All of this helps to develop critical senses while deepening curiosity. Children—as well as adults—begin to look behind the superficial, to mine for greater meaning. Above all, they develop, along the way, the crucial ability to think abstractly—because to engage in metaphor is itself to exercise such abstractions. And one cannot, after all, ever fully "walk in another person's shoes" without the capacity to imagine clearly—empathically, and in the abstract—just how those shoes would feel.

* * *

It isn't just literature. Visual artists, too, do more than mold sculpture and compose the visions in their imagination into real images on canvas or a page; through their work, they can craft minds and even futures.

"Just as sports provide students a way of learning unavailable in other disciplines, the fine arts help develop students' critical thinking skills, spatial-temporal reasoning, and help increase tolerance and cultural awareness," reads a report from the Oklahoma Policy Institute.[12]

Even more, research by the University of Arkansas, Fayetteville, in which Arkansas schoolchildren took a field trip to visit the then-new Crystal Bridges Museum in 2013, found that those who took part showed a significant increase in critical-thinking skills, capacity for historical empathy, and a marked improvement in tolerance. Students from rural or high-poverty regions had even larger gains in these areas, particularly in social tolerance.[13]

That part about "historical empathy" is crucial. As defined by the researchers, historical empathy is "the ability to understand and appreciate what life was like for people who lived in a different time and place. This is a central purpose of teaching history, as it provides students with a clearer perspective about their own time and place."[14] More importantly, the ability to experience "historical empathy" is inseparable from the ability to experience empathy—to feel what life is for people of your own time, but in a different place: the minority kids who grow up in poorer neighborhoods; the Muslim immigrants whose parents take them to mosques and who don't celebrate Christmas; the Jewish boy with the funny hat pinned to his head.

Which is why ultimately the researchers concluded that "exposure to the arts . . . affects the values of young people, making them more tolerant and empathetic. We suspect that their awareness of different people, places, and ideas through the arts helps them appreciate and accept the differences they find in the broader world."[15]

Why does this happen?

Part of the change can be explained by the intellectual process of art viewing—learning how a scene can look different depending on one's perspective, or observing the way two artists might have interpreted the same (usually biblical) scene. Looking at abstract art particularly tests the imagination: What does this look like? What if it isn't supposed to "look like" anything? Why is abstract expressionism in some ways more authentic than a painting of a sad or angry face?

Even many Old Master paintings are, in fact, little moral lessons, in which the figures symbolize ideas, like the vanitas paintings of skulls, which are not, in fact, about skulls at all, but about ephemerality, and time, and the importance of not overvaluing material things. Like literature, like poetry, they demand interpretation. (Which explains why most dictators, as well as fundamentalist Muslim and other religious groups, censor the arts; people who think critically, who explore interpretations, stand as the most perilous threats to their power.)

New technologies have shown that this, too, can be explained through the physiology of the brain, thanks to recent discoveries that looking at art stimulates "mirror neurons"—those same neurons stimulated by literature and closely associated with empathy. Neuroaestheticians like Columbia University's David Freedberg have shown, for instance, that visual art can have the same effect on the motor cortex that reading literature does. In one experiment Freedberg had subjects view an image of Michelangelo's *Expulsion from Paradise*, a panel of the Sistine Chapel masterpiece, in which Adam holds his hand out to defend himself from an angel with a sword.

Using trans-cranial magnetic stimulation to monitor the subjects' brains, Freedberg found that "just the sight of the raised wrist caused an activation of the muscle" that would flex subjects' own wrists.[16] Others have reported that viewing a Jackson Pollock canvas releases a sensation of flinging paint.

There may even be correlations between art preferences and personality: in 2015 Turkish researchers found, in accordance with earlier studies from 1973, that those who self-report as conservative prefer traditional, realist paintings, while liberals were more attracted to cubist and other abstract works.[17] Similarly psychologists at the University of London noted that "relevant qualities of more open individuals include their higher levels of imagination and creativity, their lower authoritarianism, and their higher degree of liberal attitudes and nonconventional cognitions. These traits, in turn, are believed to translate into a preference for more complex, contemporary, and challenging artistic compositions."[18]

If gray matter influences liberal or conservative political views, then the question arises whether it also affects taste in art; and if so, can training a person to enjoy abstract art also then make him more tolerant and open, as making a conservative feel safe is able to do? Can it change the composition of a person's anterior cingulate cortex—and so, his ideas, his vision, how he lives in the world?

The suggestion is that it can.

Whichever of these effects, or whatever combination of them, accounts for Jason Walters's transformation, we will never really know. But quite clearly *Schindler's List*, alongside the literature, art history, and philosophy he was discovering at that same moment, fathered, as it were, his rebirth. As literature did Maajid Nawaz.

And, it seems, Shannon Martinez, as well.

"I believe so deeply that classical, liberal arts education builds resiliency to finding resonance with the black-and-white binary thinking that internet algorithms rely upon to build and entrench divisiveness," Martinez wrote on Twitter on August 19, 2019. As a student at St. John's College, she added, "the power of engaging in discourse and ideas saved my life."

* * *

Shannon and I are far from alone in advocating education in the arts as a weapon against violence and terror. The Center on Global Counterterrorism Cooperation in Abu Dhabi notes, importantly, that "highly educated individuals have gone on to commit acts of violent extremism"—or, in other words, that simply being well educated is not enough. What makes the difference, they say, is early education programs that include "sports, drama, theater and art to stretch imaginations, promote critical thinking and strategizing, build team spirit and collaboration, and develop cultural knowledge to challenge extremist narratives."[19]

UN Human Rights Council special rapporteur Karima Bennoune went even further. In a 2017 statement to the Human Rights Council in Geneva, she declared "Arts, education, science and culture are among the best ways to fight fundamentalism and extremism. They are not luxuries, but critical to creating alternatives, making space for peaceful contestation, promoting inclusion, and protecting youth from radicalization. . . . Restrictions to and violations of artistic freedom . . . undermine efforts to counter extremism and fundamentalism."[20]

James Gilligan, too, emphasizes the importance of higher education and the arts in reducing recidivism among violent criminals. "Over a 25-year period," he writes, "more than 200 inmates, most of whom were serving time for the most serious violent crimes, including murder, rape, and armed robbery, had received a college degree and then left prison, and not one had been returned for a new crime."[21] Consequently he further recommends after-school programs for at-risk youth—who not surprisingly commit most of their (violent) crimes after the end of the school day—that would include classes in art, music, and drama. Such programs aren't just logical, says Gilligan. They've also been successful. Indeed, according to Iranian researchers, who confront family and community violence regularly, "art therapy is an effective intervention to reduce anger and its dimension. . . . Imagination and art work can help transform destructive aggression into constructive strength."[22]

This last, to be clear, is not about learning art appreciation and reading Dostoevsky, but rather about creating art, writing stories, composing music—activities art therapists for decades have known provide healing for trauma victims (such as abused children) and others. Such programs, Gilligan believes, enable "those who have been violent to adopt non-violent means for developing the feelings of self-esteem and self-respect, for being respected by others, and of being able to take legitimate and realistic pride in their skills and knowledge and achievements"[23]—and restore their humanity.

In place of shame, then, pride. In place of fear, openness. In place of narcissism, empathy. In place of rage, humanity.

* * *

If we are going to restore that sense of humanity in children in communities both at home and abroad, then there needs to be more attention paid to the joy of reading and art appreciation, and a renaissance in education to include an emphasis on literature and the arts—not just in secondary and tertiary education but beginning in the first grade. We will have to insist on funding public art projects and museums as part of an essential aspect of ensuring human rights, social equality, community respect and collaboration, and empathy for others. (In the process, perhaps parents might encourage their children to put more time and energy into reading and less into pointing cameras at their own faces.)

And while, as Jean Twenge suggests, we must also do away with the notion that "everyone is special" and everyone "deserves" a prize—whether they win or try or don't—we must also expand the world of opportunities for children, particularly in underprivileged communities, to excel: a lousy third baseman might prove an extraordinary pianist; a fumbling soccer player could have talents as a ballerina; the odd skinny kid with the big ears and the glasses who always calls out the wrong answer in science class might discover his inner Rembrandt or Picasso or Matisse.

Moreover, the results of the Crystal Bridges project make clear the profound effect that exposure to art, even once, can have on a child's thinking and understanding of the world and his or her place in it. And other studies in the ways reading fiction inspires empathy underscore the importance of literature in our lives. In light of all this, it is no coincidence that the areas of the world—and of our country—where literacy is comparatively low and where access to literature and the arts (via museums, galleries, theaters, or even primary education) is scarce, are more misogynistic, more polarized, and more violent. It was not for nothing that Kurt Vonnegut once declared, "Practicing an art, no matter how well or badly, is a way to make your soul grow."[24]

* * *

In truth, there are gaps in Jason Walters's story. His father, he says, became involved in drugs and drinking after the marriage fell apart. While he insists to me that there was no violence in his childhood home, there are also reports that his mother feared him enough to seek refuge, with his two younger sisters, in a battered women's shelter. He denies that he was bullied as a child, but people who knew him in those years have said he often was. His extremism, he says, was based on devotion to his religion; but devotion to Allah would not explain the hand grenade he made and then threw at police officers during the standoff in The Hague in the hours before his arrest—a grenade he learned to build while training for jihad in Pakistan. "Come and get me," he called out to them as they surrounded his home in The Hague. "I've been waiting for you for years!"[25]

When I ask him about these inconsistencies, Jason refuses to respond. What he does say is that his childhood was often frustrating. "It's not easy being smarter than your parents," he says. He often found himself having to explain things to them, a position of power further cemented, most likely, when he became the "man of the house" after his parents separated. In his trajectory to extremism, he saw himself as being "in the forefront . . . a part of history."[26]

This seems still to be his goal. But unlike the man he used to be, Jason Walters no longer seeks glory through violence, honor through martyrdom, identity in ideology, in hate. Now he told a Dutch journalist in 2018, "I feel I am the artist of my own life."[27]

* * *

I am walking West to Lexington when I see him: huddled in a doorway, his face shining and clean shaven, a heavy coat and hood to keep him warm. In a second's time, or even less, I realize who he is; I recognize him and do not, and then again I do, am surprised and unsurprised, and not completely certain.

"Yes," he says. "It's me. I knew I'd run into you."

When my eye first catches Rick's face, in the instant I recognize him and then don't, he shuffles, shifts, avoids my view, turns his head down. Is that because he does not want me to recognize him, or simply a coincidence, not having seen me yet at all? Surely had he not wanted me to see him he would not park himself across the street from where I live, standing, in fact, in exactly the same place he stood when our eyes first met almost forty years ago.

We became friends.

We became lovers.

There were good days and bad days and some hideously ugly days. He wanted too much vodka. I wanted too much freedom. There were demands and threats and a night I dialed 911.

Does he threaten you? The dispatcher asked me.

Yes.

Are you afraid of him?

Yes.

Does he have a weapon?

I don't think so.

Would he use one?

I don't know.

It does not occur to me that there are knives in the kitchen. It does not occur to me to say that his bodily strength is a weapon in itself.

"Please," I say.

The dispatcher tells me she can send someone around. *"But if he hasn't done anything to you, there's nothing they can do."*

"If he hasn't done anything to you, there is nothing they can do." Does he have to kill me before anyone will stop him?

When the police come, a man and a woman, the woman takes me to the bedroom to talk privately.

You need to think, she says, *if you really want to live like this.*

* * *

I was lucky: Rick didn't have a gun. But other domestic abusers do, and they use them to kill approximately five hundred women in America every year; statistics released in 2018 showed that a woman was shot and killed by a former or current partner every sixteen hours.[28] What's more, mass shootings and terror attacks worldwide have made clear that a domestic abuser with a weapon is more likely than anyone else to commit mass murder.[29]

For that to change, we need to sound the alarm, both domestically and abroad, on family abuse. We need to recognize the words of writer and activist Soraya Chemaly: "It's violence in homes, and tolerance, societal tolerance for violence in homes, that is the necessary precursor to all this public violence."[30] Even more, we need to look more closely at families, communities, and cultures that oppress women, bearing in mind Valerie Hudson and Hillary Clinton's determination that, as Hudson writes, "the best predictor of a state's peacefulness is not its level of wealth, or its level of democracy, or whether it is Islamic or not. The very best predictor of a state's peacefulness is its level of violence against women."[31] It is, after all, no coincidence that Donald Trump's most fervent supporters, particularly among the alt-right, seek to curb women's rights—including the right to abortion—and simultaneously are more militaristic in response to foreign terror attacks and generally more aggressive in response to feeling threatened; and it is similarly no coincidence that women are most abused and oppressed in the most severely violent and turbulent countries—such as those in the Middle East, greater North Africa, and parts of Southeast Asia—and in the most virulent, combative regions of our own.[32]

Because of this, we—and by "we" I mean not just governments but civilians everywhere—must actively search out and support initiatives for women's freedom and education worldwide, knowing that the emancipation of women is the key to freedom for us all: freedom from violence, freedom from warfare, and freedom, at last, from terror.

* * *

There are also practical measures Americans in particular have failed to enact, and it is impossible to take on the culture of violence without them. In the United States, for instance, perpetrators of sexual assault—but not domestic violence—are placed on a warning list for twenty years. They face restrictions on where they are allowed to live. They are required to inform neighborhood residents of their sex offender status. They forfeit, permanently, their right to bear arms. They are required to report every one to three years to local police, report any change of address to the authorities, and provide law enforcement agencies with the names of their internet service providers, all online screen names, and email accounts.

But those convicted of domestic abuse face none of these things. True, according to a law passed in 1996, they, too, forfeit their Second Amendment rights—as do those with restraining orders against them—but as Margaret Talbot noted in the *New Yorker* after the Pulse nightclub massacre, "The federal law and similar state laws are spottily enforced. These regulations are only effective if states put in place a screening process for potential gun buyers, to see if they have restraining orders against them— and many states have not." In addition, she adds, "Some states have laws that allow police to seize firearms when responding to domestic-violence incidents, but most do not." Further, "Municipal nuisance ordinances across the country allow landlords to evict tenants who have frequently called 911—a punishment that falls particularly hard on victims of domestic violence."[33]

What does happen to a domestic abuser? He might go to jail, and he might forfeit child custody rights, and he might have to pay a fine. But if, as on that night with Rick, there are no visible bruises, no weapons in sight, chances are none of this will happen. And as is well known, victims often retract their statements after an arrest, fearing the repercussions once the abuser is released. We lie: to protect ourselves, to protect our fantasies, to protect the mirage of a love that we know, but cannot bear to know, does not exist.

But here is what *should* happen, if any of this is going to change. Domestic abusers must not only lose their right to bear arms but—like sexual abusers—be required to report in regularly to law enforcement agencies, and have their internet activities monitored. Alarms should be raised whenever a domestic abuser turns up in so-called closed Facebook groups about guns, violence, right-wing hate, Islamist ideology, and misogyny. In such cases, in fact, Facebook, along with other social media companies, should be compelled to intervene. Above all, any laws that punish victims for seeking help must be struck down.

We also need resources to address familial violence and abuse in countries like Somalia, Pakistan, Afghanistan, Saudi Arabia, and elsewhere—including the United States. We must actively and consistently pressure Saudi Arabia, Iran, and other countries to bring their misogynistic laws into the twenty-first century. To do that, we will need further support for organizations like the Center for Democracy and Human Rights in Saudi Arabia, the Organization for the Freedom of Women in Iraq, and U.S.-based groups like the Tahirih Justice Center, which focuses on family abuse among immigrants, largely those from Southeast Asia, the Middle East, and North Africa; and to push global organizations like Amnesty International to take a harder stance on these matters. We need to work with Western allies to insist that imams in our own communities address these issues, and remove those imams who continue to advocate beating wives and children, which—shockingly—many still do.

Similarly there are artists bravely working in areas of the world where patriarchy, violence, and terrorism are rampant, and where they risk not only censorship but prison, torture, even death. Noted the Human Rights Council's Karima Bennoune, "Artists . . . are targeted both because creativity and expression per se are seen as a threat by fundamentalists and extremists, but also because artists often resist and offer alternatives to fundamentalist and extremist agendas."[34] These are the writers, painters, musicians, filmmakers, and poets, the galleries and publishers, the underground bookstores and music halls in Tehran and Baghdad, in Ankara and Kashmir. They need Western support—financially, politically, historically, and morally. So much of the future of these countries, these cultures, relies on them. They are the "open," democratic, empathic ones. They are the ones who fight the violence, the oppression, the patriarchal order. They are the ones who fight for knowledge, for poetry, for justice. They are the Enlightenment, and our world, quite literally, will not survive without them.

*　*　*

Still, this does not address the larger, cultural issues. Yes, encouraging youth to find self-worth through pride and dignity—and not honor or shame based on their gender, religion, geography, or position—is key to inspiring cultural change, as are endeavors to foster and nurture empathy. But even expertise in art appreciation and theater, for instance, was not enough to keep Charlie Sheen from repeatedly beating his various wives, or celebrity London art dealer Joseph Nahmad from allegedly pounding his ex-girlfriend's head against the wall of his multimillion-dollar home, or choking her from time to time.[35] Boris attended the same elite private school I did; in fact we became friends in English Lit.

Which is why even if countries across the globe increase arts education and access to museums and theater and literature, and so, inspire empathy; even if philosophic discourse becomes part of every Western and even Middle Eastern school curriculum, inspiring reason; even if classes in writing and painting and music and dance and drama are offered as replacements to violence as outlets for expression; even if domestic abuse and the oppression of women are demeaned, devalued, and condemned, so much more will still be needed to end the malignant narcissism, the need for attention, the victim chic, the longing for the romantic warrior hero, and so, the shame, the terror, the violence.

It is, for instance, well past time to do away with the "I am special" upbringing of children in the West, and to discourage the coronation of young boys—along with the enslavement of young girls—in the Middle East and North Africa region (MENA) and other honor cultures world-wide. This includes putting pressures on governments abroad to end child marriage, and criminalizing child marriage here at home, where several states permit marriage with parental permission at any age. It is equally past time to call an end to victimhood culture, that cousin of pathological narcissism that seeks vengeance and control in the face of insult and that finds such insult in any gesture that fails to demonstrate sufficient piety and honor.

Or put another way: if we hope to end extremism in our communities, we must end the extremism in the ways we raise our children. They are neither little gods nor tiny devils. They need be neither worshipped nor destroyed. Whatever their gender. Wherever they are born. Wherever they are raised.

At the same time, we in the West will have to take a harder look at the realities in which we live, as the policewoman confronted me that day, by asking ourselves if we really want to live like this.

In that moment, standing in my bedroom, the world as I had lived it broke open, shattered into pieces to the floor. And then—I could almost even see it—the shards rebuilt themselves around me, vivid and clear. There was no more refusing to believe. There was no more finding solace in the good times. There was no more blaming humid summer afternoons, the possibility of his headache, the words I must have misspoken, the dress I should not have worn—or should have. The only curtains that mattered were the ones I had drawn over my own eyes, merely to keep on living a romantic fantasy that had suddenly grown dark.

Now, they didn't merely open. I reached up and pulled them down.

* * *

At the start of this book I said that there is only one distinction between an abuser or violent criminal (such as a mass shooter) and a terrorist: the terrorist has a cause, and that cause is at once larger than he is and all of what he is. Call that cause what you will: Religious conquest. Racial supremacy. National liberty (which is why some call terrorists "freedom fighters"). It is that cause that drives him, not to violence itself but to the ultimate violent act that is the climax, the zenith, the glory of his dream.

But a cause doesn't only fuel terror: a cause inspired Martin Luther King to seek racial justice; Susan B. Anthony to lead the fight for women's right to vote; students in Parkland, Florida, to initiate a national march for gun safety. But a cause also stands behind the creation of humanitarian endeavors like UNICEF and War Child. The success of a mission doesn't rest on the power of its armies and the destructive violence of its might. It is a victory won on passion, with compassion as its arsenal and humanity as its guide.

And compassion, as philosopher Eric Hoffer wrote, "is probably the only antitoxin of the soul. Where there is compassion even the most poisonous impulses remain relatively harmless. . . . In the chemistry of man's soul, almost all noble attributes—courage, honor, hope, faith, duty, loyalty, etc—can be transmuted into ruthlessness. Compassion alone stands apart from the continuous traffic between good and evil proceeding within us."[36]

None of which is to say that these ideas alone will change the world, or end the horrors of terrorism in our lives. Many of them, too, will take a generation to realize, maybe even more than two or three. But the knowledge of these connections—of narcissism and shame, of shame and violence, of violence and honor, of honor and narcissism, of narcissism and violence, of violence and shame—and *understanding* of these connections, of this complex, intricately patterned web, will give us the power to overcome them all.

Because if we can change the thinking, and end the shame-rage cycle while teaching and instilling empathy, we will have made a major step toward peace.

* * *

It is September 11, 2019, as I write from a room in New York City, where the towers fell, where the blood colored the carpet floors, where I ran from a gun I never knew was even there, where lovers became knights and knights became villains and the sorrow and the hate still leave shadows on the pavements of the city.

And yet: I am hopeful. There is no time for mourning, and I have learned there is no time for fear. The hours, however few or many, call for comfort in the arts, for tenderness, for the sun outside the windows, and the promise that they bring.

I am not naive enough to think that we will ever reach a true utopia of peace in every home, and peace across the world.

But it's a cause to strive for.

APPENDIX A

Following the Links of Terrorism and Violence

	Death of father or mother	Divorce or abandonment by parent	Bodybuilding/ wrestling/ military	Domestic abuse (perpe- trator or victim)	Plastic surgery
Mohammed Atta (9/11 hijacker)			x	X (Mohammed Atta and other 9/11 hijackers)	
Andreas Baader (founder, leader Baader-Meinhoff Gang)	x				
Abdel Bary (UK rap star who went to Syria)		x (father imprisoned and extradited to U.S. during Bary's childhood)			
Scott Beierle (yoga studio shooter)			x	x	
Jake Bilardi (Australian convert, joined Jabhat al Nusra, died in suicide bombing)	x (mother died during Bilardi's childhood)	x		x	

	Death of father or mother	Divorce or abandonment by parent	Bodybuilding/ wrestling/ military	Domestic abuse (perpetrator or victim)	Plastic surgery
Osama bin Laden (9/11 mastermind)	x	x	x	x	
Safaa Boular (British terrorist)		x		x	
Mohammed Bouyeri (Dutch Hofstadgroep member, killed filmmaker-writer Theo van Gogh)	x (mother died during his early adulthood, two years before he radicalized)			x	
Robert Bowers (Pittsburgh Tree of Life Synagogue shooter)	x	x		x	
Anders Breivik (white supremacist who massacred 77 people)		x	x	x	x
Gregory Bush (shot two blacks in Kentucky)				x	
Syad Rizwan Farook (San Bernardino shooter)		x		x	
James Alex Fields (Charlottesville white supremacist march; killed activist Heather Heyer)	x			x	
Nidal Hasan (Fort Hood shooter)			x	x (emotional abuse)	

	Death of father or mother	Divorce or abandonment by parent	Bodybuilding/ wrestling/ military	Domestic abuse (perpetrator or victim)	Plastic surgery
Christopher Paul Hasson (white supremacist, member of Coast Guard, former Marine, accused of plotting numerous attacks)			x		
Colleen LaRose (Jihad Jane) (plotted various attacks, including murder of Mohammed cartoonist)	x			x	
Samantha Lewthwaite (suspected of executing/ planning numerous attacks worldwide; considered one of the most dangerous terrorists in the world)		x		x	
Germaine Lindsay (7/7 bomber)	x			x	
Shannon Martinez (former white supremacist)				x (raped, emotional abuse)	
Omar Mateen (security guard, Pulse nightclub shooter)			x	x	
Timothy McVeigh (Oklahoma City bomber)		x	x		
Man Haron Monis (took hostages at Lindt café, Sydney, Australia)				x	
Zacarias Moussaoui (9/11 hijacker)				x	

	Death of father or mother	Divorce or abandonment by parent	Bodybuilding/ wrestling/ military	Domestic abuse (perpetrator or victim)	Plastic surgery
James Nichols (Oklahoma City bomber)		x		x	
Terry Nichols (Oklahoma City bomber)		x	x	x	
Abu Nidal (Palestinian ANO leader)		x		x	
Mohammed Omar (founder of Taliban)	x		x	x	
Christian Picciolini (former white supremacist)				x	
Dylann Roof (Charleston SC, church shooter)		x		x	
Cesar Sayoc (sent pipe bombs to opponents of Donald Trump)			x	x	x
Mubin Shaikh (former Islamist extremist)			x	x	
O. J. Simpson (accused of killing his wife)		x	x	x	
Richard Spenser (alt-right leader)				x	
Brendan Tarrant (Christchurch, New Zealand, mosque shooter)	x	x	x	x	
Tamerlan Tsarnaev (Boston Marathon bomber)			x	x	
Jason and Jermaine Walters (members of Dutch terrorist Hofstadgroep; Jermaine later joined ISIS in Syria.)		x		x (rumored)	

APPENDIX B

Statistics

WORLDWIDE

According to the World Health Organization, men who were victims of child maltreatment are three to four times more likely to perpetrate intimate partner violence.[1]

A UN study found that in 2017, "Women killed by intimate partners or family members account for 58 per cent of all female homicide victims reported globally."[2]

UNITED STATES

In the United States approximately twenty people are abused by an intimate partner every minute. This comes to more than ten million men and women every year.[3]

In addition one in four women and one in nine men have experienced severe physical or sexual violence, or stalking.[4]

One in four women and one in seven men have experienced severe violence, such as burning, beating, or strangling.[5]

On a typical day more than twenty thousand phone calls are received by domestic violence hotlines.[6]

The presence of a gun in the home during domestic violence increases the risk of homicide by 500 percent.[7]

A 2018 UN report found that "in 2017 nearly 60 percent of female victims of deliberate homicide were killed by a family member, a rate of 137 women killed each day."[8]

One-third of women murdered in the United States are killed by their domestic partners, largely in the South, according to a 2014 report.[9]

Among Muslim women in the United States, 53 percent reported having experienced abuse at home; among non-Muslim women, the number was 33 percent.[10]

FRANCE

In 2018 France recorded 121 murders of women—or one woman every three days. According to the BBC, "in Western Europe, France is said to be among the countries with the highest rate of women killed by their partner, with 0.18 victims per 100,000 women according to 2017 Eurostat figures. This compares with a rate of 0.13 in Switzerland, 0.11 in Italy and 0.12 in Spain, but is less than Germany (0.23)."[11] Over two hundred thousand women between the ages of eighteen and seventy-five in France suffer physical or sexual assaults every year at the hands of current or ex-partners.[12]

UNITED KINGDOM

In London alone, 78,814 domestic abuse cases were recorded by the Metropolitan police in 2018.[13] Nearly 250,000 London residents have suffered domestic abuse in their lifetime; 5.9 percent of women and 2.9 percent of men.[14]

THE NETHERLANDS

Between 2015 and 2018, 747,000 men and women eighteen years of age or older have been the victims of domestic abuse, according to a government report. About a third of those victims admitted to having also perpetrated abuse themselves.[15]

Approximately 119,000 children (under 18) are subjected to child abuse each year, or about 3 percent of Dutch children.[16]

INDIA

In India one in three women has experienced sexual or physical violence in the home.[17]

In rural India 54 percent of women between the ages of forty to forty-nine support domestic violence. In urban areas 46.8 percent approve.[18]

TURKEY

A study of 1,481 Turkish women found that 41.3 percent had experienced domestic violence. More than 89 percent of those had been the victim of abuse from their husband.[19]

SAUDI ARABIA

According to a 2009 UN General Assembly report, "A study conducted in 2003–04 showed that 52.6 per cent of men interviewed abused their wife for 'misconduct'; an act that 52.7 per cent of the male respondents accept as 'the appropriate way to deal with women's misconduct.'" The report also noted that "husbands or ex-husbands, followed by close relatives (predominantly fathers and brothers), are the most common perpetrators of violence against women within the family. The NSHR [National Society for Human Rights] received complaints concerning physical and psychological violence, sexual harassment, defamation and insults. Data from the National Program for Family Safety shows that physical violence is the most common form of violence reported, which in 60 percent of cases is caused by husbands, followed by brothers and fathers."[20]

In the same report the authors note that "the Human Rights Commission and the NSHR have received complaints relating to abuse of power by husbands or other family members, such as: the denial of education, health or inheritance to wives and children; denying a wife the possibility to see her children; confiscating official documents such as identity cards in order to prevent women from travelling or accessing services; and the abandonment of wives and their children."[21]

Rape is not included in the Saudi Arabian criminal code.[22]

A 2018 report on the countries of the Arab League noted, "Published evidence suggests that physical, sexual, and emotional violence against adolescents is widespread in the Arab region. In many studies, prevalence rates exceeded other regional or global estimates, including rates of violent discipline, fighting, and intimate partner violence against adolescent girls."[23]

SUDAN

In 2016 the UN's Human Rights Council Mission to the Sudan reported: "The Special Rapporteur was informed that domestic violence is widespread, pervasive and remains largely invisible, due to the absence of reporting mechanisms and statistics as well as a lack of adequate policies and programs. The Special Rapporteur heard numerous accounts of domestic violence, both directly from victims and also from service providers. The description of weapons used, including rocks, and the injuries sustained by women, including permanent damage to the eyes, were underpinned by statements about the lack of access to assistance, whether from family, friends, neighbors or State authorities. Seeking redress from the police and the courts, including seeking a divorce, was an exercise in futility for most women."[24]

As in Saudi Arabia, women who report being raped are often treated as criminals themselves, subject to flogging or even a death sentence. [25]

APPENDIX C

Violence at Home, Violence in the World

Although it is the treatment of women, and not religious background, that both reflects honor culture and affects the violence or militarism of a society, it is worth noting that, as Valerie Hudson observes, "In Yemen, Egypt and Libya and throughout the Middle East, North and West Africa, and Central and South Asia, increasingly virulent forms of Islam are severely curtailing the rights of women and, by extension, further destabilizing already fragile states."[1] The numbers bear this out. Traditions of arranged marriage, female genital mutilation, and honor violence account for much of this.

The statistics listed are the most recent available.

VIOLENCE BY COUNTRY

Most violent countries, 2020

1. Afghanistan[2]
2. Syria
3. South Sudan
4. Yemen
5. Iraq
6. Somalia
7. Central African Republic
8. Libya
9. Congo
10. Russia

11. Pakistan
12. Turkey
13. Sudan
14. Ukraine
15. North Korea

Most violent countries, 2019

1. Afghanistan[3]
2. Syria
3. South Sudan
4. Yemen
5. Iraq
6. Somalia
7. Central African Republic
8. Libya
9. Congo
10. Russia
11. Pakistan
12. Turkey
13. Sudan
14. Ukraine
15. North Korea

VIOLENCE AGAINST WOMEN BY COUNTRY

Most Dangerous Countries for Women, 2018

1. Yemen[4]
2. Afghanistan
3. Syria
4. Pakistan
5. South Sudan

6. Iraq
7. Democratic Republic of Congo
8. Mali
9. Libya
10. Sudan

Most Dangerous Countries for Women, 2019

1. Yemen[5]
2. Afghanistan
3. Syria
4. Pakistan
5. South Sudan
6. Iraq
7. Democratic Republic of Congo
8. Central African Republic
9. Mali
10. Libya

VIOLENCE BY STATE

Most Violent States, 2018

1. Alaska[6]
2. New Mexico
3. Tennessee
4. Arkansas
5. Nevada
6. Louisiana
7. Alabama
8. Missouri
9. South Carolina
10. Arizona

Most Violent States, 2016

1. Louisiana[7]
2. Alaska
3. Tennessee
4. Delaware
5. Nevada
6. Arkansas
7. Missouri
8. Florida
9. South Carolina
10. Arizona

VIOLENCE AGAINST WOMEN BY STATE

States with Most Domestic Abuse Cases, 2017

1. Alaska[8]
2. Louisiana
3. Nevada
4. Oklahoma
5. South Carolina
6. New Mexico
7. South Dakota
8. Georgia
9. Tennessee
10. Texas

States Where Women Are Most Likely to Be Murdered by Men, 2015

1. Alaska[9]
2. Nevada
3. Louisiana
4. Tennessee
5. South Carolina

6. Arkansas
7. Kansas
8. Kentucky
9. Texas
10. New Mexico and Missouri (tie)

WORST STATES FOR QUALITY OF LIFE FOR WOMEN

Ratings based on average of women's economic well-being and health and safety rank

1. Louisiana[10]
2. Mississippi
3. Arkansas
4. Alabama
5. Oklahoma
6. South Carolina
7. Idaho
8. West Virginia
9. Texas
10. Georgia

Ratings based on health and safety rank only

1. Arkansas
2. Oklahoma
3. Mississippi
4. Nevada
5. West Virginia
6. Louisiana
7. Tennessee
8. Alabama
9. South Carolina
10. Alaska

NOTES

INTRODUCTION

1. Susan Heitler, PhD, "What Domestic Batterers Can Teach Us about Terrorism," *Psychology Today*, September 10, 2011.
2. Soraya Chemaly, "Sex and World Peace: Or, What Little Girls Have to Do with Our Wars," Huffington Post, October 12, 2012.
3. Heitler, "What Domestic Batterers Can Teach Us about Terrorism."
4. Also referred to as "malignant narcissism."
5. Anne Manne, "Narcissism and Terrorism: How the Personality Disorder Leads to Deadly Violence," *Guardian*, June 8, 2015, https://www.theguardian.com/world/2015/jun/08/narcissism-terrorism-violence-monis-breivik-lubitz-jihadi-john.
6. Personal conversation with Otto Kernberg, MD, director of the Personality Disorders Institute at the New York–Presbyterian Westchester Behavioral Health Center and professor of psychiatry at Weill Cornell Medicine, July 9, 2015.
7. M. I. Singer, D. B. Miller, S. Guo, K. Slovak, and T. Frieson, "The Mental Health Consequences of Children's Exposure to Violence," Cleveland OH: Cuyahoga County Community Health Research Institute, Mandel School of Applied Social Sciences, Case Western Reserve University, 1998. As cited by Jeffrey L. Edleson, "Problems Associated with Children's Witnessing of Domestic Violence," VAW National Online Resource Center on Violence Against Women, April 1999, https://vawnet.org/sites/default/files/materials/files/2016-09/AR_Witness.pdf.
8. David Rutledge, "How 'Jihadi Cool' Draws Young Brits from the Suburbs to the Battlefield," interview with Raffaello Pantucci, "The Religion and Ethics Report," ABC Radio National, September 2, 2005, https://www.abc.net.au/radionational/programs/religionandethicsreport/jihadi-cool-from-the-suburbs-to-the-battlefield/6743680.
9. Robin Morgan, *The Demon Lover: The Roots of Terrorism* (New York: Washington Square Press, 2001), location 6125. Kindle.
10. Morgan, *The Demon Lover*, location 119.
11. Dana Ford, "Michelle Knight on Ariel Castro: 'He Said That He Had Puppies,'" CNN.com, May 6, 2014, https://www.cnn.com/2014/05/05/us/michelle-knight-interview/index.html.
12. Patricia Evans, *The Verbally Abusive Relationship* (New York: Simon & Schuster, 2010), 107.

I. THE NARCISSIST

1. Serge Schmemann, "U.S. ATTACKED: President Vows to Exact Punishment for 'Evil,'" *New York Times*, September 12, 2001.

2. Adam Robinson, *Bin Laden: Behind the Mask of the Terrorist* (New York: Arcade Publishing, 2002).

3. Chris Suellentrop, "Abdullah Azzam: Godfather of Jihad," *Slate*, April 16, 2002.

4. Kate Zernike and Michael T. Kaufman, "The Most Wanted Face of Terrorism," *New York Times*, May 2, 2011, https://www.nytimes.com/2011/05/02/world/02osama-bin-laden-obituary.html.

5. Zernike and Kaufman, "The Most Wanted Face of Terrorism."

6. Zernike and Kaufman, "The Most Wanted Face of Terrorism."

7. From documents recovered from bin Laden's compound, known collectively as "Bin Laden's Bookshelf," Office of the Director of National Intelligence, http://www.dni.gov/index.php/resources/bin-laden-bookshelf?start=1, accessed March 2016.

8. Zernike and Kaufman, "The Most Wanted Face of Terrorism."

9. Office of the Director of National Intelligence, "Bin Laden's Bookshelf."

10. Jerrold M. Post, MD, "Killing in the Name of God: Osama bin Laden and Al Qaeda," in The Counterproliferation Papers, Future Warfare Series, no. 18, USAF Counterproliferation Center, Maxwell Air Force Base, AL, 2002, p. 8.

11. Cited in *Frontline*, "Osama bin Laden v. the U.S.: Edicts and Statements," https://www.pbs.org/wgbh/pages/frontline/shows/binladen/who/edicts.html, accessed March 10, 2020.

12. Zernike and Kaufman, "The Most Wanted Face of Terrorism."

13. O. F. Kernberg, "The Narcissistic Personality Disorder and the Differential Diagnosis of Antisocial Behavior," *Psychiatric Clinics of North America* 12, no. 3 (1989): 553–70; Julian Borger, "Saddam, Tell Me about Your Mum," *Guardian*, November 14, 2002.

14. Personal email from A. H. Esman, MD, to author.

15. Anne Manne, *The Life of I: The New Culture of Narcissism* (Melbourne, Australia: Melbourne University Press, 2014), 241; Jerrold M. Post, paraphrased in Andrew Maykuth, "Bin Laden a 'Malignant' Personality Who Commands Attention, CIA Expert," *Philadelphia Inquirer*, November 10, 2004.

16. James Gilligan, *Preventing Violence* (New York: Thames and Hudson, 2001), location 417. Kindle.

17. Gilligan, *Preventing Violence*, location 397. Kindle.

18. Manne, "Narcissism and Terrorism."

19. Author interview with Otto Kernberg, July 9, 2015, New York.

20. Cited in Peter Giesen, "Jihad blijkt opvallend vaak een familieaangelegenheid," *Volkskrant*, March 23, 2016.

21. Jon Henley, "Anders Behring Breivik Trial: The Father's Story," *Guardian*, April 13, 2012.

22. Sally Jacobs, David Filipov, and Patricia Wen, "The Fall of the House of Tsarnaev," *Boston Globe*, December 13, 2013, https://www.bostonglobe.com/metro/2013/12/15/the-fall-house-tsarnaev/lg5Q3XqtbOOQR1ZCWgB1sK/story.html.

23. Deborah Sontag, David M. Herszenhorn, and Serge F. Kovaleski, "A Battered Dream, Then a Violent Path," *New York Times*, April 27, 2013.

24. Jacobs, Filipov, and Wen, "The Fall of the House of Tsarnaev."

25. Jacobs, Filipov, and Wen, "The Fall of the House of Tsarnaev."

26. Sontag, Herszenhorn, and Kovaleski, "A Battered Dream, Then a Violent Path."

27. Christopher Lasch, *The Culture of Narcissism* (New York: W. W. Norton and Co., 1978), 85.

28. Lasch, *The Culture of Narcissism*, 84.

29. "PrimeTime: McVeigh's Own Words," ABC News, March 29, 2001, http://abcnews.go.com/Primetime/story?id=132158&page=1.

30. Kim Sendgupta, "Married Couple among Amman Bombers," *Independent*, November 12, 2005.

31. Charlotte Kemp, "My Bizarre and Terrifying Childhood with My Father, Osama bin Laden," *Daily Mail*, October 28, 2009.

32. Guy Lawson, "Osama's Prodigal Son: The Dark, Twisted Journey of Omar Bin Laden," *Rolling Stone*, January 20, 2010.

33. Jim Yardley, "Portrait of a Terrorist," *New York Times*, October 10, 2001.

34. Hans Werdmölder, *Generatie op Drift* (Arnhem, Netherlands: Gouda Quint, BV, 1990).

35. Werdmölder, *Generatie op Drift*, 5.

36. Lodewijk Dros, "Gids Voor De Moslim," *Volkskrant*, April 21, 2004, https://www.trouw.nl/nieuws/gids-voor-de-moslim~ba6628ec/.

37. Daniel Goleman, "The Roots of Terrorism Are Found in Brutality of Shattered Childhood," *New York Times*, September 2, 1986.

38. Russell Myers, "Ex-wife of Egypt Air Hijacker Says She Endured 'Marriage of Hell' with Fake Suicide Bomber," *Daily Mirror*, March 31, 2016.

39. Michael Janofsky with Sara Rimer, "A Troubled Life Unfolds: A Special Report.; Simpson: 'Baddest Cat,' a Polished Star, or Both?" *New York Times*, June 25, 1994.

40. Daily News Wire, "Evidence Depicts OJ as Brute, Diary Cites Beatings, Threats," Philly.com, January 12, 1995.

41. Scott Michaels, "Inside the Mind of OJ Simpson," ABC News, September 18, 2007.

42. Josh Meyer, "Police Records Detail 1989 Beating That Led to Charge," *Los Angeles Times*, June 17, 1994.

43. Michael Janofsky with Sarah Rimer, "A Troubled Life Unfolds," *New York Times*, June 26, 1994.

44. Kenneth B. Noble, "Prosecution Says Simpson Abused Wife for 17 Years," *New York Times*, January 12, 1995.

45. Letter from Nicole Simpson, accessed from Court TV Online at https://web.archive.org/web/20081227003930/http://www.courttv.com/casefiles/simpson/new_docs/nicoleletter.html, accessed on April 11, 2016.

46. Noble, "Prosecution Says Simpson Abused Wife for 17 Years."

2. THE SHAME AND THE POWER

1. James Gilligan, "Shame, Guilt, and Violence," *Social Research* 70, no. 4 (winter 2003): 1149–80.

2. Bridget Kendall, "What Drives Women to Extreme Acts?" BBC World News, July 28, 2015, https://www.bbc.com/news/world-33600267.

3. Jane C. Hu, "To Deradicalize Extremists, Former Neo-Nazis Use a Radical Method: Empathy," *Quartz*, November 9, 2018, https://qz.com/1457014/to-deradicalize-extremists -former-neo-nazis-use-a-radical-method-empathy/.

4. Farhana Qazi, *Invisible Martyrs* (Oakland CA: Berrett-Koehler Publishers, 2018), 57.

5. Voltairenet.org, "Proclamation of the Caliphate," July 1, 2014, https://www.voltairenet .org/article184550.html, accessed June 1, 2019. See also, "The Return of Khilafah," *Dabiq*, July 5, 2014, 3.

6. Central Intelligence Agency, "'Face' Among the Arabs," September 18, 1995, https://www .cia.gov/library/center-for-the-study-of-intelligence/kent-csi/vol8no3/html/v08i3a05p _0001.htm.

7. Gilligan, "Shame, Guilt, and Violence," 3.

8. Thomas Friedman, "The Humiliation Factor," *New York Times*, November 9, 2003.

9. Lindsay Dodgson, "Feeling Intense Shame Can Turn Some People into Narcissists— Here's How," *Business Insider*, March 20, 2018, https://www.businessinsider.com/how -shame-can-create-a-narcissist-2018-3/.

10. Dodgson, "Feeling Intense Shame."

11. Scott Shane, "The Enduring Influence of Anwar al-Awlaki in the Age of the Islamic State," Combatting Terrorist Center at West Point, July 2016, https:// ctc.usma.edu/the-enduring-influence-of-anwar-al-awlaki-in-the-age-of-the-islamic -state/.

12. Paul R. Pillar, "Scott Shane's 'Objective Troy,'" *New York Times Book Review*, September 8, 2015.

13. Mark Zaslav, "Narcissism—The Shame-Negating Personality," *The Neuropsychotherapist*, February 4, 2017, https://www.thescienceofpsychotherapy.com/narcissism-the-shame -negating-personality/ (italics in original).

14. Peter Jansson, "Shame a Common Cause for Male Violence," doctoral thesis, Jönköping University, October 2016.

15. Jansson, "Shame a Common Cause for Male Violence."

16. Jansson, "Shame a Common Cause for Male Violence."

17. Halim Barakat, "The Arab Family and the Challenge of Change," in *The Arab World* (Berkeley CA: University of California Press, 1993), http://www.academia.edu/10810736 /The_Arab_Family_and_the_Challenge_of_Change.

18. Umm Salihah, "An Islamic Perspective on Child-Rearing and Discipline," *New York Times*, January 12, 2011, https://parenting.blogs.nytimes.com/2011/01/12/an-islamic -view-of-parenting/.

19. Barakat, "The Arab Family and the Challenge of Shame."

20. Seth Meyers, PsyD, "The Disturbing Link Between Narcissism and Sadism," *Psychology Today*, July 8, 2016, https://www.psychologytoday.com/us/blog/insight-is-2020/201607 /the-disturbing-link-between-narcissism-and-sadism.

21. Ken Sullivan and William Wan, "Troubled. Quiet. Macho. Angry. The Volatile Life of the Orlando Shooter," *Washington Post*, June 17, 2016.

22. Sullivan and Wan, "Troubled. Quiet. Macho. Angry."

23. Sullivan and Wan, "Troubled. Quiet. Macho. Angry."

24. Adam Goldman, Joby Warrick, Max Bearak, "'He Was Not a Stable Person': Orlando Shooter Showed Signs of Emotional Trouble," *Washington Post*, June 12, 2016.

25. Yasmine Mohammed, *Unveiled: How Western Liberals Empower Radical Islam* (Victoria, Canada: Free Hearts Free Minds, 2019), 145 (used with permission).

26. Mohammed, *Unveiled*.

27. Gilligan, "Shame, Guilt, and Violence."

3. HONOR SOCIETY

1. Central Intelligence Agency, "'Face' Among the Arabs."

2. S. G. Smith, J. Chen, K. C. Basile, L. K. Gilbert, M. T. Merrick, N. Patel, M. Walling, and A. Jain, "The National Intimate Partner and Sexual Violence Survey (NISVS): 2010–2012 State Report." Atlanta GA: National Center for Injury Prevention and Control, Centers for Disease Control and Prevention, 2017, https://www.cdc.gov/ violenceprevention/pdf/nisvs-statereportbook.pdf, accessed July 26, 2019. See also U.S. Department of Health and Human Services, Administration for Children and Families, Administration on Children, Youth and Families, Children's Bureau (2018). "Child Maltreatment 2016," https://www.acf.hhs.gov/cb/research-data-technology/ statistics-research/child-maltreatment, accessed July 25, 2019; Alissa Scheller, "At Least a Third of all Women Murdered in the U.S. Are Killed by Male Partners," Huffington Post, December 6, 2017, https://www.huffpost.com/entry/men-killing-women-domesti _n_5927140; Alexandra Klausner, "The Wife-Killer Map of America: THIRD of all Women Murdered in the U.S. Are Killed by Their Partners Who Most Likely Live in the South, Reveals Study," *Guardian*, October 10 2014, https://www.dailymail.co.uk /news/article-2787329/That-s-no-Southern-gentleman-Study-finds-THIRD-women -murdered-U-S-killed-male-partners-likely-live-South-gun.html.

3. S. L. Bloom, "Commentary: Reflections on the Desire for Revenge," *Journal of Emotional Abuse* 2, no. 4 (2001): 61–94; October 12, 2008, http://dx.doi.org/10.1300 /J135v02n04_06.

4. Bloom, "Commentary: Reflections on the Desire for Revenge," 86.

5. Sandra Mackey, *Passion and Politics: The Turbulent World of the Arabs* (New York: Plume/ Penguin, 1994), 26–27.

6. Khalida Brohi, *I Should Have Honor* (New York: Random House, 2018), location 84. Kindle.

7. *Post* Staff, "Aiya Altameemi Beating: Parents Who Padlocked Daughter to Bed for Talking to Boy Take Plea Deal," Huffington Post, November 7, 2012, https://www .huffpost.com/entry/aiya-altameemi-beating-padlocked-talking-to-boy_n_2089763.

8. "Shame" finds its roots in the Teutonic word *skem*, which means "to cover."

9. Sharifa Alkhateeb, "Ending Domestic Violence in Muslim Families," National Resource Center on Domestic Violence, https://vawnet.org/sites/default/files/materials/files/2016 -09/EndingDVMuslimFamilies.pdf, accessed March 17, 2020.

10. Morgan, *The Demon Lover*, location 117.

11. Daniel Pipes, foreword to *The Smarter Bomb: Women and Children as Suicide Bombers* by Anat Berko (Lanham MD: Rowman and Littlefield, 2012), x.

12. Berko, *The Smarter Bomb*, 109, 80.

13. Dominic Casciani, "The Radicalisation of Safaa Boular: A Teenager's Journey to Terror," BBC News, June 4, 2018, https://www.bbc.com/news/uk-44359958.

14. Casciani, "The Radicalisation of Safaa Boular."

15. Wolfie James, "Seven Reasons Why Alt-Right Men Are the Hottest," May 27, 2017, AltRight.com, https://altright.com/2017/03/27/7-reasons-why-alt-right-men-are-the -hottest/.

16. TOI Staff, "Austrian Girls Who Joined ISIS 'Want to Come Home,'" *Times of Israel*, October 11, 2014, https://www.timesofisrael.com/austrian-girls-who-joined-is-want-to -come-home/.

17. Lizzie Dearden, "Isis Austrian Poster Girl Samra Kesinovic 'Used as Sex Slave' Before Being Murdered for Trying to Escape," *The Independent*, December 31, 2015, https://www .independent.co.uk/news/world/middle-east/isis-austrian-poster-girl-samra-kesinovic -used-as-sex-slave-before-being-murdered-for-trying-to-a6791736.html.

18. Author interview with Dov Cohen, June 23–24, 2019.

19. Sabrina Tavernise, "With His Job Gone, an Autoworker Wonders, 'What Am I as a Man?'" *New York Times*, May 27, 2019, https://www.nytimes.com/2019/05/27/us/auto -worker-jobs-lost.htmlg.

20. Richard Nisbett, Dov Cohen et al., "Insult and Aggression in the Culture of Honor," *Journal of Personality and Social Psychology* 70, no. 5 (1996): 945–60.

21. Christian Picciolini, *Romantic Violence: Memoirs of an American Skinhead* (Chicago IL: Goldmill Goup, LLC, 2015), 65.

22. Picciolini, *Romantic Violence*, 64.

23. Picciolini, *Romantic Violence*, 64.

24. Picciolini, *Romantic Violence*, 124.

25. Picciolini, *Romantic Violence*, 81.

26. Jacobs, Filipov, and Wen, "The Fall of the House of Tsarnaev."

27. Casciani, "The Radicalisation of Safaa Boular."

28. Casciani, "The Radicalisation of Safaa Boular."

29. Ryan P. Brown et al., "Culture, Masculine Honor, and Violence Against Women," *Personality and Social Psychology Bulletin* 44, no. 4 (2017): 538–49 (italics in original).

30. Brown et al., "Culture, Masculine Honor, and Violence Against Women."

31. University of Michigan, "Psychologist Discusses Cultures of Honor, Traditions of Violence," *Michigan News*, May 23, 1997, https://news.umich.edu/psychologist-discusses -cultures-of-honor-traditions-of-violence/.

32. ADL Center on Extremism, "When Women Are the Enemy: The Intersection of Misogyny and White Supremacy," Anti-Defamation League, 2018, https://www.adl.org/media /11707/download.

33. ADL Center on Extremism, "When Women Are the Enemy."

34. Brown et al., "Culture, Masculine Honor, and Violence Against Women."

35. Leonie Cooper, "The 25 Best Country Music Songs of All Time," NME, April 15, 2018, https://www.nme.com/blogs/nme-blogs/25-best-country-music-songs-time-1951105.

36. Hu, "To Deradicalize Extremists, Former Neo-Nazis Use a Radical Method: Empathy," (italics in original).

37. Personal conversation with Shannon Foley Martinez via Skype, May 9, 2019.

38. Steven Hendrix, "He Always Hated Women. Then He Decided to Kill Them," *Washington Post*, June 7, 2019, https://www.washingtonpost.com/graphics/2019/local/yoga -shooting-incel-attack-fueled-by-male-supremacy/?utm_term=.d1e0558b31ff.

4. EMPATHY

1. Transcript of Ariel Castro's statement to the court, August 1, 2013, http://transcripts .cnn.com/TRANSCRIPTS/1308/01/ng.01.html.

2. Bloom, "Commentary: Reflections on the Desire for Revenge."

3. James C. Ballenger, Second Competency Evaluation report of Dylann Roof, January 1, 2017, 12, https://bloximages.newyork1.vip.townnews.com/postandcourier.com/content/ tncms/assets/v3/editorial/1/4d/14d50c5a-35c3-11e7-a5e5-87d6dd34667b/59137e82453c2 .pdf.pdf.

4. "Laatste Woord Mohammed B," transcript of sentencing statement, *Volkskrant*, August 9, 2005, https://www.volkskrant.nl/nieuws-achtergrond/laatste-woord-mohammed-b -b8643c96/.

5. UNICEF, "Behind Closed Doors: The Impact of Domestic Violence on Children" (West Sussex, UK: Body Shop for UNICEF, 2006).

6. Rachel Dissell, "Ariel Castro Files: Kidnapper and Rapist Tells of Abuse as a Child, Says Never Suicidal," *Cleveland Plain Dealer*, May 5, 2014.

7. Personal conversations with Shannon Martinez via Skype, June–July 2019.

8. National Coordinator, Terrorisme Bestrijding en Veiligheid, Algemene Inlichting en Veiligheidsdienst Minderjarigen bij ISIS, The Hague, Netherlands, 2017, 8–10, 13, https://www.njb.nl/Uploads/2018/3/Nota--Minderjarigen-bij-ISIS-.pdf, accessed May 1, 2017; March 12, 2020. Also see Charlotte McDonald-Gibson, "What Should Europe Do with the Children of ISIS?" *New York Times*, July 23, 2017, https://www.nytimes .com/2017/07/23/opinion/isis-children-european-union.html.

9. Ford, "Michelle Knight on Ariel Castro."

10. Tracy Egan Morrisey, "Charlie Sheen's History of Violence Toward Women," Jezebel .com, March 2, 2011, https://jezebel.com/charlie-sheens-history-of-violence-toward -women-5774374.

11. Richard Nisbett and Dov Cohen, *Culture of Honor: The Psychology of Violence in the South*, (Boulder CO: Westview, 1996), 86.

12. Berko, *The Smarter Bomb*, 4.

13. Personal conversations with Yasmine Mohammed, June–July 2019.

14. Jeff Dunetz, "'The Street Was Covered with Blood and Bodies,' The Sbarro Bombing," JewishPress.com, August 11, 2017, https://www.jewishpress.com/blogs/the-lid-jeffdunetz /the-street-was-covered-with-blood-and-bodies-the-sbarro-bombing/2017/08/11/.

15. Raanan Ben-Sur, "Sbarro Terrorist 'Not Sorry,'" YnetNews.com, March 27, 2006, https://www.ynetnews.com/articles/0,7340,L-3232591,00.html.

16. Ballenger, Second Competency Evaluation report of Dylann Roof, 9.

17. Marc Fisher and Joel Achenbach, "Boundless Racism, Zero Remorse: A Manifesto of Hate and 49 Dead in New Zealand," *Washington Post*, March 15, 2019, https://www .washingtonpost.com/national/boundless-racism-zero-remorse-a-manifesto-of-hate-and -49-dead-in-new-zealand/2019/03/15/3d407c64-4738-11e9-90f0-0ccfeec87a61_story .html?utm_term=.5e98de8b54cd.

18. George Simon, "Shame, Guilt, Regret, Remorse and Contrition," blog post, DrGeorgeSimon.com, November 7, 2014, https://www.drgeorgesimon.com/shame-guilt-regret -remorse-and-contrition/.

19. Gilligan, "Shame, Guilt, and Violence."

20. Julie Hirschfield Davis, "Trump Calls Some Unauthorized Immigrants 'Animals' in Rant," *New York Times*, May 16, 2018, https://www.nytimes.com/2018/05/16/us/politics /trump-undocumented-immigrants-animals.html. See also, Abigail Simon, "People Are Angry Trump Used This Word to Describe Undocumented Immigrants," *Time*, June 19, 2018, https://time.com/5316087/donald-trump-immigration-infest/; Donald Trump, Twitter post, https://twitter.com/realDonaldTrump/status/1009071403918864385?s= 20, accessed March 11, 2020.

21. L. Schulze, I. Dziobek, A. Vater et al., "Gray Matter Abnormalities in Patients with Narcissistic Personality Disorder," *PubMed* 47, no. 10 (October 2013): 1363–69; https:// doi.org/10.1016/j.jpsychires.2013.05.017; Epub June 15, 2013.

22. Max-Planck-Gesellschaft, "I'm OK, You're Not OK: Right Supramarginal Gyrus Plays an Important Role in Empathy," *ScienceDaily*, October 9, 2013, www.sci-encedaily.com/releases/2013/10/131009133057.htm.See also Giorgia Silani, Claus Lamm, Christian C. Ruff, and Tania Singer, "Right Supramarginal Gyrus Is Crucial to Overcome Emotional Egocentricity Bias in Social Judgments," *Journal of Neuroscience* 25 (September 2013), https://doi.org/10.1523/jneurosci.1488-13 .2013.

23. Fritz Breithaupt and Andrew B. B. Hamilton, *The Dark Sides of Empathy* (Ithaca: Cornell University Press, 2019); Jonathan Lambert, "Does Empathy Have a Dark Side?" NPR.

com, April 12, 2019, https://www.npr.org/sections/health-shots/2019/04/12/712682406 /does-empathy-have-a-dark-side.

24. Lambert, "Does Empathy Have a Dark Side?"

25. Eliana Aponte, "The Dark Side of Empathy," *The Atlantic*, September 25, 2015.

26. Hendrix, "He Always Hated Women. Then He Decided to Kill Them."

5. THE ABUSER

1. Valerie Hudson et al., *Sex and World Peace* (New York: Columbia University Press, 2012), location 1820. Kindle.

2. Gilligan, *Preventing Violence*, location 509.

3. Gilligan, "Shame, Guilt, and Violence," 1149–80.

4. Gilligan, "Shame, Guilt, and Violence."

5. Rachel Louise Snyder, "*No Visible Bruises* Upends Stereotypes of Abuse, Sheds Light on Domestic Violence," *Fresh Air*, May 7, 2019, https://www.npr.org/sections/health -shots/2019/05/07/721005929/no-visible-bruises-upends-stereotypes-of-abuse-sheds -light-on-domestic-violence.

6. Gilligan, "Shame, Guilt, and Violence."

7. Dan Barry, Serge F. Kovaleski, Alan Blinder, and Mujib Mashal "'Always Agitated, Always Mad': Omar Mateen, According to Those Who Knew Him," *New York Times*, June 18, 2016, https://www.nytimes.com/2016/06/19/us/omar-mateen-gunman-orlando -shooting.html.

8. Shane Harris, Brandy Zadrozny, and Katie Zavadski, "The Unhinged Home That Raised Orlando Killer Omar Mateen," *Daily Beast*, June 18, 2016, https://www.thedailybeast .com/the-unhinged-home-that-raised-orlando-killer-omar-mateen.

9. Personal conversations with Yasmine Mohammed, June–July 2019.

10. Tatiana Elghossain et al., "Prevalence of Key Forms of Violence Against Adolescents in the Arab Region: A Systematic Review," *Journal of Adolescent Health* 64, no. 1 (January 1, 2019): 8–19.

11. Elghossain et al., "Prevalence of Key Forms of Violence Against Adolescents in the Arab Region."

12. Ramola Talwar Badam, "'Spare the Rod': Arab World Needs to Change Attitudes Towards Physical Child Discipline," *The National*, November 20, 2017, https://www .thenational.ae/uae/spare-the-rod-arab-world-needs-to-change-attitudes-towards-physical -child-discipline-1.677407.

13. Harry Enten, "Americans' Opinions on Spanking Vary by Party, Race, Region and Religion," FiveThirtyEight.com, September 15, 2014, https://fivethirtyeight.com/features /americans-opinions-on-spanking-vary-by-party-race-region-and-religion/.

14. Bloom, "Commentary: Reflections on the Desire for Revenge."

15. "Trauma as a Precursor to Violent Extremism," START Research Brief, April 2015, https://www.start.umd.edu/pubs/start_cstab_TraumaAsPrecursortoViolentExtrem-ism_April2015.pdf. By contrast START found that in the general U.S. population,

28 percent of American adults reported having been physically abused; 20.7 reported childhood sexual abuse; and 12.4 percent reported childhood neglect.

16. Hudson et al., *Sex and World Peace*, location 1929. Kindle.

17. Jessica Stern, "Holy Avengers—The Rise of Religious Terrorists," *Financial Times* [UK] Arts & Weekend, June 12, 2004, https://www.belfercenter.org/publication/holy-avengers.

18. Borger, "Saddam, Tell Me About Your Mum," *Guardian*, November 14, 2002.

19. "Andreas Baader and Gudrun Ensslin," Encyclopedia.com, https://www.encyclopedia.com/books/encyclopedias-almanacs-transcripts-and-maps/baader-andreas-and-ensslin-gudrun, updated February 28, 2020.

20. Dennis Balcolm, "Absent Fathers," *Journal of Men's Studies* (June 1998): 287.

21. Jason Yates Sexton, *The Man They Wanted Me to Be* (Berkley CA: Counterpoint, 2019), 136. Kindle.

22. Joshi Herrmann, "Abdel Bary: The Rising Rap Star Who Rejected Drugs and Chose Jihad Instead," *Evening Standard*, August 15, 2014, https://www.standard.co.uk/lifestyle/london-life/abdel-bary-the-rising-rap-star-who-rejected-drugs-and-chose-jihad-instead-9671093.html.

23. Maajid Nawaz, with Tom Bromley, *Radical: My Journey Out of Islamist Extremism* (Guilford CT: Lyons Press, 2013), location 162. Kindle.

24. Personal conversation with Shannon Foley Martinez, July 2019.

25. Anne Manne, "Narcissism and Terrorism," accessed July 4, 2019.

6. THE ABUSED

1. "What Is Gaslighting?" National Domestic Violence Hotline web page, May 29, 2014, https://www.thehotline.org/what-is-gaslighting/.

2. Business Digest, *New York Times*, August 20, 2001, https://www.nytimes.com/2001/08/20/business/business-digest-778540.html?searchResultPosition=2.

3. Gilligan, "Shame, Guilt, and Violence."

4. Neil A. Louis, "Moussaoui's Childhood Is Presented as Mitigating Factor," *New York Times*, April 18, 2006.

5. UNICEF, "Behind Closed Doors."

6. Personal conversation with Mubin Shaikh via Skype, July 9, 2019.

7. J. Liebschutz, J. B. Savetsky, R. Saitz, N. J. Horton, C. Lloyd-Travaglini, and J. H. Samet, "The Relationship between Sexual and Physical Abuse and Substance Abuse Consequences" *Journal of Substance Abuse Treat* 22, no. 3 (2002): 121–28.

8. Bloom, "Commentary: Reflections on the Desire for Revenge."

9. This anecdote first appeared in "If I Could Close My Eyes, a Story of Love, Pain, Hope, and Release," in *Diane* magazine, September 2006.

10. Berko, *The Smarter Bomb*, x.

11. Berko, *The Smarter Bomb*, 24–25.

12. Qazi, *Invisible Martyrs*, 51.

13. Lucy Kafanov, "How All-Female ISIS Morality Police 'Khansaa Brigade' Terrorized Mosul," NBC News, November 20, 2016, https://www.nbcnews.com/storyline/isis -uncovered/how-all-female-isis-morality-police-khansaa-brigade-terrorized-mosul -n685926.
14. Brown et al., "Culture, Masculine Honor, and Violence Against Women."
15. Author interview with Dov Cohen, June 23–24, 2019.
16. Picciolini, *Romantic Violence*, 210–11.
17. As cited in Manne, Afterword, *The Life of I*, updated edition (Melbourne, Australia: Melbourne University Press, 2015).
18. Personal conversations with Yasmine Mohammed, 2018–2019.
19. Jerrold Post, *Narcissism and Politics: Dreams of Glory* (New York: Cambridge University Press, 2015), 218.
20. Picciolini, *Romantic Violence*, 228.
21. Personal conversation with Ayaan Hirsi Ali, Amsterdam, April 2003 (emphasis hers).
22. Personal conversation with Yasmine Mohammed via Skype, June 18, 2019 (emphasis hers).

7. TERROR, HONOR, VIOLENCE

1. Khalida Brohi, *I Should Have Honor.*
2. Phyllis Chesler, "Worldwide Trends in Honor Killings," *Middle East Quarterly* (Spring 2010): 3–11, https://www.meforum.org/2646/worldwide-trends-in-honor-killings. Quote taken from personal email correspondence with Dr. Chesler, April 29, 2011.
3. Brohi, *I Should Have Honor*, location 76. Kindle.
4. Saeed Kamali Dehghan, "Ameneh Bahrami: Was I Right to Pardon the Man Who Blinded Me with Acid?" *Guardian*, April 26, 2015, https://www.theguardian.com/world /2015/apr/26/ameneh-bahrami-interview-iran-acid-attack-blinded.
5. Douglas Jehl, "For Shame: Arab Honor's Price: A Woman's Blood," *New York Times*, June 20, 1999.
6. Bob Mitchell and Noor Javed, "I Killed My Daughter . . . with My Hands," *Toronto Star*, June 16, 2010, https://www.thestar.com/news/crime/2010/06/16/i_killed_my _daughter__with_my_hands.html.
7. Mitchell and Javed, "I Killed My Daughter . . . with My Hands."
8. Canadian Press, "Chronology of Events in the Shafia Murders," CTV News, January 29, 2012, https://www.ctvnews.ca/chronology-of-events-in-the-shafia-murders-1 .760520.
9. Christie Blatchford, "I Would Do It Again: Court Hears Horror of Alleged Honor Killings," *National Post*, October 20, 2011, https://nationalpost.com/opinion/christie -blatchford-i-would-do-it-again-court-hears-horror-of-an-alleged-honour-killing.
10. Masoeme Abbrin, "Eerwraak: De Namus Gebroken," *Trouw*, August 28, 2003, https:// www.trouw.nl/nieuws/eerwraak-de-namus-gebroken~bbc22d8a/.

11. This paragraph appeared previously in Abigail R. Esman, "Dead Silence," *The Daily*, November 8, 2011.

12. Jehl, "For Shame: Arab Honor's Price."

13. Rhea Wessel, "Interview [with Serap Cileli]: Forced Marriage in Germany," *World Politics Review*, February 1, 2007, https://www.worldpoliticsreview.com/trend-lines /516/interview-forced-marriage-in-germany.

14. Amnesty International, "You Shall Procreate—Attacks on Women's Sexual and Reproductive Rights in Iran," March 2015, https://www.amnesty.org/download/Documents /MDE1311112015ENGLISH.pdf.

15. U.S. Department of State, "Country Reports on Human Rights Practices for 2016" (section 6), March 7, 2017, https://www.state.gov/country-reports-on-human-rights -practices-for-2016/.

16. Nisbett and Cohen, *Culture of Honor: The Psychology of Violence in the South*, 2.

17. As cited in: UK Home Office, *Country Policy and Information Note, Iran: Honour Crimes Against Women*, October 2017, https://www.ecoi.net/en/file/local/1416949/1226 _1508940013_cpin-iran-honour-crimes-october-2017-ex.pdf.

18. Dan Bilefsky, "How to Avoid Honor Killing in Turkey? Honor Suicide," *New York Times*, July 16, 2006, https://www.nytimes.com/2006/07/16/world/europe/16turkey .html.

19. Personal email and phone conversation with Jesse Krimes, April 2015.

20. John Twomey, "Thugs Force Man to Drink Acid for Affair with Muslim Woman," *Sunday Express*, July 24, 2009, https://www.express.co.uk/news/uk/115992/Thugs-force -man-to-drink-acid-for-fling-with-Muslim.

21. Personal email correspondence with Dr. Chesler, April 29, 2011.

22. "30 jaar cel voor Almelose Turk om eerwraakmoord op dochter," *Trouw*, July 16, 2004. https://www.trouw.nl/nieuws/30-jaar-cel-voor-almelose-turk-om-eerwraakmoord-op -dochter-bf1929e7/.

23. Chesler, "Worldwide Trends in Honor Killings."

8. THE WOMEN

1. Personal conversation with Shannon Foley Martinez via Skype, May 9, 2019.

2. Eric Hoffer, *The Passionate State of Mind*, 1951, section 29.

3. Eric Hoffer, *The True Believer* (New York: Harper Collins e-books, 2011), chapter 2.

4. Brohi, *I Should Have Honor*, 109.

5. Anne Speckhard and Ardian Shajkovci, "American-Born Hoda Muthana Tells All About Joining ISIS and Escaping the Caliphate," *Homeland Security Today*, April 23, 2019, https://www.hstoday.us/subject-matter-areas/counterterrorism/american-born-hoda -muthana-tells-all-about-joining-isis-and-escaping-the-caliphate/.

6. Katrin Bennhold, "Jihad and Girl Power: How ISIS Lured Three London Girls," *New York Times*, August 17, 2015, https://www.nytimes.com/2015/08/18/world/europe/jihad -and-girl-power-how-isis-lured-3-london-teenagers.html.

7. Personal conversation with Yasmine Mohammed via Skype, June 18, 2019.

8. James Longman, "Female Muslim Converts Drawn to the Islamic State," BBC.com, January 29, 2015, https://www.bbc.com/news/uk-31027457.

9. "Jihadgangers zijn relatief vaak bekeerlingen; 45 procent is van Marokkaanse komaf," *Volkskrant*, July 5, 2017, https://www.volkskrant.nl/nieuws-achtergrond/jihadgangers-zijn-relatief-vaak-bekeerlingen-45-procent-is-van-marokkaanse-komaf-bb147bf6/.

10. "Laura Passoni, repentie du jihad, raconte ses neuf mois passés au cœur de l'Etat islamique," FranceInfo TV, September 29, 2016, https://www.francetvinfo.fr/monde/proche-orient/offensive-jihadiste-en-irak/temoignage-9-mois-en-syrie_1848285.html (author's translation).

11. Anne Speckhard, "ICSVE's New 'Breaking the ISIS Brand' Video Clip: The Promises of ad-Dawlah to Women," (transcript) International Center for the Study of Violent Extremism, May 5, 2017, https://www.icsve.org/icsves-new-breaking-the-isis-brand-video-clip-the-promises-of-ad-dawlah-to-women/.

12. Personal conversation with Carla Rus, December 14, 2005.

13. Personal conversation with Afshin Ellian, Leiden, Netherlands, 2007.

14. Zack Adesina and Oana Marocico, "Is It Easier to Get a Job If You're Adam or Mohammed?" BBC News, February 6, 2017, https://www.bbc.com/news/uk-england-london-38751307. See also, Ianthe Sahadat, "Als je solliciteert kun je nog beter een strafblad hebben dan een buitenlandse achternaam," *Volkskrant*, July 5, 2017, https://www.volkskrant.nl/nieuws-achtergrond/als-je-solliciteert-kun-je-nog-beter-een-strafblad-hebben-dan-een-buitenlandse-achternaam-b1c19ae1/.

15. Abigail Esman, "The Real Jihadist Threat No One Is Watching," Investigative Project on Terrorism, July 17, 2017, https://www.investigativeproject.org/6415/the-real-jihadist-threat-no-one-is-watching.

16. Qazi, *Invisible Martyrs*, 12 (italics in original).

17. Qazi, *Invisible Martyrs*, 14.

18. Kiriloi M. Ingram, "More than 'Jihadi Brides' and 'Eye Candy': How Dabiq Appeals to Western Women," International Centre for Counter-Terrorism, August 12, 2016, https://icct.nl/publication/more-than-jihadi-brides-and-eye-candy-how-dabiq-appeals-to-western-women/.

19. Caitlin Moscatello, "British ISIS Bride Reportedly Recruiting Women to Marry Islamic State Militants," Glamour.com, September 8, 2014, https://www.glamour.com/story/british-bride-of-isis-reported.

20. As cited in "Al Qa'ida Women's Magazine: Women Must Participate in Jihad," Memri.org, September 7, 2004, https://www.memri.org/reports/al-qaida-womens-magazine-women-must-participate-jihad#_edn1.

21. Qazi, *Invisible Martyrs*, 12 (italics in original).

22. Seyward Darby, "The Rise of the Valkyries," *Harper's*, September 2017, https://harpers.org/archive/2017/09/the-rise-of-the-valkyries/.

23. "White Nationalists Applaud as Lana Lokteff Boasts That Women Elected Trump and Hitler," AngryWhiteMen.org, March 16, 2017, https://angrywhitemen.org/2017/03 /16/white-nationalists-applaud-as-lana-lokteff-boasts-that-women-elected-trump-and -hitler/#more-27726.

24. ADL Center on Extremism, "When Women Are the Enemy."

25. Seyward Darby, "The Rise of the Valkyries."

26. Personal conversation with Carla Rus, December 2005.

27. Personal conversation with Shannon Martinez, May 9, 2019.

28. "Richard Bertram Spencer," Southern Poverty Law Center website, https://www.splcenter .org/fighting-hate/extremist-files/individual/richard-bertrand-spencer-0, accessed March 13, 2020.

29. Lyz Lenz, "You Should Care That Richard Spencer's Wife Says He Abused Her," Huffington Post UK, January 13, 2019.

30. Andrew Anglin, "What Is the Deal with WMBF Relationships?" DailyStormer.com, September 19, 2016, https://archive.is/3trgB.

31. Kenneth B. Noble, "Simpson Threw Wife into Wall, Her Sister Tells Jury," *New York Times*, February 4, 1995, https://www.nytimes.com/1995/02/04/us/simpson-threw-wife -into-wall-her-sister-tells-jury.html.

32. A 2017 CDC National Intimate Partner and Violence Survey report based on 2010–2011 figures cites the following as showing the highest twelve-month prevalence of violence or stalking by an intimate partner (listed in order of percentage): South Carolina, Kentucky, Washington, Louisiana, Illinois, Alabama, Nevada, Arkansas, Minnesota, https://www.cdc.gov/violenceprevention/pdf/NISVS-StateReportBook .pdf, accessed March 14, 2020. In addition, a 2017 U.S. Department of Health and Human Services report cited Kentucky and Indiana for having the highest child abuse rates, with Arkansas rated number one in child fatalities (U.S. Department of Health and Human Services, Administration for Children and Families, Administration on Children, Youth and Families, Children's Bureau, 2019), Child Maltreatment 2017, https://www.acf.hhs.gov/cb/research-data-technology/statistics-research/child -maltreatment, accessed July 25, 2019. For official rates of domestic homicide and rape, see Ryan Brown and Kiersten Baughman, "Culture, Masculine Honor and Violence Toward Women," in: *Personality and Social Psychology Bulletin*, December 2017.

9. THE TIES THAT BIND

1. Personal conversation with Yasmine Mohammed via Skype, July 16, 2019.

2. Mark Berman, "What the Police Officer Who Shot Philando Castile Said about the Shooting," *Washington Post*, June 21, 2017, https://www.washingtonpost.com/news/ post-nation/wp/2017/06/21/what-the-police-officer-who-shot-philando-castile-said -about-the-shooting/.

3. Morgan, *Demon Lover*, location 6665. Kindle.

4. Kevin Sack and Alan Binder, "Jurors Hear Dylann Roof Explain Shooting in Video: 'I Had to Do It,'" *New York Times*, December 9, 2016, https://www.nytimes.com/2016/12/09/us/dylann-roof-shooting-charleston-south-carolina-church-video.html.

5. Cycle of Violence, Women's Center—Youth and Family Services of California, https://www.womenscenteryfs.org/index.php/get-info/prevention/education/14-cycle-of-violence, accessed March 14, 2020.

6. Email correspondence with Shannon Martinez, May 13, 2019.

7. Picciolini, *Romantic Violence*, 230.

8. Picciolini, *Romantic Violence*, 94–95.

9. Personal conversation with Carla Rus, December 14, 2005.

10. Pete Simi et al., "Trauma as a Precursor to Violent Extremism," START, National Consortium for the Study of Terrorism and Responses to Terrorism, April 2015, https://www.start.umd.edu/pubs/START_CSTAB_TraumaAsPrecursortoViolentExtremism_April2015.pdf.

11. Andrew Higgins, "A Surly Misfit with No Terror Links Turned a Truck into a Tank," *New York Times*, July 15, 2016, https://www.nytimes.com/2016/07/16/world/europe/a-surly-misfit-with-no-terror-links-turned-a-truck-into-a-tank.html.

12. Nawaz, *Radical*, location 69. Kindle.

13. Webpage capture of Robert Bowers's Facebook page, http://archive.is/1zr9J, accessed October 27, 2018.

14. Yates Sexton, *The Man They Wanted Me to Be*.

15. Gilligan, "Shame, Guilt, and Violence."

16. Jacquelyn C. Campbell et al., "Risk Factors for Femicide in Abusive Relationships," *American Journal of Public Health* 93, no. 7 (July 2003).

17. Abigail Esman, *Radical State: How Jihad Is Winning Over Democracy in the West* (Santa Barbara CA: Praeger, 2010), 8.

10. PEACE AT HOME, PEACE IN THE WORLD

1. Personal conversation, February 13, 2015.

2. Brown and Baughman, "Culture, Masculine Honor, and Violence toward Women."

3. Ryan Brown et al., "School Violence and the Culture of Honor," *Psychological Science* 20, no. 11 (November 2009).

4. Collin D. Barnes, Ryan Brown, and Lindsey L. Osterman, "Don't Tread on Me: Masculine Honor Ideology in the U.S. and Militant Responses to Terrorism," *Personality and Social Psychology Bulletin* 38, no. 8 (2012).

5. Barnes, Brown, and Osterman, "Don't Tread on Me."

6. Barnes, Brown, and Osterman, "Don't Tread on Me."

7. Barnes, Brown, and Osterman, "Don't Tread on Me" (italics in original).

8. Brohi, *I Should Have Honor*, ix.

9. Gul Tuysuz, "7 Times Turkish President 'Mansplained' Womanhood," CNN.com, June 9, 2016, https://edition.cnn.com/2016/06/09/europe/erdogan-turkey-mansplained

-womanhood/index.html. Despite Erdogan's politics and religiously inspired rule, it is perhaps also worth noting that the centuries of warfare and aggression in the Ottoman Empire ceased after Ataturk's reforms, which ended sharia law and gave women equal rights to education and employment and within ten years, the right to vote. Modern Turkey's nearly one hundred years of peace distinguishes the country from the rest of the Middle East.

10. M. Steven Fish, "Islam and Authoritarianism," *World Politics* 55, no. 1 (October 2002): 4–37, http://www.jstor.org/stable/25054208.

11. Michelle Goldberg, "Norway Massacre: Anders Breivik's Deadly Attack Fueled by Hatred of Women," *Daily Beast*, July 25, 2011, https://www.thedailybeast.com/norway -massacre-anders-breiviks-deadly-attack-fueled-by-hatred-of-women.

12. As cited in Harry Hurt III, *The Lost Tycoon* (New York: Norton, 1993).

13. Marie Brenner, "After the Gold Rush," *Vanity Fair*, September 1, 1990.

14. Nancy Collins, "Donald Trump Talks Family, Women in Unearthed Transcript," *Hollywood Reporter*, October 13, 2016, https://www.hollywoodreporter.com/news/donald -trump-women-unearthed-1994-primetime-interview-nancy-collins-938176.

15. Bandy Lee et al., *The Dangerous Case of Donald Trump: 37 Psychiatrists and Mental Health Experts Assess a President* (New York: Thomas Dunne Books, 2017).

16. Eli Harman, "White Sharia," *Heritage and Destiny*, September–October 2017.

17. "'White Sharia' and Militant White Nationalism," Southern Poverty Law Center, November 27, 2017, https://www.splcenter.org/hatewatch/2017/11/27/white-sharia -and-militant-white-nationalism.

18. "'White Sharia' and Militant White Nationalism."

19. ADL Center on Extremism, "When Women Are the Enemy," accessed September 10, 2019.

20. Daryl Johnson, Southern Poverty Law Center, "Doomsday Desperation," August 17, 2017, https://www.splcenter.org/hatewatch/2017/08/17/doomsday-desperation.

21. "Why 3 Anti-Islam Activists Were Denied Entry Into the UK," BBC.com, March 14, 2018, https://www.bbc.com/news/blogs-trending-43393035.

22. ADL Center on Extremism, "When Women Are the Enemy."

23. Personal conversation with Shannon Foley Martinez via Skype, May 9, 2019.

24. David Futrelle, "The 'Alt-Right' Is Fueled by Toxic Masculinity—And Vice Versa," NBCnews.com, April 1, 2019, https://www.nbcnews.com/think/opinion/alt-right-fueled -toxic-masculinity-vice-versa-ncna989031.

25. Eli Saslow, *Rising Out of Hatred: The Awakening of a Former White Nationalist* (New York: Doubleday, 2018).

26. Sara Sidner, *Anderson Cooper 360*, August 4, 2019, http://transcripts.cnn.com/TRAN-SCRIPTS/1908/04/se.01.html.

27. Gilligan, "Shame, Guilt, and Violence," 1, 149.

28. Picciolini, *Romantic Violence*, iii.

29. Hoffer, *The Passionate State of Mind*.

30. Picciolini, *Romantic Violence*, 303.

31. As noted by Maajid Nawaz, for instance, in *Radical*. See also, Esman, *Radical State*.

32. Hudson et al., *Sex and World Peace*, location 1823. Kindle.

33. Hudson et al., *Sex and World Peace*, location 2077. Kindle.

34. Janey Stephenson, "The Correlation between Domestic Violence and Terror Is Distressingly Stark," *The Debrief*, March 29, 2017.

35. Morgan, *The Demon Lover*, location 315. Kindle.

11. CULTURE OF TERRORISM

1. Richard Parker, "Was Trump's El Paso Visit a Turning Point?" *New York Times*, August 8, 2019.

2. Paul P. Murphy et al., "Dayton Shooter Had an Obsession with Violence and Mass Shootings, Police Say," CNN.com, August 7, 2019, https://www.cnn.com/2019/08/05 /us/connor-betts-dayton-shooting-profile/index.html.

3. Erin Ailworth, Georgia Wells, and Ian Lovett, "Lost in Life, El Paso Suspect Found a Dark World Online," *Wall Street Journal*, August 8, 2019.

4. Ailworth, Wells, and Lovett, "Lost in Life."

5. Colin Drury, "Grinning Trump Gives Thumbs-up with Baby Whose Parents Were Shot Dead in El Paso Terror Attack," *Independent*, August 9, 2019, https://www.independent .co.uk/news/world/americas/trump-melania-baby-el-paso-thumbs-up-hospital-parents -mass-shooting-a9049086.html.

6. Josh Dawsey and John Wagner, "During El Paso Hospital Visit, Trump Compared His and O'Rourke's Crowd Sizes at Political Rallies, Video Shows," *Washington Post*, August 8, 2019, https://www.washingtonpost.com/politics/during-el-paso-hospital -visit-trump-compared-his-and-orourkes-crowd-sizes-at-political-rallies-video-shows /2019/08/08/573a3e68-b9eb-11e9-bad6-609f75bfd97f_story.html.

7. Jean M. Twenge and W. Keith Campbell, *The Narcissism Epidemic* (New York: Atria Books, 2009).

8. Jean Twenge, *Generation Me, Revised and Updated: Why Today's Young Americans Are More Confident, Assertive, Entitled—And More Miserable Than Ever Before* (New York: Atria Books, 2014), 63.

9. Twenge, *Generation Me*, 68.

10. Twenge, *Generation Me*, 68–69.

11. Twenge and Campbell, *The Narcissism Epidemic*.

12. Post, *Narcissism and Politics*, location 72.

13. Charles Murray, Southern Poverty Law Center listing, https://www.splcenter.org/ fighting-hate/extremist-files/individual/charles-murray.

14. Twenge and Campbell, *The Narcissism Epidemic*.

15. Bradley Campbell and Jason Manning, "The New Millennial 'Morality': Highly Sensitive and Easily Offended," *Time*, November 17, 2017, https://time.com/4115439/student -protests-microaggressions/.

16. Central Intelligence Agency, "'Face' Among the Arabs."

17. Zoe Williams, "Me! Me! Me! Are We Living through a Narcissism Epidemic?" TheGuardian.com, March 2, 2016, https://www.theguardian.com/lifeandstyle/2016/mar/02/narcissism-epidemic-self-obsession-attention-seeking-oversharing.

18. D. W. Sue, *Microaggressions in Everyday Life: Race, Gender and Sexual Orientation* (Hoboken: Wiley and Sons, 2010).

19. Bradley Campbell and Jason Manning, *The Rise of Victimhood Culture: Microaggressions, Safe Spaces, and the New Culture Wars* (Los Angeles: Palgrave McMillan, 2018).

20. Clover Linh Tran, "CDS Appropriates Asian Dishes, Students Say," *Oberlin Review*, November 6, 2015.

21. John Villasenor, "Views among College Students Regarding the First Amendment: Results from a New Survey," Brookings Institute, September 18, 2017, https://www.brookings.edu/blog/fixgov/2017/09/18/views-among-college-students-regarding-the-first-amendment-results-from-a-new-survey/.

22. Conor Friedersdorf, "The Rise of Victimhood Culture," *Atlantic*, September 11, 2015, https://www.theatlantic.com/politics/archive/2015/09/the-rise-of-victimhood-culture/404794/.

23. Emily Shire, "Victims and Microaggressions: Why 2015 Was the Year Students Lost Their Minds," *Daily Beast*, December 27, 2015, https://www.thedailybeast.com/victims-and-microaggressions-why-2015-was-the-year-students-lost-their-minds.

24. Campbell and Manning, "The New Millennial 'Morality.'"

25. Olga Khazan, "How White Supremacists Use Victimhood to Recruit," TheAtlantic.com, August 15, 2017, https://www.theatlantic.com/science/archive/2017/08/the-worlds-worst-support-group/536850/.

26. Khazan, "How White Supremacists Use Victimhood to Recruit."

27. Picciolini, *Romantic Violence*.

28. "The Inconvenient Truth," online statement from El Paso shooter Patrick Crusius. This manifesto was posted online just prior to the attack. I was able to access it immediately after. Within hours, however, a public outcry ensued, demanding that the text be removed from the Internet so as to avoid influencing or inciting others and to deny the killer the narcissistic gratification of an audience. Within days, the manifesto had been removed entirely.

29. Ian Buruma, "Final Cut," *The New Yorker*, December 27, 2004, https://www.newyorker.com/magazine/2005/01/03/final-cut-2.

30. Elizabeth Harris and Joseph Goldstein, "Park's Rules on Scarves Are Cited in a Melee," *New York Times*, August 30, 2011.

31. Stern, *Holy Avengers*.

32. "What Is Jihadism?" BBC.com, December 11, 2014, https://www.bbc.com/news/world-middle-east-30411519.

33. Cornelia Riehle, "European Terrorism Situation and Trend Report 2019," European Union Agency for Law Enforcement Cooperation (EUROPOL), 2019, 8–9, https://

eucrim.eu/news/eu-terrorism-situation-and-trend-report-2019/, accessed August 3, 2019.

34. "Operation Inherent Resolve: Lead Inspector General Report to the United States Congress," Washington DC: U.S. Department of Defense, August 2019, https://media.defense.gov/2019/Aug/06/2002167167/-1/-1/1/Q3FY2019_LEADIG_OIR_REPORT.PDF.

35. Glen Carey, "Al Qaeda Is as Strong as Ever after Rebuilding Itself, U.S. Says," *Bloomberg*, August 1, 2019.

36. Christian Taylor, "Al-Qaida Is Stronger Today than It Was on 9/11," *The Conversation*, July 3, 2019, https://theconversation.com/al-qaida-is-stronger-today-than-it-was-on-9-11-117718.

37. Eric Tlozek, "Al Qaeda Was Forgotten during the Rise of Islamic State, but the Terrorist Group Is More Dangerous than Ever," ABC News, July 30, 2019, https://www.abc.net.au/news/2019-07-31/al-qaeda-was-forgotten-but-the-terror-group-is-more-dangerous/11365230.

38. Carl Bernstein, *Fear: Trump in the White House* (New York: Simon and Schuster, 2018), epigraph.

39. For the studies see, Ryota Kanai et al., "Political Orientations Are Correlated with Brain Structure in Young Adults," *Current Biology* 21 (April 26, 2011): 677–80; and H. Hannah Nam et al., "Amygdala Structure and the Tendency to Regard the Social System as Legitimate and Desirable," Nature Human Behaviour 2 (February 2018): 133–38, https://www.nature.com/articles/s41562-017-0248-5.pdf. Quote is found in Kanai et al., "Political Orientations Are Correlated with Brain Structure in Young Adults."

40. H. Hannah Nam et al., "Amygdala Structure and the Tendency to Regard the Social System as Legitimate and Desirable," 133.

41. H. Hannah Nam et al., "Amygdala Structure and the Tendency to Regard the Social System as Legitimate and Desirable" (emphasis added).

42. Hilary Brueck, "These Key Psychological Differences Can Determine Whether You're Liberal or Conservative," *Business Insider*, April 19, 2018.

43. Hilary Brueck, "A Yale Psychologist's Simple Thought Experiment Temporarily Turned Conservatives into Liberals," *Business Insider*, October 21, 2017, https://www.businessinsider.com/how-to-turn-conservatives-liberal-john-bargh-psychology-2017-10.

44. Koran (Surah Al-Haj) 22:19.

45. Hilary Breuck, "Scientists Have Discovered Two Simple Psychological Differences that Make You Liberal or Conservative," *Business Insider*, February 3, 2018, https://www.businessinsider.com/liberals-and-conservatives-process-disgust-and-empathy-differently-2018-1.

46. Koran, 9: 28, and Koran, 98:6.

47. Hadith, Al-Bukhari 7/541, no. 835; Muslim, 3/160, no. 5268.

48. Hadith, Al-Bukhari 4:47.

49. "Beyond Red and Blue: The Political Typology," Pew Research Center, June 2014, https://www.people-press.org/2014/06/26/the-political-typology-beyond-red-vs-blue/.

50. Alexandra Klausner, "Wife Killer Map of America: THIRD of All Women Murdered in the U.S. Are Killed by Their Partners Who Most Likely Live in the South, Reveals Study," *Daily Mail*, October 9, 2014. See also, Evan Comen, "The Most and Least Literate States," *24 Wall Street*, updated January 11, 2020, https://247wallst.com/special -report/2018/09/07/most-and-least-literate-states/2/0.

51. "When Men Murder Women" (Washington DC: Violence Policy Center, September 2018), http://vpc.org/studies/wmmw2018.pdf. See also Mike Bronson, Posie Boggs, Jennifer Jones, "How to Close Alaska's Literacy Gap with Other States," *Anchorage Daily News*, October 31, 2015.

52. Mohammed S. Shiraz, "The Impact of Education and Occupation on Domestic Violence in Saudi Arabia," *International Journal of Social Welfare* 25 (2016): 339–46.

53. Bilgur Erten and Pinar Keskin, "For Better or Worse? Education and the Prevalence of Domestic Violence in Turkey," *American Economic Journal* 10, no. 1 (January 2018).

54. "Violence and Socioeconomic Status," American Psychological Association, https:// www.apa.org/pi/ses/resources/publications/violence, accessed August 16, 2019.

55. Naureen Chowdhury Fink et al., "The Role of Education in Countering Violent Extremism," CGCC, December 2013, https://globalcenter.org/wp-content/uploads/2013/12/ Dec13_Education_Expert_Meeting_Note.pdf.

56. Indeed, in February 2020, British classicist Mary Beard set off a debate about whether nudes in art were "soft porn for the elite" that should be removed from museum walls (https://www.historyextra.com/period/modern/mary-beard-bbc-series-shock -nude-nakedness-interview-art-history-naked/), while the director of the Van Gogh Museum in Amsterdam considered the question of whether an Edgar Degas drawing of a nude bather should be exhibited in a "multicultural society"—suggesting it might be too offensive to Muslims (Roelf Jan Duin, "Directeur Van Gogh: Past naakt nog in een museum?" Het Parool, February 10, 2020, https://www.parool.nl/kunst-media /directeur-van-gogh-past-naakt-nog-in-een-museum-baa86583/).

57. Peggy McGlone, "Trump's Budget Eliminates NEA, Public TV, and Other Cultural Agencies. Again," *Washington Post*, February 12, 2018.

58. Brian Kisida and Daniel H. Bowen, "New Evidence of the Benefits of Arts Education," Brookings Institute, February 12, 2019, https://www.brookings.edu/blog/brown-center -chalkboard/2019/02/12/new-evidence-of-the-benefits-of-arts-education/.

59. John Bayley, "Tackle Youth Violence by Ending Illiteracy," *Guardian*, September 1, 2008.

60. Baoguo Shi, Xiaoqing Cao et al., "Different Brain Structures Associated with Artistic and Scientific Creativity: A Voxel-Based Morphometry Study," *Nature*, February 21, 2019.

61. "The Creative Brain Is Wired Differently," *Neuroscience News*, January 23, 2018, https:// neurosciencenews.com/creativity-networks-8355/.

62. Jared Yates Sexton, *The Man They Wanted Me to Be*, 117–18. Kindle.

63. Amnesty International, "Iran: Tortured Filmmaker and Musicians Face Imminent Arrest amid Crackdown on Artists," March 1, 2016, https://www.amnesty.org/en/latest /news/2016/03/iran-tortured-filmmaker-and-musicians-face-imminent-arrest-amid -crackdown-on-artists/.

64. "Iran Arrests Theater Artists Over Shakespeare Production," Radio Free Europe, September 10, 2018.

65. Cara Anna, "Afghans Restore Art Shattered by Taliban as Peace Deal Nears," Associated Press, August 20, 2019.

12. TOWARD A SOLUTION

1. Esther Voet, "Jason Walters Spreekt," *Nieuw Israelietisch Weekblad*, June 4, 2018, published as "Former Jihadi Jason Walters Speaks," The Investigative Project on Terrorism, July 15, 2018, https://www.investigativeproject.org/7487/former-jihadi-jason-walter-speaks (author's translation).

2. Voet, "Jason Walters Spreekt."

3. Nawaz, *Radical*, location 189. Kindle.

4. Nawaz, *Radical*, location 204. Kindle.

5. David Comer Kidd and Emanuele Castano, "Reading Literary Fiction Improves Theory of Mind." *Science*, October 18, 2013, https://science.sciencemag.org/content/342/6156 /377.

6. Liz Bury, "Reading Literary Fiction Improves Empathy, Study Finds," *Guardian*, October 8, 2013, https://www.theguardian.com/books/booksblog/2013/oct/08/literary-fiction -improves-empathy-study.

7. Anne Murphy Paul, "Your Brain on Fiction," *New York Times*, March 17, 2012, https:// www.nytimes.com/2012/03/18/opinion/sunday/the-neuroscience-of-your-brain-on -fiction.html.

8. Murphy Paul, "Your Brain on Fiction."

9. Sarah Kaplan, "Does Reading Fiction Make You a Better Person?" *Washington Post*, July 22, 2016, https://www.washingtonpost.com/news/speaking-of-science/wp/2016 /07/22/does-reading-fiction-make-you-a-better-person/.

10. Kaplan, "Does Reading Fiction Make You a Better Person?"

11. T. S. Eliot, "The Burial of the Dead," from *The Wasteland: A Facsimile and Transcript of the Original Drafts, including the Annotations of Ezra Pound.* (New York: Harcourt Brace, 1971), 7.

12. Rebecca Fine, "Fine Arts Education Matters: How Shrinking Budgets Deepen Inequalities," Oklahoma Policy Institute, December 18, 2018, https://okpolicy.org/fine-arts -education-matters-how-shrinking-budgets-deepen-inequalities/.

13. Jay P. Greene, Brian Kisida et al., "Arts Education Matters: We Know, We Measured It," *Education Week*, December 2, 2014, https://www.edweek.org/ew/articles/2014/12 /03/13greene.h34.html?r=924562112.

14. Jay P. Greene, Brian Kisida, and Daniel H. Bowen, "The Educational Value of Field Trips," *Education Next*, September 16, 2013.

15. Greene, Kisida et al., "Arts Education Matters."

16. Abigail Tucker, "How Does the Brain Process Art?" *Smithsonian*, November 2012, https://www.smithsonianmag.com/science-nature/how-does-the-brain-process-art-80541420/.

17. Recep Oz et al., "A Study on Individuals' Art Preferences According to Their Personality Traits via Computer Aided Web Site," *American Journal of Educational Research* 3, no. 8 (2008): 1052–56.

18. Tomas Chamorro-Premuzic, Charlotte Burke, and Anne Hsu, "Personality Predictors of Artistic Preferences as a Function of the Emotional Valence and Perceived Complexity of Paintings," *Psychology of Aesthetics, Creativity and the Arts* 4, no. 4 (2010): 196–204.

19. "The Role of Education in Countering Violent Extremism," Center on Global Counterterrorism Cooperation, December 2013, https://globalcenter.org/wp-content/uploads/2013/12/Dec13_Education_Expert_Meeting_Note.pdf.

20. Report of the Special Rapporteur in the Field of Cultural Rights, UN Human Rights Council 34th Session, February 27–March 24, 2017, UN Human Rights Council, *Report of the Special Rapporteur in the Field of Cultural Rights*, February 23, 2017, A/HRC/34/56, available at: https://www.refworld.org/docid/58af045e4.html.

21. Gilligan, *Preventing Violence*, location 1580. Kindle.

22. Ramin Alavinezhad, Masoumeh Mousavi, Nadereh Sohrabi, "Effects of Art Therapy on Anger and Self-Esteem in Aggressive Children," *Procedia: Social and Behavioral Sciences* 113 (2014): 111–17.

23. Gilligan, *Preventing Violence*, location 1892. Kindle.

24. Kurt Vonnegut, *A Man without a Country* (New York: Seven Stories Press, 2005), 24.

25. Juncal Fernandez-Garayzabal, "An Interview with Jason Walters, Former Salafi Jihadist," Light upon Light, https://www.lightuponlight.online/an-interview-with-jason-walters-former-salafi-jihadist/, accessed September 1, 2019.

26. Juncal Fernandez-Garayzabal, "An Interview with Jason Walters."

27. Janny Groen, "Deze man wilde sterven als martelaar, deradicaliseerde, en wil nu helpen Islamisten te begrijpen," *Volkskrant*, September 28, 2018, https://www.volkskrant.nl/nieuws-achtergrond/deze-man-wilde-sterven-als-martelaar-deradicaliseerde-en-wil-nu-helpen-islamisten-te-begrijpen~b38864cd/.

28. "New Domestic Violence Report Finds More than 525 Women Shot and Killed Every Year by Intimate Partners," Brady Center to Prevent Gun Violence, October 12, 2018, https://www.globenewswire.com/news-release/2018/10/12/1620737/0/en/New-Domestic-Violence-Report-Finds-More-Than-525-Women-Shot-and-Killed-Every-Year-By-Intimate-Partners.html.

29. "The Relationship between Domestic Violence and Mass Shootings," *All Things Considered*, October 7, 2017, https://www.npr.org/2017/10/07/556405489/the-relationship-between-domestic-violence-and-mass-shootings. See also, "In Texas and Beyond, Mass Shootings Have Roots in Domestic Violence," https://www.npr.org/sections/

health-shots/2017/11/07/562387350/in-texas-and-beyond-mass-shootings-have-roots-in
-domestic-violence https://www.npr.org/sections/health-shots/2017/11/07/562387350/
in-texas-and-beyond-mass-shootings-have-roots-in-domestic-violence, accessed March
22, 2020; Steph Black, "The Link Between Mass Shootings and Domestic Violence"
Jewish Women International (n.d.), https://www.jwi.org/articles/the-link-between
-mass-shootings-and-domestic-violence, accessed March 15, 2020.

30. Janine Jackson, "Tolerance of Violence in Homes Is the Necessary Precursor to Public
Violence," FAIR.org, November 17, 2019, https://fair.org/home/tolerance-of-violence
-in-homes-is-the-necessary-precursor-to-public-violence/.

31. Hudson et al., *Sex and World Peace*, location 4705. Kindle.

32. Hillary Clinton, Statement at 2013 Women in the World Summit, April 15, 2013,
https://awpc.cattcenter.iastate.edu/2017/03/09/2013-women-in-the-world-summit
-april-5-2013/.

Also see Organisation for Economic Cooperation and Development (OECD),
"Violence Against Women" (indicator), doi: 10.1787/f1eb4876-en, accessed March 13,
2020; Eric W. Dolan, "Testing the Hillary Doctrine: Study Finds Lack of Women's
Rights Linked to Anti-American Terrorism" *PsyPost*, April 17, 2017 https://www.psy-
post.org/2017/04/testing-hillary-doctrine-study-finds-lack-womens-rights-linked-anti
-american-terrorism-48759. For the World Health Organization map of countries by
prevalence, see http://gamapserver.who.int/mapLibrary/Files/Maps/Global_Violence
_Against_Women_2010.png?ua=1 (accessed March 13, 2020); for an interactive map
and chart by country, see OECD, "Violence Against Women," https://data.oecd.org
/inequality/violence-against-women.htm, accessed March 13, 2020. For information
on most violent countries, see Institute for Economics and Peace, "Global Peace Index
2019: Measuring Peace in a Complex World," June 2019, http://visionofhumanity.org/
reports; "Most Violent Countries Population (2020-02-17)," World Population Review,
http://worldpopulationreview.com/countries/most-violent-countries/.

33. Margaret Talbot, "Terror Begins at Home," *New Yorker*, June 16, 2016, https://www
.newyorker.com/news/daily-comment/terror-begins-at-home.

34. Report of the Special Rapporteur in the Field of Cultural Rights, UN Human Rights
Council.

35. Anny Shaw, "London Art Dealer Joseph Namad Spared Jail after Banging Ex-Partner's
Head against Wall during Drunken Row," *Art Newspaper*, August 1, 2019.

36. Hoffer, *The True Believer*, section 139.

APPENDIX B

1. World Health Organization Violence and Injury Prevention Statement, World Health
Organization, https://www.who.int/violence_injury_prevention/violence/global_cam-
paign/16_days/en/index7.html, accessed July 10, 2019.

2. United Nations, "Global Study on Homicide" (Vienna, Austria: United Nations Office
on Drugs and Crime, 2018).

3. National Coalition Against Domestic Violence, NCADV.org statistics https://ncadv .org/statistics, accessed July 6, 2019.

4. National Coalition Against Domestic Violence, NCADV.org statistics.

5. National Coalition Against Domestic Violence, NCADV.org statistics.

6. National Coalition Against Domestic Violence, NCADV.org statistics.

7. National Coalition Against Domestic Violence, NCADV.org statistics.

8. "UN Urges Countries to End Marital Rape and Close Legal Loopholes," *Global Citizen*, June 25, 2018.

9. Klausner, "Wife-Killer Map of America."

10. Allison Celik and Bushra Sabri, "801 Muslims Speak Up to Stop Family Violence," Project Sakinah, 2011, http://projectsakinah.org/Resources/Surveys/2011-Survey/Survey -Results.

11. "France Announces Anti-Femicide Measures as 100th Killing Recorded," BBC.com, September 3, 2019, https://www.bbc.com/news/world-europe-49571327.

12. "In France, a Woman Is Killed by Partner or Ex-Partner Every Three Days," *France24/ AFP*, July 10, 2019.

13. Sarah Marsh, "Domestic Abuse Offences in London Rise 63% in Seven Years," *Guardian*, February 27, 2019.

14. Marsh, "Domestic Abuse Offences in London Rise 63% in Seven Years."

15. "Huiselijk en Seksueel Geweld Factsheet 2019" (Utrecht: Movisie, 2019), 1; https:// www.huiselijkgeweld.nl/publicaties/factsheets/2019/02/25/huiselijk-geweld-feiten-en -cijfers-2019, accessed October 3, 2019.

16. "Huiselijk en Seksueel Geweld Factsheet 2019," 3.

17. Sheikh Saaliq, "Every Third Woman in India Suffers Sexual, Physical Violence at Home," News 18, February 8, 2018, https://www.news18.com/news/india/the-elephant-in-the -room-every-third-woman-in-india-faces-domestic-violence-1654193.html.

18. Saaliq, "Every Third Woman in India Suffers Sexual, Physical Violence at Home."

19. F. Basar and N. Demirci, "Domestic Violence against Women in Turkey," *Pakistan Journal of Medical Sciences* 34, no. 3 (2018): 660–65; doi:10.12669/pjms.343.15139.

20. UN Human Rights Council, "Report of the Special Rapporteur on Violence against Women, Its Causes and Consequences (addendum)," UN Mission to Saudi Arabia, April 14, 2009, A/HRC/11/6/Add.3, available at https://www.refworld.org/docid/49f8448a2 .html.

21. "Report of the Special Rapporteur on Violence against Women."

22. "Report of the Special Rapporteur on Violence against Women."

23. T. Elghossain et al., "Prevalence of Key Forms of Violence Against Adolescents in the Arab Region: A Systematic Review," *Journal of Adolescent Health* 64 (2019): 8–19.

24. "Report of the Special Rapporteur on Violence against Women, Its Causes and Con- sequences on Her Mission to the Sudan," UN Human Rights Council, April 2016, https://www.refworld.org/docid/57615e974.html.

25. "Report of the Special Rapporteur on Violence against Women."

APPENDIX C

1. Valerie M. Hudson and Patricia Leidl, *The Hillary Doctrine: Sex and American Foreign Policy* (New York: Columbia University Press, 2015), 154.

2. "Most Violent Countries Population (2020-02-17)," World Population Review, http://worldpopulationreview.com/countries/most-violent-countries/, accessed March 16, 2020.

3. "Global Peace Index 2019," http://visionofhumanity.org/app/uploads/2019/06/GPI-2019-web003.pdf, accessed March 15, 2020.

4. "Women Peace and Security Index," *National Geographic*, https://www.nationalgeographic.com/culture/2019/10/peril-progress-prosperity-womens-well-being-around-the-world-feature/, accessed March 14, 2020.

5. "Women Peace and Security Index," *National Geographic*, https://giwps.georgetown.edu/the-index/, accessed March 16, 2020.

6. Samuel Stebbins, "Dangerous States: Which States Have the Highest Rates of Violent Crimes and Most Murders," *USA Today*, January 13, 2020, https://eu.usatoday.com/story/money/2020/01/13/most-dangerous-states-in-america-violent-crime-murder-rate/40968963/.

7. Thomas C. Frohlich, Samuel Stebbins, and Michael B. Sauter, "America's Most Violent (and Peaceful) States," *USA Today*, July 29, 2016, https://www.usatoday.com/story/money/business/2016/07/29/americas-most-violent-and-peacefulstates/87658252/.

8. John MacDonald, "Top 10 States with the Most Domestic Abuse Cases," October 19, 2017, https://www.aggressivelegalservices.com/domestic-abuse-cases-worst-states/.

9. "When Men Murder Women: An Analysis of 2015 Homicide Data," (Washington DC: Violence Policy Center, 2017), http://www.vpc.org/studies/wmmw2017.pdf, accessed March 16, 2020.

10. Adam McCann, "Best and Worst States for Women," Wallet Hub, March 2, 2020 https://wallethub.com/edu/best-and-worst-states-for-women/10728/.